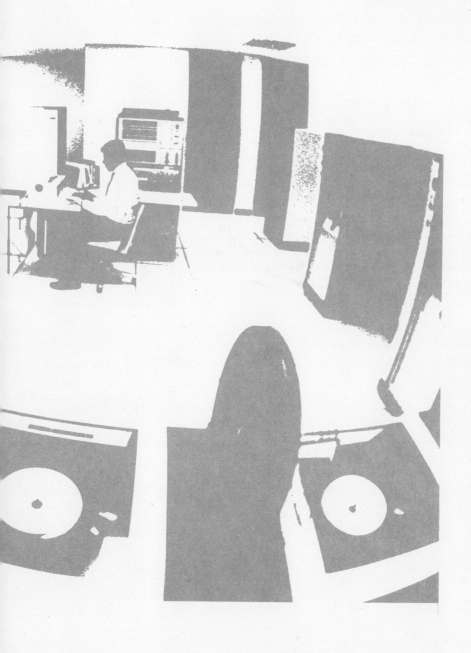

The Program Development Process

The Program Development Process

Part 1
THE INDIVIDUAL PROGRAMMER

J. D. ARON
IBM Corporation

▲▲ ADDISON-WESLEY PUBLISHING COMPANY
Reading, Massachusetts • Menlo Park, California
London • Amsterdam • Don Mills, Ontario • Sydney

ISBN 0-201-14451-4
ABCDEFGHIJ-HA-7987654

To the memory of Ascher Opler
who was the founding spirit of
The Systems Programming Series

THE SYSTEMS PROGRAMMING SERIES

*The Program Development Process
Part I—The Individual Programmer — Joel D. Aron

The Program Development Process
Part II—The Programming Team — Joel D. Aron

The Design and Structure of Programming Languages — John E. Nicholls

Mathematical Background of Programming — Frank Beckman

Structured Programming — Harlan D. Mills
Richard C. Linger

An Introduction to Database Systems — C. J. Date

Compiler Engineering — Patricia Goldberg

Interactive Computer Graphics — Andries Van Dam

Sorting and Sort Systems — Harold Lorin

Recursive Programming Techniques — William Burge

Compilers and Programming Languages — J. T. Schwartz
John Cocke

*Published

Foreword

The field of systems programming primarily grew out of the efforts of many programmers and managers whose creative energy went into producing practical, utilitarian systems programs needed by the rapidly growing computer industry. Programming was practiced as an art where each programmer invented his own solutions to problems with little guidance beyond that provided by his immediate associates. In 1968, the late Ascher Opler, then at IBM, recognized that it was necessary to bring programming knowledge together in a form that would be accessible to all systems programmers. Surveying the state of the art, he decided that enough useful material existed to justify a significant codification effort. On his recommendation, IBM decided to sponsor The Systems Programming Series as a long term project to collect, organize, and publish those principles and techniques that would have lasting value throughout the industry.

The Series consists of an open-ended collection of text-reference books. The contents of each book represent the individual author's view of the subject area and do not necessarily reflect the views of the IBM Corporation. Each is organized for course use but is detailed enough for reference. Further, the Series is organized in three levels: broad introductory material in the foundation volumes, more specialized material in the software volumes, and very specialized theory in the computer science volumes. As such, the Series meets the needs of the novice, the experienced programmer, and the computer scientist.

Taken together, the Series is a record of the state of the art in systems programming that can form the technological base for the systems programming discipline.

The Editorial Board

Preface

The process of building a program system involves the application of tools and techniques for program design within a framework of procedural controls. The right tools and techniques are essential to achieve programs of high quality, reliability, and serviceability. The procedural controls ensure that the program will be delivered on time and within budget while meeting all the functional and performance specifications. It is the purpose of this book and its companion volume, Part 2 (published separately) to discuss the development of program systems as a process, tying together all technical and procedural aspects of the problem.

A brief review of the changing nature of the programming development process in Chapter 1 explains the increasing need over the years for better planning and control procedures. Chapter 2 introduces some useful concepts which establish the point of view of the system programmer or system manager involved in developing a program end product.

The remainder of Part I discusses the procedure followed by a good individual programmer. These examples of good programming practice are valid for programming activities of any size. They are grouped in Part 1 for two purposes: (1) to help the individual programmer and (2) to provide standards of programming development which will be assumed in Part 2.

Part 2, *The Programming Team,* covers the activities of a group. When several good programmers get together to work on a small system, the performance of the group may deteriorate unless a new set of activities is defined to coordinate the group. Interactions which did not exist for a programmer working along will now affect the operation, in some cases constraining, in other cases increasing productivity. The management of these interactions at various stages in the development process must adapt to the characteristics of the system at each state. Examples taken from actual experience are used throughout the text to illustrate various points. In each case, the example has been simplified to be useful. Characteristically, real systems are too large and complex to be described in a text or to be used as case studies. For this reason, there are no exercises in the book. Any meaningful student exercise would be a book-sized problem in itself. Trivial exercises would mislead the reader into thinking systems are simpler than they are in real life. The best way to learn the principles of program system development is to get involved in a development project. Then, this book will be a self-explanatory guide to the steps in the process. For the classroom, a case study guide will be provided. Case studies are far inferior to on-the-job training because they omit too much detail but, being based on factual cases, they do have the advantage of realism.

Part 1 is aimed at the individual programmer working alone or as a member of a team. It teaches the procedural aspects of programming that make for effective results. Because it covers the *process* of programming, the volume supplements the usual *technology* training each programmer requires. Part 2 explains how team projects work. It shows why individuals have to conform to the rules and regulations found in any organized activity. By stressing the system aspects of the programming process and assuming that the reader knows the guidelines of Part 1, Part 2 teaches how the large program systems needed in today's environment can be built. To further emphasize the teamwork needed on large projects, the case studies allow groups of programmers and other team members to play out their roles in a classroom training environment.

Gaithersburg, Maryland   J.D.A.

Contents

Contents of Part 2

THE PROGRAMMING TEAM

CHAPTER 17
PLAN DOCUMENTS

Technical Plan
Resource Plan
Test Plan
Documentation Plan
Implementation Plan
Support Plan
Maintenance Plan

CHAPTER 18
RESOURCE MANAGEMENT

Resource Planning
  Requirements
  Impact of the Resource Plan
  Resources to be Considered
Estimating
  Purpose of Estimate
  Methods of Estimating
  Factors Affecting the Estimate
Budgeting
  Converting an Estimate into a Budget
  Contingencies, Burdens, Risks
  Budget vs. Actual
  Control of Expense Elements
Scheduling
  Project Length vs. Workload
  Schedule Documents
  Milestones and Checkpoints
  Coordinating Schedules with Performance
  Scheduling for Procedural Delays

CHAPTER 19
INTERFACE MANAGEMENT

Responsibility for Managing Interfaces
Configuration Control Group
  Baseline Control
  Change Control
  Work Breakdown Structure
  Deliverable End Items
Project Reviews
  Value of Reviews
  Types of Reviews
  Setting Up a Review

1
History of the Program Development Process

A phenomenon of the computer age has been the amazing growth in the number of programmers needed in spite of rapid improvements in tools to increase each programmer's productivity. This growth is seen in the larger and larger groups working on important program systems, as well as in the number of programmers supporting each installed computer. As in all things, increasing size leads to disproportionately increasing complexity; therefore, much programming activity is now directed toward the management of complexity instead of toward designing efficient instruction sequences. The emphasis on management rather than technology represents a major change in the nature of programming since the 1950s.

The motivation for the first commercial computers was the need to solve scientific calculations, such as those arising in aircraft and nuclear-reactor design problems. The designers of these machines discovered the benefits of storing programs the same way data was stored. Stored programs permitted a sequence of instructions to be modified according to the circumstances of the problem being solved. The stored-program concept made it possible for a programmer to turn a general-purpose computer into a hardware/software system[1] which would act like a special-purpose machine especially engineered to solve a given problem.

---

1. Keywords such as *system* are defined in Chapter 2.

1.1   FIRST STAGE

In an early paper on the computer of the Princeton Institute for Advanced Study (IAS), Von Neumann and Goldstine [1] introduced the basic programming concepts needed to make the IAS "Johnniac" an effective tool for problems in numerical computation. Unfortunately, this paper was not widely distributed, nor were such other reports and books as Wilkes, Wheeler, and Gill's [2] work on EDSAC. The latter volume introduced labor-saving devices, such as subroutine libraries, to help programmers.

The lack of attention paid to these publications may be due to several factors. First, many computer users were engineers and/or mathematicians, for whom programming was a necessary but uninteresting chore; they did not see programming as a challenging intellectual activity. Second, the language of programming was new, poorly developed, and hard to understand. Third, the problems important enough to warrant use of a digital computer tended to have straightforward programming solutions; therefore, no literature search was made before coding started. For example, a meteorological problem designed to run on an IBM 701 first had to be limited to fit the small memory of the 701. The equations of motion of the atmosphere had to be analyzed by a meteorologist/numerical analyst to produce a set of difference equations. A step-by-step mathematical procedure was designed to solve the difference equations, and finally, a sequence of computer instructions was written to translate the procedure into machine language. Only the first step involved "meteorology." A literature search, if needed, would have to cover only meteorology and numerical analysis since the actual programming, or "coding," was trivial when the problem was properly set up. It is no wonder that computer users in that environment considered "programming" a subject of limited professional interest.

1.1.1   Business Applications

The first major step toward recognition of programming as a special category of professional activity came when decimal arithmetic computers were installed in business applications. The people assigned to program these machines were, for the most part, former machine operators and administrative personnel. They had no training in mathematics and were often frightened by equations and Boolean symbols. They were knowledgeable in their problem area but had no experience in setting up logical procedures explaining the step-by-step handling of transactions in the area. For this group, there was no counterpart of the meteorologist to tell them what had to be done. They had to dig in themselves and (a) define the problem, (b) describe how the problem was to be handled, and (c) convert the description into

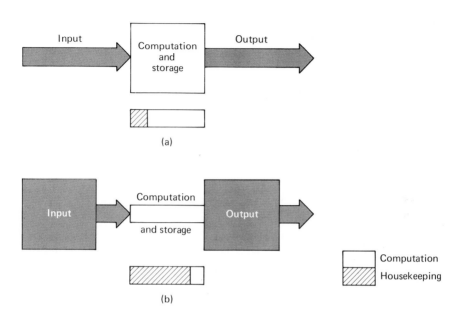

Fig. 1.1 Characteristics of scientific versus business applications: (a) scientific computation; (b) business data processing.

a program. The program they produced was quite different from a scientific program (Fig. 1.1) in that it was heavy on input/output and light on arithmetic. The scientist would submit a small amount of data to initialize a large computation involving many intermediate results and a brief statement of final results. This required a fast computer with lots of memory. The business programmer, on the other hand, would handle many input records—each fairly short—and produce many output reports with only a small amount of arithmetic to compute control totals or discount rates or trend lines, etc. A slow computer with a small memory was adequate because its throughput would be limited by input/output device speeds in any case. An analysis of a business data processing program would very likely show that the bulk of the instructions were for *housekeeping*—for initializing the program before each transaction, for checking input/output error signals, for analyzing transaction routing codes, etc. More important, the business application maintained large files of data, such as master payroll data, customer address lists, inventories. These files had to be updated periodically and preserved for long periods. The size of the master files was large compared with the input transaction file, so that most input/output processing was due to handling the master files.

1.1.2   Programming Aids

To cope with the complexities of the business environment (which is logically more complicated than the scientific environment because there are so many independent decision points and no mathematical relationships to unify them), business programmers began to look for ways to make the job of writing an *application program* easier. First, they wanted to be able to use decimal numbers; binary machine manufacturers produced decimal arithmetic subroutines. Second, they wanted to be freed of the need for worrying about where the job sat in the computer; symbolic assembly programs, relocatable loaders, and optimal assemblers were produced. Third, they wanted to avoid the tedious programming needed to handle input/output; the Input Output Control Systems (IOCS) were provided. Later, file-handling systems became available. To meet programmer needs, the new activity of *systems programming* was born.

1.2   INDIVIDUAL RESPONSIBILITY

Note that up to this point it has been sufficient to talk about the programmer in the singular. In the first stage of programming development, individual programmers worked on individual applications. Where several programmers were working together, each usually had a clearly defined task, depending very little on the others. Each program was the creation of one person. Its quality and efficiency depended more on the mental agility and technique of the programmer than on the tools available (Fig. 1.2). Except when using a macro assembler, programmers communicated directly with the computer in its language and took advantage of its capabilities and idiosyncracies. The advantage of this way of working was that the programmer's entire energy could be devoted to the problem without distraction. The disadvantages were that one programmer's results may have been too cryptic to be of use to others, and an individual programmer could tackle problems only of a limited size. The method worked, apparently, because the problems suited to first-generation machines with limited memory and inefficient bulk storage were all within the size limits one person's mind could span.

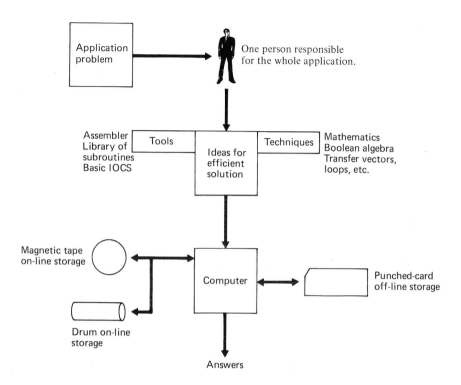

Fig. 1.2 Programming: first stage.

1.3   SECOND STAGE

As larger computers were introduced, larger problems were tackled. If a problem appeared too big for one person to handle, it would be given to a small team. Often the whole team would contribute to program definition and to the design of a program structure to solve the problem, but the actual programming would be subdivided into relatively independent tasks. The team would discuss objectives and develop specifications among themselves to avoid difficulties when the separate sections of the program were assembled into a single programming system.

To facilitate the programming task and to make better use of the hardware, new systems programming tools and techniques were generated (Fig. 1.3). Whereas, formerly, simple subroutines were placed in common libraries, from which they could be obtained on call, the second-generation programmers stored whole programs in the library. In 1954, you would go

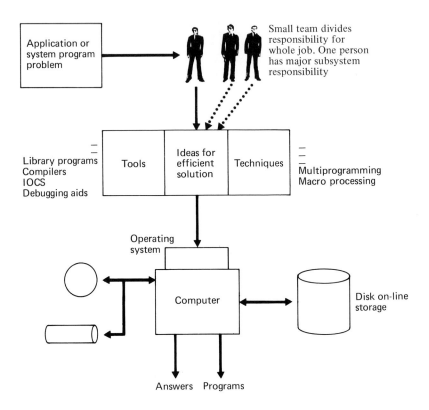

Fig. 1.3 Programming: second stage.

to the library for a sine subroutine or a double-precision arithmetic subroutine. In 1961, you would still expect those subroutines to be there, but you would also look for a sort package (which would automatically generate a good sort program for a file of a given size and structure) or a report program generator (which would generate programs to edit data and rearrange it to fit a given format for a printed report).

1.3.1 Languages

Whereas, formerly, an assembly language allowed you to substitute a symbolic name for a numeric operation code, address, or data entry, you could now write your source program in a language more like English. Such a language as FORTRAN was a programming language, but it minimized references to any particular computer so that the programmer could concentrate on the problem to be solved.

A new kind of program, called a *compiler*, was now needed to translate the higher-level FORTRAN statements into machine language. The compiler was the first important system program to place a curtain between the programmer and the machine. It relieved the programmer of the need for specifying machine-dependent instructions. But the higher-level language also tended to be inefficient when translated into some important functions. As a result, many programs written in higher-level languages—though easier to write, debug, read, and maintain—took longer to execute and used more storage than similar programs written in assembly language. The loss of efficiency was important at the time because machine time was a relatively costly resource. However, the long-term trend, already in evidence in 1960, was for programming cost to increase relative to machine cost. Soon the loss of machine throughput was less costly than inefficient use of programming talent, so most users gradually switched to higher-level languages. Typically, only users in specialized areas where execution times or memory were critical (such as airborne and spaceborne computers, real-time process control computers, very small machines, very large numerical computations) continued to write in assembly language and to hand-optimize their code.

Less sophisticated improvements in languages involved macro assemblers. Used very much like assemblers, the macro assembly program allowed the use of single statements to represent whole subroutines and still gave the programmers access to detailed machine features. Sometimes the macro assembler made it possible to defer initialization of the subroutine until the program was executed (by the use of symbolic parameters which were assigned actual values as the program processed input data). The macros were often supplied by the computer vendor but, since they were easy to write and could be readily added to a macro assembler, they could also be written by the user to fit his particular needs.

1.3.2 Performance

Although the language improvements were introduced at a time when primary bulk storage was on magnetic tape or drum, they did not hit their stride until such large-volume secondary (or bulk) units as disks and drums became available. Random-access speed and capacity made it practical to compile large programs. Yet the speed was still very slow compared with that realized with core storage, the main computer memory. Consequently, the bigger and faster computers were often idle while waiting for data to be transmitted from bulk storage. The answer to this problem was to increase

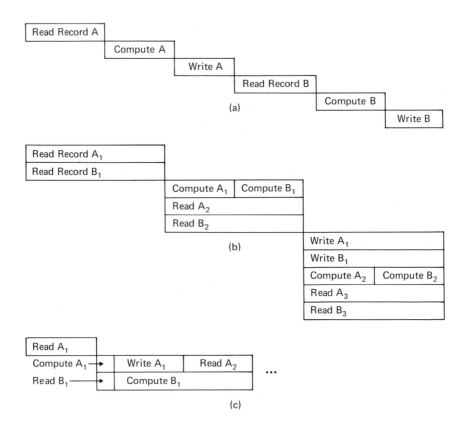

Fig. 1.4 Rudimentary multiprogramming: (a) unoverlapped operation; (b) overlapped operation with four I/O channels; (c) multiprogrammed scientific/business programs with one channel.

the computer workload by some rudimentary multiprogramming. For example, a large data processing job could be split in half so that each half resided in a separate storage unit. One record from each unit would be retrieved simultaneously, cutting the average access time in half. If the arithmetic operations were short, all the computing could be made to overlap the access time. The amount of overlap depended on the number of independent channels available for input and output and the ratio of I/O time to compute time (Fig. 1.4). In some instances, it was more convenient to overlap a business application (high I/O demands) with a stream of scientific applications (heavy computer loads). In either case, the result was better utilization of the expensive computing resource.[2]

To accommodate the higher number of I/O operations, more than one I/O channel had to be attached to the computer. In addition, a set of software buffers were established in the computer. Each buffer was an area of memory assigned to receive an input record or to hold a record for shipment to an output device. The synchronization of more than two buffers or disk access arms became a frequent source of program errors because the sequencing of many events, each of which may contain innate errors and each of which may create a condition that causes errors in its successor, is very difficult to visualize. The IOCS system program was expanded to handle buffer scheduling and its associated error processing because an IOCS written by I/O experts to handle general cases was more reliable than the I/O programs generated by the average programmer. But in shielding the user from the actual movement of records within the machine, IOCS became a second important curtain layer between the programmer and the machine.

1.3.3 Operating Systems

A third, even more impenetrable, curtain began to close in this time period. It was the operating system [3]. It grew in response to two needs.

1. The increasing speed of computers made it uneconomical to require manual setup of each job. It became evident that lost time due to setup could exceed useful computing time. The operating system permitted many jobs to be set up in batch before they reached the computer. Under operating-system control, the entire batch would be executed without stopping except for error correction or tape-file mounting.

2. The proliferation of system programs required the integration and coordination of the tasks called for in each job. The operating system monitored the calls and links to all system and application programs under its control.

1.4 SYSTEM PROGRAMS AND THEIR IMPACT

The introduction of a new term, *system program,* was changing the nature of programming. In 1955, programmers communicated directly with the

---

2. A special case of multiprogrammed operation overlapped the slow card reader, punch, and printer devices with computing jobs; for instance, many output reports would be recorded on tape at high speed and printed later when the computer was doing scientific work. The term *spooling,* used to refer to this procedure, is derived from *s*imultaneous *p*eripheral *o*peration *on-l*ine.

computer through instructions they wrote, for the most part. In 1961, they communicated with the machine through an intermediary, the operating system. The instructions they wrote now made up only a portion of the instructions used in getting the job done. They would use many programming support tools, such as compilers, before they had a program to execute. They would use such tools as debugging aid packages—whose only raison d'être was to make the "curtain" programs more manageable if not transparent. They would use library programs to save effort, and they would use IOCS and operating system services to save confusion as well as effort. More personal time would go into decisions related to the management of these technological resources, and, unfortunately, less would be devoted to solving the original problem in the purest sense. Programmers would become dependent on the quality and availability of the systems programs built by others. And to their distaste, they would see a new class of problems arise—systems programming problems—which drew attention away from the application area in order to generalize the systems programs to support more and more users. The production of new system programs began to use substantial amounts of time on computers that had originally been procured to produce answers to application problems.

System programs were intended to help programmers write application programs which solved user problems. System programs possessed a degree of generality not found in typical application programs. It was sufficient that an application program solve a specific problem on a specific machine. Thus the highway engineering earthwork computation (which calculated the cubic yards of dirt to be cut or filled to form a roadbed) would be written one way in Louisiana, which is essentially flat and where an IBM 650 decimal computer was used, but another way in Colorado, which has steep grades and where a Bendix G15 binary computer was used. This gave each state a tailored solution. Such an arrangement made no sense in system programming. System programs were written so as to be useful to as many people as possible. Although they would run on only one class of machines, they had to be flexible enough to run on any configuration of hardware devices allowed on the machine. In addition, they had to support a very wide range of problem specifications. As generic programs, they were relatively insensitive to the user's environment, i.e., a FORTRAN compiler would compile FORTRAN programs written by a biological research scientist just as it would a program written by an accountant.

By supplying general-purpose system programs, a vendor could increase the productivity of programmers and simultaneously reduce their workload. Therefore, the system program became a marketing tool as well as a technological tool. And the product being offered gradually changed from a hardware system—described in terms of microseconds per arithmetic operation—

to a hardware/software system—described in terms of *throughput,* or the amount of work the system could do.

1.5   CLASSES OF PROGRAMMERS

During the second stage, several distinct classes of programmers were formed: application programmers, system programmers, and, in smaller numbers, hardware diagnostic programmers and special hardware programmers (the optimal assembly language programmers of airborne-type machines). The skills of the first two groups were similar; they had to know how to program general-purpose computers in a variety of languages. The last two groups were also similar; they had to know some hardware logic design and the assembly language for a particular machine. Good people in any of the four groups were generally able to work with the technology in a different group without much trouble. Nevertheless, the points of view of the groups differed considerably. *Application programmers* were first and foremost problem solvers. For them, system programs were a means to an end. *System programmers* thought in terms of getting the best performance out of a machine for a very generalized function. They frequently had no feel for how their product would ultimately be used. *Diagnostic programmers* were concerned with proving the reliability and serviceability of a machine; they may have had no knowledge of either the application or system programs that would run on the machine. *Special hardware programmers* saw themselves as members of a project team building a system in which the computer played a small but important role. Their programming orientation was to reduce the number of instructions and data words needed to handle a straightforward computation.

    The main interaction between groups was that between the application and system programmers. The fact that they had different points of view led to poor communication between them and, in turn, increased the need for programmers to spend time on management and administrative tasks. The strength of the management structure they set up was supposed to protect them from the errors or omissions caused by uncertainty in the communications environment. In the final analysis, the management structure was the key to satisfying the user.

1.6   THIRD STAGE

The computer industry continued to grow at an explosive rate during the 1960s as the third generation of computers reached the market. The growth was not uniformly distributed across user classes. Scientific users, who tended to acquire the strongest programmers, had entered the field early, and most of them had first- or second-generation computers. As they grew up to larger, third-generation machines, they stressed productivity aids and throughput, and they invested in training their own staff to achieve it. But as a group, the highly sophisticated scientific users were becoming a smaller and smaller portion of the market. Far greater numbers of business users were becoming customers. As before, these users had limited technological training and relied on the vendor to simplify the use of computers as well as to provide tools for their efficient use. Many business users were very small and were getting their first computer without any trained staff at all. As a whole, the average skill level of programmers was falling. The productivity of programmers would have deteriorated, had it not been for compensating factors.

- Programming education was more effective.
- System programs were more helpful.
- User organizations shared their know-how.
- Machine costs were going down fast enough to make average programs cost-effective.

One of the reasons productivity was maintained and, in many cases, improved was that ever-increasing functions were assigned to the system program. Thus, presumably, application programmers would concentrate on the application problem. The efforts to achieve such a division of effort were not entirely successful. Because so much was assigned to the system program, it became so big that it was unmanageable. Its complexity was then passed on to the user, who, instead of finding the system program a boon, found it a burden. However, he had to use it because the design of operating systems had reached the stage where the average programmer could no longer reach the hardware. The system programs that made the solution of very large problems feasible were imposed on small problems as well. Every programmer found a larger and more complex set of tools and techniques to be learned and understood. Every program needed more programmers, with the usual disproportionate increase in complexity due to sheer project size. This led to pressure to redesign and improve the system programs. A vicious circle had been created, and it could be broken only by better management of the program development process (Fig. 1.5).

Changes in the development process took several forms.

- Technological changes resulting from the design of new hardware features.
- Technological changes resulting from a deeper insight into data processing requirements.

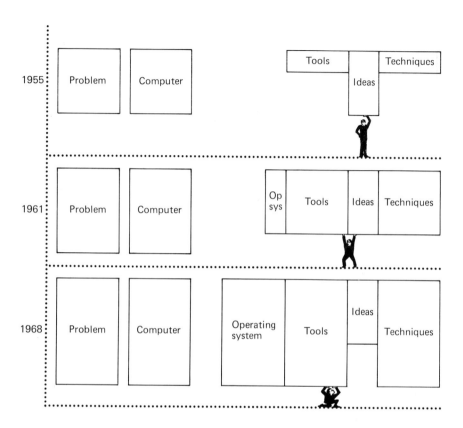

Fig. 1.5 Changing nature of programming.

- Management, organization, and administrative changes recommended by experienced managers, usually influenced by principles of engineering management.

The rate at which changes were implemented varied according to management's ability to recognize the value and the relevance of a new idea. It also depended on how deeply involved a group was in a project. Many managers preferred to defer changes until they had fulfilled their commitments—a normally conservative approach when working to a tight deadline.

The sheer size of many projects, such as air traffic control, airline reservations handling, space missions, and construction of new operating systems, came to dominate the development process. In every dimension—manpower, tools, techniques, problem complexity, hardware features, even geographic

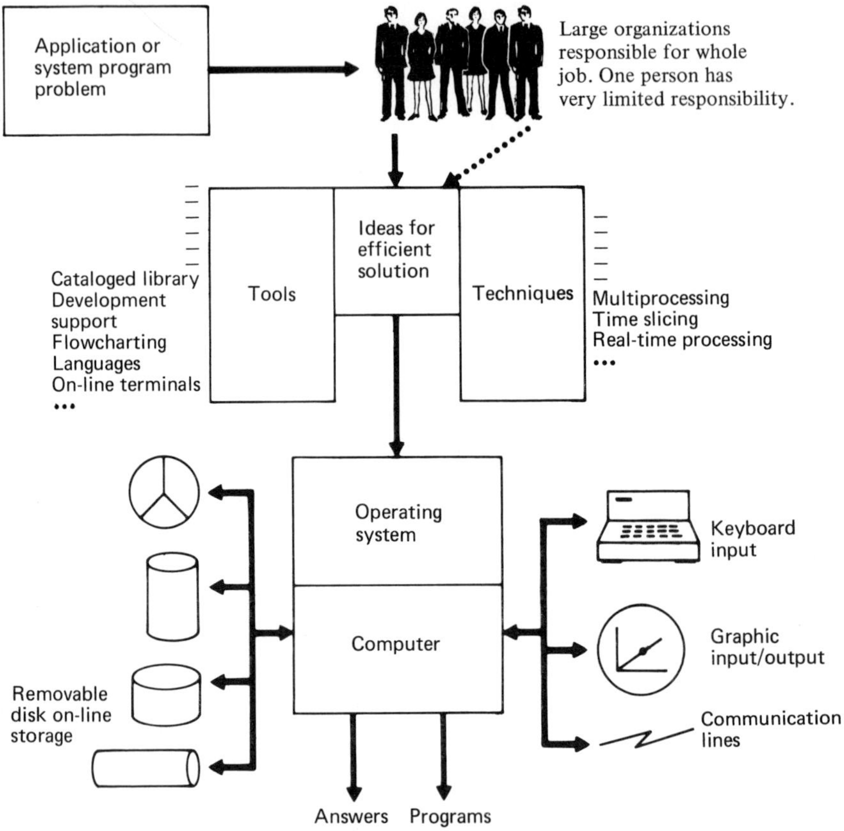

Fig. 1.6 Programming: third stage.

dispersion of resources—third-stage projects were so large they challenged the management skill of the best managers (Fig. 1.6).

1.6.1 Hardware Technology

The new hardware features that contributed to changes in the program development process included:

- Improved bulk storage devices with removable disk packs, which allowed the programmer to handle very large files without calling for additional hardware.

- Communications attachments that allowed many devices (tele-typewriters, telephones, typewriters, and computers) to transfer data from remote locations to the central computer.

- Manual input devices, including typewriters, which permitted data and programs to be entered directly into the computer without being punched into cards.

- Graphic displays, which allowed data and answers to be edited on-line, without waiting for a computer printout.

- Read-only storage devices, which, though normally hidden from the programmer, permitted changes to the instruction repertoire of the computer. (*Microprogrammers* prepare instructions for read-only stores.)

- Measurement devices that could be attached to a running computer to determine how efficiently it was being used.

- Computer and memory features that allowed multiple processors to work on a single problem.

As these components were added, they led to a gradual shift away from centralized batch systems to an increasing number of on-line systems with the consequence that, today, hardware/software systems must be described in terms of not only cost and throughput but also *response time*. In fact, program systems must now be able to measure their own performance in order to provide an acceptable response to the user.

1.6.2   Software Technology

The magnitude of the programming required by a large application caused users to devote more of their time to this topic than to the hardware they would need. Lumping all their problems together, they began to refer to *software* when they were talking about any system aspect that was not hardware or management. Thus application programs, system programs, analyses, temporary support tools, models, etc., became software. The term had appeal: it offered an appropriate contrast to hardware. Software was less tangible, more yielding, easier to modify than hardware. However, these very attributes led to severe problems. By accepting hardware as fixed and immutable, users forced the software to absorb all the changes needed to make the hardware fit the problem. More and more work fell on the system and application programmers, and as the jobs grew larger, this work load got harder to control. So many of the requirements placed on the programmers were due to hardware or other nonprogramming problems that there was no coherent logical thread to the programming.

During the third stage, the pressures on programmers narrowed down to three areas.

1. Programmers could not cope with the intellectual burden of the tools and techniques they had to work with. There was a desperate need to unify and simplify the programming process.
2. Programmers with simple problems had to be relieved of the weight of full-blown system programs.
3. System programmers needed tools that supported groups as well as individuals.

New procedures plus improved programmer support combine to reduce these pressures. As explained in the following paragraphs, these changes are leading to a fourth stage of program development.

1.7 STANDARDS

Programming standards are used mainly to achieve consistent, manageable processes and products. They are designed for efficiency in the long run—sometimes at the expense of local optimization.

Standards are intended to get people to use the best-known method for doing a task. While they discourage the use of less effective alternatives, they impede the development of new alternatives. But they also simplify training. Some standards are technical; they affect the design and implementation of a program. For example:

- Top-down programming—Programmers can be directed to design their program by first defining files and major component structure and then adding calls to more detailed subelements. This approach is logical and preserves the integrity of design in a large system.

- Structured programming—By following mathematically valid rules, programmers will generate programs that are easy to read and to test.

- Using library programs—If programmers will search for existing programs that satisfy a set of requirements, considerable new programming effort can be avoided.

- Using a standard high-level language—The use of one version of a high-level language on a project can speed up programming, improve communications, and reduce training time.

Some standards affect the procedures used to control a program development. For example:

- Activity networks—The requirement that a chart be drawn showing all the activities to be completed in the project, as well as the interactions among activities, provides an excellent tool for ensuring the completeness of a project plan and the validity of the schedule.

- Phase review—Formal procedures for obtaining management and technical approval at the end of a task avoid false starts and permit timely decision-making.

- Configuration management—Constructing a baseline specification and establishing a control procedure to authorize changes to the baseline are necessary in the control of a large system.

- Machine room standards—Better service can be obtained from a central computer facility if all users follow standard procedures for job submission, priority assignment, and usage forecasting.

When properly used, standards simplify an individual programmer's job by eliminating the need for tradeoff studies and by making automated tools such as a flowchart generator available. Standards also establish a uniform basis for groups of programmers to work together without confusion or misunderstanding.

1.8 COMPUTER SCIENCE

To raise the base of technical understanding still higher requires education in computer science. Degrees in computer science were rare prior to 1968 but were offered by many schools after that. By following the leadership of the Association for Computing Machinery [4], these schools have been able to structure courses that give a graduate thorough grounding in the fundamentals of computing and system programming that would take years to acquire through on-the-job training. Programmers who enter the business with computer science degrees are equipped to cope with substantially more technical information than their peers without equivalent background.[3]

The subjects taught in computer science courses do not necessarily constitute a "science." Except for courses borrowed from other subject areas, such as physics and mathematics, most computer science courses stress the practice of programming rather than basic principles. There is, in fact, a question whether basic principles of programming exist to any significant extent. Until principles are discovered, computer education will have more the character of an engineering curriculum than of a science curriculum [5]. Nevertheless, programmer effectiveness depends, in part, on raising the level of conventional knowledge to a common plateau for all programmers.

---

3. Managers must take the disparate backgrounds of their employees into account when they organize a programming team. It is not a simple matter to integrate a computer science graduate into an organization structured around nonscientists.

1.9   LANGUAGES FOR DESIGNING PROGRAMS

A major thrust toward unifying the programming process in the design and coding phases involves the concept of languages as the embodiment of a programming system. Computation languages, as mentioned, were constructed to permit the programmer to work in a form close to natural language. They are capable of describing procedures, data files, hardware devices, and time-controlled sequences. By the use of algebraic or symbolic notation they can be concise, and by the use of full text they can be readable [6]. Experience has shown that they are useful tools for writing programs. Why not use them for designing program systems? After all, a program system is no more than a set of interrelated, time-controlled procedures operating on a set of data files and hardware devices. In the 1950s the programming languages were not intended to be used for system design and would probably have been too clumsy for that purpose. More recently, it has been suggested that a single language be used to describe the structure of a program system, the instruction sequence in the programs, and, in some cases, the hardware logic to execute the instructions. A subset of the language would also be used to command and query the system during execution. The appeal of this approach is its unity. A high degree of automation can be envisaged, since only one translator would be needed to produce all levels of design and implementation. The translator could even be used to design the logic of a special-purpose machine for running the program system and, with an automated factory, could build the machine. At this writing such pervasive power does not exist in any language,[4] but it is clear that, should such a language be developed, it would increase programmer effectiveness and reduce the burden of tools and techniques. Its probable effect on the business decisions of computer and software companies is completely unknown.

1.10   COMPUTER SERVICE AND ACCESSIBILITY

Programmers prefer to get their machine time when they ask for it, with no delays at either the input side or the output side of the machine room. When the programmers share a single machine, there is contention for service to the extent that no programmer is satisfied. Techniques for improving the service range from simply increasing machine capacity (which is wasteful of computing resources) to shortening the delays in the turn-

---

4. Languages such as APL and AED, described in [6], have been proposed as existing candidates for total-systems programming. So has English although it suffers severely from unavoidable verbosity and ambiguity. Alternatively, proposals to build APL or PL/I machines would bring the hardware level up closer to the programmer's language level.

around cycle. Delays can be reduced by having couriers or using remote entry terminals to speed up transmission of jobs from programmer to machine. They can be further reduced by time-sharing, so that the computer serves many programmers, each of whom has a remote entry terminal. Time-sharing is attractive but not necessarily effective, since it may make communication among the programmers difficult, leading to errors. This is particularly true when the group activity lasts many months. In such projects the programmers are overly dependent on the time-sharing system.[5] On the other hand, an interactive time-sharing system usually relieves the programmer of the need to manipulate the operating system. The programmer communicates through simple commands to the interactive system, which in turn takes care of all instructions to other system programs.

An alternative approach to the service problem is to manage the programming project in such a way as to increase the utility of a fixed amount of computer time. This can be done by the following procedures.

- Reducing the impact of long turnaround by teaching programmers to do more than one program unit at a time, so that they always have work in progress.

- Reducing the impact of long turnaround by teaching programmers to do more logical analysis of their programs between computer runs. This reduces the number of runs needed to debug a program.

- Laying out a usage-requirements schedule that uses priorities, three-shift operation, and a peak-averaging implementation plan to reduce overlapping demands on the computer.

- Providing systems support personnel in the computer room to eliminate programming and operating problems that can be detected on the spot.

- Minimizing traffic jams by keeping programmers out of the computer room.

1.11   DEVELOPMENT-SUPPORT SYSTEMS

It was pointed out earlier that language improvements have been proposed as the key to building a base for computer science or engineering. As the third stage of programming progressed, it was clear that system programs

---

5. This comment is applicable to programmers. Many people who use terminals occasionally to solve problems are free to use other methods if the computer is unavailable. Instead of thinking of the people who use interactive terminals for problem-solving as programmers, think of them as engineers, managers, librarians, accountants, physicists, etc., who use a computer in their work. They should not have to know much about programming, since a well-designed computer-assisted training aid can be built into the interactive system.

were beginning to dominate the programming business. This provided counterevidence to the language proposal, since most successful languages were unable to express the functions used in system programs (pointer manipulation, list-processing, syntax procedures) in a convenient form. They were also weak in regard to linking together and testing large programs. Fortunately, third-stage studies showed that there was no theoretical bar to expressing these functions. They had previously been omitted because individual programmers had seen no need for them. Since these functions were most important in projects being programmed by a group, languages for system programming had to facilitate group activity. This required, in addition to readability, features for linking program units and for segregating tested units from units in process. The latter requirements call for a library maintenance and control system in addition to a compiler.

Another feature proven useful in time-shared problem-solving systems, such as BASIC and APL/360, is the ability to interact with the program in process. The problem solver can write a sequence of instructions and immediately assign values to the variables and execute the sequence. This procedure catches errors in logic as they occur. Applying this technique to system programming is harder (although when it exists, the same symbiosis occurs for expert programmers) because incremental execution of a large program frequently calls for information not currently available to existing interpreters and compilers.

Support of this type is again a blend of technical and managerial procedures. The development-support tools (listed below) range from simple manual procedures to elaborate automated systems, and they are used for various parts of the project.

- A *time-sharing system* by itself permits individual programmers to code and debug efficiently.

- A *job-control system* by itself can collect and label all completed programs. Then it can monitor changes to each program and ensure that the changes have been authorized.

- *An automatic program-analysis and documentation system* fills a need of the group by getting individuals to explain their programs in a way that others can understand.

- The development of a *model* of the system program and its associated hardware helps ensure the completeness of the design. It can then be used to simulate the performance of the system. By maintaining the model and replacing its parts with actual program units as the project progresses, one can predict system performance with a high degree of accuracy. The addition of a *statistics-gathering device* (software or hardware) permits measurement of the actual operating program to evaluate its performance.

■ A *program-support library* combining most of the previous features spans the life of the project. Initially, it captures the system specifications in a form that can be stored in the computer. It can also store information on assignments of individuals and interactions between people and programs. Later, it gathers the programs as they are written, either off-line or on-line, and edits them to see that they conform to specifications and standards. By manual or automated means it controls who can inspect, modify, or use the programs. It collects administrative data, including statistics on performance of people and programs. Finally, it maintains the authorized version of the completed system.

It is quite possible to implement each concept in a variety of ways to fit a budget. The one factor they all have in common is the constraint they place on a programmer's individuality. They call for the individual to conform to rules which benefit the group. As it turns out, though, the constraints affect only how a programmer uses resources shared by others. Individual creativity regarding the way an assigned unit of programming is written is seldom affected.

1.12 MANAGEMENT TRENDS

The fact that both technical and managerial solutions exist to a system programming problem reemphasizes the changing nature of programming. First-stage programmers faced only the complexity of a problem statement. Third-stage programmers also have to face the complexity of interactions among many variables, some of which are poorly understood and some of which are mutually inconsistent. Bringing order out of chaos is a management function; therefore the system programming job is increasingly oriented to management-like functions.

The evolution of the program development process from an individual activity to a group activity involving complex technology was by no means obvious. It was a sequence of subtle natural-seeming changes. Analysis of the changes was often due to the need for explaining a major project failure. As a result, most management decisions were made to correct mistakes rather than to prepare for the future.

1.12.1 Fitting the Problem to the Programmer

Managers concentrated first on getting projects under control and eliminating unnecessary complexities. The methods available were aimed at fitting the problem to the programmer (Fig. 1.7). Taking a cue from hardware engineers, software managers recognized the need for a baseline specification for the job to be done. The procedures could be copied from similar procedures used in building large hardware systems—with perhaps the best

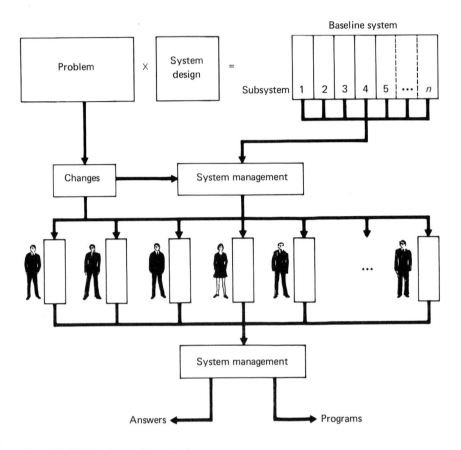

Fig. 1.7 Fitting the problem to the programmer.

guide being the "configuration management" procedures used by the U.S. Department of Defense (DOD) and the National Aeronautics and Space Administration (NASA) [7].

Implementation of the procedures is not trivial. First, to specify a baseline, one must assume mutual agreement between the programming group and the user. But since programs are hard to specify in detail and because many users lack the ability to spell out their requirements, mutuality may not be achievable. Second, because there are so many people involved in a programming project, each of whom interprets the specification uniquely, the specification is too fluid to be a real baseline. Third, the programmers can contact the user and negotiate changes outside the scope of the baseline. Control of these problems is achieved by introducing a new function of *system management.* The system management team calls for the problem to be subdivided into functional units by the designers. Great care is exerted to make each unit self-sufficient, communicating with other units or data files only through well-defined interfaces that are clearly covered in the baseline specification. Now, with a standard organization,[6] each individual can be given an assignment small enough to handle and carefully isolated from the rest of the system. When it is time to reassemble the program units into a system, the system management team is responsible for controlling the interactions. This ensures that there are no omissions or illogical links in the design. Only the system management group has the authority to change the baseline, and by funneling all user contacts through its office, the group can limit changes to those which are technically and economically feasible.

The system management approach works for the following reasons.

- It reduces the workload of the individual programmer by limiting each assignment to a single unit of the system.
- It identifies and monitors communication points in the system where interactions can occur.
- It identifies and explicitly adopts or rejects changes to the specified job.
- It separates management of system structure (the interactions) from internals (the program units).
- It makes each individual's responsibility clear.

The method also prevents surprise when it incorporates frequent reviews of project status. All this is accomplished at the cost of the system management umbrella superimposed on the basic development organization. Programmers are still asked to know all the tools and techniques available, although for practical purposes they do not. Instead, they use a small subset of the current technology. If the subset is applicable to the job, they will perform well; otherwise, their programs will be below average.

1.12.2   Fitting the Programmer to the Problem

At the same time that managers of ongoing projects have been resorting to system management techniques to control their jobs, another approach has been proposed for new projects. The object of the alternative is to fit the programmer to the job, i.e., to make it possible for one person to do

---

6. A standard organization is a pyramid with the most experienced people at the top and the junior people at the bottom. The number of people at each experience level is inversely proportional to their experience. Each pyramid is headed by one manager, who sets objectives, resolves conflicts, and directs activities.

a large job more or less the way it was done in the first stage of programming development. For this purpose, it would be necessary to compress the entire technology, which is now too large for one person to handle, to a manageable size. The compression must not leave out anything; therefore it must depend on summarizing basic principles rather than preserving technical details. Formalization of "computer science" or "software engineering" would obviously contribute to this goal. And, as is true with a physicist or a nuclear reactor engineer, the programmer would have to be a very special individual, capable of assimilating and applying the science and technology. It is also true that, just as a nuclear reactor engineer can call on a construction specialist to build a shielding enclosure, the programmer should be able to call on an operating system specialist or a language specialist to provide needed expert support at the detail level. The Chief Programmer Team approach is based on this reasoning.

A standard organization pushes performance to the bottom of the pyramid while retaining management responsibility at the top. By contrast, a Chief Programmer Team is organized so as to focus responsibility for performance as well as management on the programmer in charge. The typical team consists of the following members [8].

1. Chief Programmer—a highly qualified programmer of great breadth, able to take full personal responsibility (see Fig. 1.2) for defining, programming, testing, and installing a large system.

2. Backup Programmer—a highly qualified programmer, who works with the Chief on the design of the system nucleus and code sections of the program as directed. The main role, however, is to support the Chief by providing models, test cases, and analyses that verify the design.

3. Librarian—a nonprofessional assistant to the Chief Programmer, whose duties are similar to those of a secretary but include the handling of programs as well as correspondence. In particular, the Librarian performs all the clerical tasks associated with the development support system.

The team may also include a system analyst/programmer, whose job is to determine user requirements and program user-oriented functions. Other programmers can be added on large jobs to code specific functions, such as mathematical routines. Such assignments reduce the Chief's workload but do not relieve him of responsibility for each line of delivered code. External support for the team can be provided by a project manager, who handles business aspects of the project, and experts, available on call, who can handle specific in-depth technical questions.

As shown in Fig. 1.8, the Chief Programmer Team takes on the whole problem as a unit. When they encounter a need for support, they use an

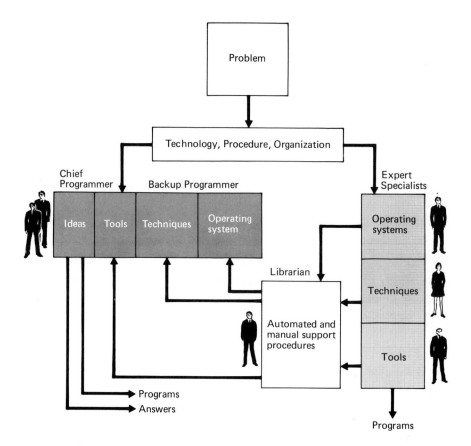

Fig. 1.8 Fitting the programmer to the problem.

existing support tool or they call on the expert specialists. As much of the project and its support as possible is automated. To avoid getting the programmers involved in the mechanics of the automated system, the Librarian is the interface with the machine.

A Chief Programmer Team should probably not exceed six people. Larger groups lead to a hierarchy of managers, with associated communication problems. A key element of the Chief Programmer approach is the minimization of system interactions by focusing all design and implementation on one person. If this element is lost, the group rapidly turns into a standard pyramid. The limited size of the Chief Programmer Team places an upper limit on the size of the problem the team can undertake. However, the limit is indeterminate because it depends on the skill of the team, the stability and analytic simplicity of the problem, and the tools and techniques that are applicable. A Chief Programmer Team will usually expect to accomplish the same results as a standard organization two to five times as large. Since it is unlikely that any major project will be done twice, making comparison of the approaches possible, a valid ratio may never be obtained. On the other hand, Figs. 1.2 through 1.8 show that the *ideas* needed to solve a system programming job of any size have offered a constant level of challenge to the programmer over the years. There should be no obstacle to the Chief Programmer's understanding of any job that is feasible for a larger organization. Understanding does not imply that implementation is feasible. Mastery of the applicable tools and techniques is also required. From this discussion, it appears that the system management and Chief Programmer approaches will coexist in the fourth stage of program development.

1.13 FOURTH STAGE

The fourth stage of program development is the stage of the mid-1970s. System programming has advanced to the point where normal business controls and measurements can be applied. Improvements in programming effectiveness should be measured against such goals as the following [9].

- Reduced dollar costs and/or higher profits
- Increased product quality and reduced maintenance
- Improved employee satisfaction and growth
- Shorter delivery schedules
- Improved position for future activities

To reduce costs, which are primarily based on programmer man-hours and computer usage, two routes can be followed.

1. Reduce man-hours and computer usage.
2. Reduce cost per hour of manpower and computer.

The first route will also contribute to shorter delivery schedules, which are often proportional to applied resources. Both routes will improve product quality and employee relations if they take advantage of the best features of system management and organization demonstrated in the 1960s.

Man and machine hours are reduced by (a) making better machine service and automated development tools available and (b) giving these tools to the programmers best equipped to use them. Thus the most productive people are made more productive. Cost per hour is reduced by defining jobs for lower-salaried employees, such as high school graduates with secretarial or limited coding skills. Quality is improved because system design

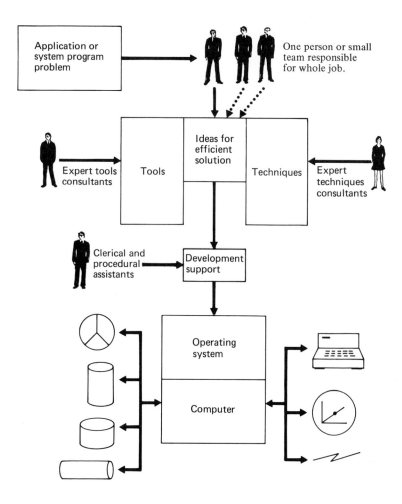

Fig. 1.9 Programming: fourth stage.

is executed by a small group of very skilled programmers rather than distributed across a large pyramid of mixed skills. Employees appreciate the results because each one has a better-defined job. In terms of personnel administration, each job is structured so that it is a challenging and respectable assignment for the person qualified to fill it. Employees' achievement will be evident to them and others, and they will find they are competing for promotion against their peers, not against more skilled employees.

In summary (Fig. 1.9), the fourth stage of program development will emphasize small teams of specialized individuals: broad-based expert programmers, narrow-based expert programmers, and subprofessional assistants. Where possible, these teams will be organized around the Chief Programmer to simplify project control. Projects too large for a Chief Programmer Team will be organized in a standard pyramid, with system management controls superimposed to control communication and interactions.[7] In both cases, maximum use will be made of standard tools and techniques designed for knowledgeable users. The fourth stage will look more like the first and second stages than like the third in that it will consist of tasks, each of which can be done by one person who is uniquely qualified to do it.

The feasibility of the fourth-generation approach depends on the ability to define intellectually manageable programs. As Professor E. W. Dijkstra pointed out in his Turing Award Lecture (on receiving the Turing Award from the Association for Computing Machinery, August 14, 1972), this can be done, "provided that we approach the task with a full appreciation of its tremendous difficulty, provided that we stick to modest and elegant programming languages, provided that we respect the intrinsic limitations of the human mind and approach the task as Very Humble Programmers" [10].

1.14   THE PLAN OF THE BOOK

In the foregoing review of the history of programming, it has been possible to highlight several trends. The most important trend has been the shift toward group activities. It is significant that the top managers in the 1970s were programmers in the 1950s and 1960s. Since that time, they have not been sufficiently involved in the details of programming to be aware of the fundamental difference between individual and group programming. Their first reaction to a reported problem is "That type of problem was easy for me to solve. Why is it so hard for you?" The fact that a given programming problem may have one solution when the program stands alone and another when the program is embedded in a system escapes notice.

To avoid confusing the reader by mixing the attributes of small and large jobs, this book is organized to treat individual jobs first. Part 1 is mostly about programming. Part 2 introduces a number of activities that are required when several people are working as a team. It is mostly about project management.

In each section, the unique features due to the size of the project will be emphasized. Obviously, many features are common to all levels of system size. In particular, the things an individual programmer must do to write

---

7. When the subsystems of Fig. 1.7 are suitable for Chief Programmer Team implementation, the standard pyramid may be a collection of teams.

a single program unit are independent of the size of the system to which that unit belongs. There are other useful concepts that help clarify why programs behave the way they do. Some of the more important of these are collected in Chapter 2. They help explain some of the jargon used later, and they establish the point of view that many software managers take toward the process they manage.

REFERENCES

1. Von Neumann, J., and H. H. Goldstine, *Planning and Coding of Problems for an Electronic Computing Instrument,* Vol. 1–3. Reprinted in A. H. Taub (ed.), *John Von Neumann: Collected Works,* Vol. 5, pp. 1–235. New York: MacMillan, 1963.

2. Wilkes, M. V., D. J. Wheeler, and S. Gill, *The Preparation of Programs for an Electronic Digital Computer, with Special Reference to the EDSAC and the Use of a Library of Subroutines.* Cambridge, Mass.: Addison-Wesley, 1951.

3. Orchard-Hays, W., "The Evolution of Programming Systems." *Proceedings of the IRE,* Vol. 49, No. 1, January 1961.

4. "Curriculum 68—Recommendations for Academic Programs in Computer Science," a report of the ACM Curriculum Committee on Computer Science. *Communications of the ACM,* Vol. 11, No. 3, March 1968.

5. "Software Engineering Education," Section 6. *Techniques in Software Engineering,* John Buxton and Brian Randell (eds), report on a conference sponsored by the NATO Science Committee, October 27–31, 1969.

6. Sammet, J. E., *Programming Languages: History and Fundamentals.* Englewood Cliffs, N.J.: Prentice-Hall, 1969.

7. Air Force Systems Command Manuals
   AFSCM 310-1 *Management of Contractor Data and Reports*
   AFSCM 375-5 *Systems Engineering Management Procedures*
   Air Force Military Standards
   MIL(USAF)STD-483 *Configuration Management Practice for Systems, Equipment, Munitions, and Computer Programs*
   These and similar manuals from other government agencies can be obtained from the Superintendent of Documents, U.S. Government Printing Office, Washington, D.C.

8. Baker, F. T., "Chief Programmer Team Management of Production Programming." *IBM Systems Journal,* Vol. 11, No. 1, 1972.

9. Sammet, J. E., "Perspective on Methods of Improving Software Development." *Software Engineering,* Vol. 1. New York and London: Academic Press, 1970.

10. Dijkstra, E. W., "The Humble Programmer." *Communications of the ACM,* Vol. 15, No. 10, October 1972.

2
Some
Useful
Concepts

This book stresses the importance of good communication as a factor in successful project development. Whenever information must be transferred between people, it is modified by the communication process. "Good communication" permits the essential message to be received and understood well enough for the receiver to appreciate the full intent of the transmitter. The most common test of communication quality is to observe whether the receiver acts the way you expected, given the information in the message. It helps for both parties to agree on the meaning of the most commonly used words. That is why in this chapter a small number of key words are defined.

This book is about the *program development process*. The process is viewed as an organized set of activities that produces a program system. In this sense, the program development process is analogous to engineering processes that produce computer hardware or bridges or buildings. But being analogous to engineering does not mean that program development is the same as hardware development. Some of the differences between software and hardware are explained below. The analogy holds in one important respect: success of the process is more a management problem than a technical problem. *Designing* a bridge takes a lot of technical know-how about stress analysis, properties of materials, load forecasting. But *building* a bridge is more concerned with recruiting, parts stockpiling, scheduling, subcontract management, budgeting, etc. The program development process *builds* program systems. Thus this book does not deal with inner details of specific programs. It deals with planning and organizing, resource management, project control, and decision-making. Sufficient data is provided on tools and techniques to show how they are used and how their use is justified, but the reader is referred elsewhere for details on how they work. On the other hand, the things a project manager must do personally are spelled out completely.

There are several places in the text where guidelines are given. They are based on "conventional wisdom," which is nothing more than the consensus of opinion of experienced people. Sometimes a guideline is backed up by some statistical data, but more often, in the poorly measured world of programming, there is no proof that the data applies to new situations. What, then, is the purpose of guidelines?

The purpose is to provide some light in the darkness. Many managers do not know where to start in laying out an organization or estimating the resources for a large job. The guidelines tell how successful experienced managers have approached the problem in the past. To the extent that the guidelines fit the current situation, they offer a conservative, achievable approach. The manager can trust them for two reasons. First, all that is really needed is a safe ballpark figure for planning purposes. With that, the manager can accept the responsibility for carrying the job to a successful conclusion. The guidelines provide that ballpark estimate.

Second, there is an underlying conceptual basis for the guidelines. They all are based on the belief that a fundamental unit of work and a basic theory of systems cause programming projects to behave the way they do. In physics, the fundamental unit is the electron and the system behavior theory is the Rutherford-Bohr model of the atom. In systems programming, no such elegant theories exist, but borrowing from other fields, programmers can consider the fundamental unit of work to be the maximum single task one programmer can handle. The system behavior theory can be the theory of organization used in the social sciences.

Some of these useful concepts will be discussed in this chapter after the key words are defined.

2.1   KEY WORDS

System: a structured aggregate of elements that satisfies a set of functional and performance specifications. The "structured" attribute means that all the elements in the system are interrelated and may interact. A picture of a system looks like an organization chart or a communications network. Each element can be separately described and may have nonsystem functions; however, within the system the element is completely described only when its interconnections with other elements are shown. A system has at

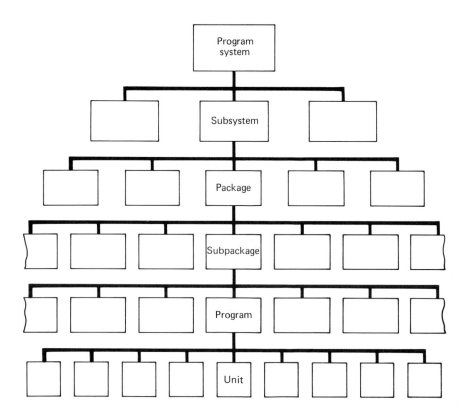

Fig. 2.1 Program system terminology.

least two elements, but the term "system" generally connotes many elements. Small collections of elements can be treated as nonsystems without much risk. Large collections are dominated by structural considerations and must be looked at as systems to be understood. All systems of interest have a purpose. In particular, program systems should have clear specifications of what they will do and how they will perform. Note that system elements need not be homogeneous. The elements of a program system project may include programs, computers, programmers, other personnel, data files, supplies, buildings, etc.

Program system: a system whose deliverable elements are computer programs and their related documentation (Fig. 2.1).

Computer system: a system whose deliverable elements are various hardware devices, interconnected to provide means for input/output, storage, arithmetic, and control.

System program: a program or a program system that is designed to make a computer system more productive or easier to use.

Application program: a program or a program system that solves a user's problem.

System of procedures: a collection of related directives, usually documented in a procedures manual. The system of procedures makes the independent activities of many individuals manageable as an ensemble. An activity is *systematic* when it follows a system of procedures.

Subsystem: a logical part of a system that is itself a system.

Data processing system: a system whose subsystems include a computer system and appropriate system and application programs.

Program: a sequence of instructions or steps that completely describes a purposeful procedure. The sense of this definition is that a program is precise and exhaustive. It is usually written in a highly stylized manner and may use a unique language. The definition obviously fits computer programs, and in the text, "program" is synonymous with "computer program." It also fits other precisely sequenced activities: television schedules, sporting events, instructions for automatic tools, etc. (One common use of the word will be avoided in this book. "Program" is used by large organizations, especially the U.S. government, to describe a major system undertaking. In this usage, "program" implies coordination of technical and financial plans with executive decisions. To avoid confusion, the term "project" will be used in the text to describe such activities.)

Computer program: a program that can be executed on a computer to transform or use data. Every computer program is a system since it is a structured aggregate of computer instructions, subprograms, etc. However, a computer program is not normally thought of as a system unless its development involves several programmers (i.e., the program is too big for one person to build) or it is intended to be part of a larger system.

> *Source program:*   a computer program written by a programmer in a programming language (which may be a machine language, a symbolic macro assembly language, or a more natural high-level language).

> *Object program:*   a computer program executable by a machine. The object program is derived from the source program by a translation process, where necessary.

Subprogram: a logical unit of a program. Subprograms may contain smaller subprograms. It is convenient to give a subprogram a name that indicates its function as well as its place in the programming system structure.

Routine: a section of a program or a subprogram that has been isolated for identification. It may or may not have a recognizable logical function. In the text, "routine" and "subprogram" will be used interchangeably when it is unnecessary to distinguish a logical unit. "Routine" may also be used in its common adjectival sense of "ordinary" or "repetitive" when no ambiguity will result.

Computer program package: a logically related collection of subprograms and routines that can be integrated and tested independent of the rest of the program. Obviously, a package is a subsystem of a program. The term is often used to refer to hierarchical levels within large subsystems. "Package" is preferred when describing computer programs. "System" is generally used for the broader concept of "programs and their environment." "Package" is also used to describe the physical, deliverable package of tapes, cards, disks, documents that is the end product of a development effort.

Program unit: the smallest defined module of a program system. If the program structure flowchart is a tree, the units are the end points of the branches. Units are normally assigned to individual programmers. Thus there is an analogy between the program tree with program units at the lowest level and the organization tree with individual programmers at the lowest level. A unit may consist of more than one program, just as an individual in an organization may be expected to perform more than one task. A program unit is a *unit of work* rather than a unit of code.

Programming: the process of defining, designing, developing, and installing programs.

   Coding: the activity of writing the source statements of a program.

   Debugging: the activity of detecting, diagnosing, and correcting errors (the "bugs") in a program. In this book, debugging is always done by the original programmer. It can be done by examination, by desk checking, or by dynamically exercising the program on a computer, using test data.

   Testing: the activity of exercising a program to determine if it is correct, that is, to see that the program gives the correct results for all the specified test conditions. In this book, testing is always done by someone other than the original programmer.[1]

---

1. Debugging is called *unit testing* in many projects. Here a distinction is made between looking for errors in your own work and looking at someone else's work. For that reason, "testing" is not used in describing unit debugging. Given a choice, managers should have programmers do their own debugging; therefore the definition used in the text implies a preferred way of proceeding.

Project: an activity organized to accomplish an assigned task. The goal of the project is usually to deliver an end product to a *user*. The user may establish an internal project organization or may purchase the product from a *vendor*. Quite often, the user has an agent, the *buyer*, who negotiates with the vendor. Thus the vendor's *customer* may be either the user or the buyer.

2.2 INDIVIDUAL CONCEPTUAL ABILITY

Concept: The maximum size of a unit of programming is determined by the programmer's conceptual ability.

A program unit is the smallest defined module of a program system, and it is usually assigned to one programmer. Surprisingly, the size of a program unit is predictable within limits. That is, when experienced programmers are asked, "How large is the typical program unit?" they give answers ranging up to about 1000 lines of assembly language source statement. Until 1972, the response fell in the range of 400–1000 lines. Since the advent of structured programming, which emphasizes style, modularity, and correctness, a consensus has developed that small units are generally better than large ones, and the range of response is shrinking to 50–200 lines. Clearly, the size of a unit is limited by its function. If a meaningful subprogram can be coded in only 10 lines, it can still be called a subprogram and assigned as a unit. The significance of the consensus regarding unit size is that it recognizes an upper limit for "good" units.

Even more striking is the fact that each designer has a personal modal value for unit size, and so has each manager. The question put to designers is "When you have completed your design and the job is ready to be assigned to individual programmers for implementation, how large do you expect the finished program to be?" Managers are asked, "When you assign tasks to your programmers, what is the average size of the program unit they produce?" To either question the usual answer—after some hesitation—is a single number, less than 1000 when discussing machine language or less than 200 when talking about higher-level languages prior to 1972. In other words, managers as a group assign programs smaller than 1000 lines, but each individual manager assigns programs of a specific characteristic size. He can calibrate his own behavior because it is reasonably repeatable.

This self-calibration is obviously useful as an estimating aid, as will be explained in Part 2. But why does it work? No one knows. One possible reason has intuitive appeal: a program unit is the largest conceptual unit that can be effectively communicated between two people. With reference to the opening paragraph of this chapter, "effective communication" involves transmission, reception, and understanding. Managers give instruc-

tions to programmers orally or in writing. A manager assigns enough work
to be certain that a programmer can take the instructions, go away for some
length of time, and return with the job done. The manager's thought runs:
"I know Joe is pretty good with this type of problem, and I expect to be
busy with other responsibilities, so I will give him a good, healthy assignment. If I am perfectly clear in my instructions, I won't have to hold his
hand for a few weeks." Thus the manager maximizes the scope of Joe's
assignment while being careful not to overload or confuse him. Designers
work in a similar way. They carry the design down to the level of detail
where any good programmer can understand how to carry a given unit to
completion. (As implied, managers are more likely to take a programmer's
actual ability into account.)

A similar phenomenon occurs in business data processing. Traditionally,
business problems are identified by accountants, personnel specialists, middle management, or other operating-level employees.[2] The problems tend
to be addressed one at a time [1]. An accountant will call in an analyst/pro-
grammer from the information systems department, explain the problem,
work out the details regarding data inputs and report outputs, and then
rely on the analyst/programmer to develop a computerized solution. There
are no system implications; the problem is treated as an isolated case. Except
for clarification of details or concurrence on procedures, there is little contact
between the user and the developer until the finished program is submitted
for acceptance. From agreement on what must be done until delivery, the
time involved is no more than 4–6 weeks. The programmer seldom needs
help. (If there are co-workers to speed up the process, it takes 4–6 program-
mer-weeks.) There appears to be a direct correlation between 400–1000 lines
of code and 4–6 weeks of programming effort.

What is happening here? The designer, manager, and accountant are
all doing the same thing. They are conceiving the maximum program unit
that they can communicate to a programmer who, understanding the requirement, can develop a program without further guidance. Why does this
lead to such small program units? First, the problem statement is limited
by the conceptual ability of the initiator. Second, communicability is limited
by the language of discourse and the two parties' fluency in the language.
Third, the interpretation placed on the problem statement is limited by the
programmer's conceptual ability. The kinds of people employed in each of
the job categories have similar educational and cultural backgrounds, and

---

2. This statement applies to those tasks that actually get programmed. Higher-
level executives often ask for seemingly simple things in vague terms, but on examination, their requests often prove to be impractical. Only after extensive analysis
and study are the implementable tasks defined by lower-level employees.

apparently they have similar conceptual limits. Therefore they have no difficulty in communicating with one another. Experiments aimed at integrating disadvantaged high school dropouts into professional programming groups showed that typical program assignments had to be carried to a lower level of detailed design before the programmers could proceed. Once they understood the assignment, however, their programming was comparable to that of college graduates working on larger units. Similar results were observed for junior programmers with impaired communications channels due to deafness or blindness.

There are a number of consequences of limited conceptual ability.

- The maximum size of a program unit should not exceed the conceptual limit of the programmer. Managers must avoid imputing to their employees their own superior ability to understand complex concepts. (This statement may sound facetious, but it is frequently true that an individual is promoted to management because of demonstrated conceptual breadth, as opposed to meticulous handling of details.)

- An assignment that is complex enough to exceed the capacity of one person will be further complicated by the burden of interface control among the assignees.

- Complex concepts cannot be understood equally well at all levels of an organization hierarchy.

- Higher-level managers must deal with abstractions which retain the important generalizations about the problem but omit details.

- Communications between various levels of an organization are subject to error because each participant has a unique concept of the job.

- Some jobs are inconceivable. That is, a job may be so big that no one can state a clear picture of it at any level of abstraction that other people can understand and work with. Inconceivable goals must be redefined in terms of conceivable goals before a project can be carried out. (In practice, this leads to the implementation of very large jobs in several phases; the first phase is delivered with basic capabilities, and later phases add enhancements.)

A corollary of individual conceptual ability is the simplicity and relatively lower potential for error that occurs when the number of concepts a programmer must understand is minimized. As indicated in Chapter 1, the tools and techniques used in programming should be logical and easy to use. If they aren't, they compete for attention with the problem to be programmed.

2.3 SPAN OF ATTENTION—SPAN OF CONTROL

Concept: A manager's span of control is limited by the number of independent, interrelated activities he or she can handle.

In his classic paper "The Magical Number Seven . . ." [2], Professor G. A. Miller showed that there are definite upper limits to an individual's perception. Stated in terms of the number of different items an individual can accurately identify, the limit is seven. Miller studied responses to various one-dimensional stimuli, such as pitch and loudness of tones, salinity of fluids, and relative position of a point on a line. He found that all the experiments leveled off in the same manner. Miller refers to this ability to discriminate up to seven things of the same type the *span of absolute judgment.* The average value for all his experiments was 6.5 categories of discrimination. When there are multiple dimensions to the experiment, such as loudness and pitch combined, a subject can recognize more categories—up to 100–150 with up to 10 dimensions of stimuli. However, the added clues are not perfect; for instance, loudness and pitch do not lead to $6 \times 5 = 30$ recognizable categories—they lead to only 8 or 9.

Miller refers to another type of test in which subjects were asked to report the number of dots in a square briefly flashed on a screen. In tests of this type, the subjects were always accurate when there were no more than six dots in the pattern. When there were more than six, they made errors. This breakpoint, again at the number seven, is called the *span of attention.* For numbers within their span of attention, subjects *know* the answer; outside their span of attention, they have to *estimate* (leading to errors) or *count* (consuming a lot of time).

If we carry these concepts over into the development process, it is possible to establish the span of control that is appropriate for most managers. The results published by Miller can be compared with empirical results published in management literature. For example, Colonel L. F. Urwick recommends that no supervisor be asked to manage more than five, or at most six, subordinates whose work interlocks [3]. He bases this principle on rules of thumb established in military organizations and large corporations. Experience had shown that *teamwork* involves the coordination of the independent but interrelated activities of all the team members. Furthermore, managers knew they were overloaded when the team began to miss objectives or when internal cliques began to form to the detriment of the team as a whole. The overload condition occurred when, on the average, the manager had more than seven people. Again, the magical seven appears. V. A. Graicunas, a friend of Urwick, explains the limit on the span of management control another way. Graicunas tabulated all the relationships that can exist in an organization of M subordinates. He treats each possible relationship—i.e., manager-employee, employee-employee, and employee-group of employees—as an influence on the manager's decision. He counts an employee's attitude toward each peer as a separate issue. The total number of relationships is a measure of the complexity of the manager's job. The formula Graicunas derived [4] for the number of relationships is

$$R = M(2^{M-1} + M - 1).$$

Thus a manager with five subordinates has 100 possible relationships, one with eight subordinates has 1080, and one with twelve has 24,708, according to Graicunas. Other estimates of complexity ignore relationships between employee and employee group on the basis that they are too subtle to be significant. This approach still leaves

$$R = \frac{M(M+1)}{2}.$$

The span of control problem leads to the recommendation, in programming organizations, that a first-level manager have 4–8 programmers. There may be several nonprogrammers as well (such as a secretary). The guideline attempts to ensure that, at any given time, the manager has a manageable span of attention. That is, the manager can always recognize all the things that are going on and can discriminate among them to identify those that are currently in need of attention.

The guideline is especially applicable in systems programming because, by its nature, systems programming is a team activity. Each programmer operates on his or her own initiative, doing a complex intellectual task. Yet all of the programmer's work is affected by what the other team members are doing. This is the hardest type of team to manage because the content of the work is simultaneously complex and intangible. Fortunately, tasks can be assigned in such a way that the important interactions are spread out in time among team members. Thus the manager may never be faced with more than two or three independent, interrelated intellectual activities to manage simultaneously. Sometimes, the job will subdivide nicely and there will be few important interactions, so that one manager can control 8–12 programmers. It is risky to organize this way, however, because such a large group lacks the flexibility to respond to a crisis without losing control.

The value of these guidelines is that, when coupled with the unit of work described in Section 2.2, they provide a rational basis for estimating the resources required to build a programming system.

2.4 COMPLEXITY

Concept: The complexity of a system is proportional to the square of the number of its units.

Graicunas's observation—that a manager must take into account not only the direct manager-employee relationships but also the attitudes that each employee holds toward other team members—stresses the importance of interpersonal relations to management decisions. One might assume that planning and controlling inanimate programs is a lot simpler than managing people because there are no interpersonal relations. That is not true, however. In a program system, it is possible for every program unit to interact with every other. The units can exchange or share data. They can pass control information back and forth. And, when programs are poorly designed or when transient computer errors are present, they can change one another. A good design minimizes these interactions, as is shown in Volume 2, but it may not reduce the number enough to make the system manageable.

The simplest measure of complexity for program systems requires the assumption that there can be one path from any element to any other. The potential number of interactions is

$$I = \frac{N(N-1)}{2},$$

where N is the number of units in the system. Since program systems can have very large N, their complexity can easily get out of hand. Miller teaches that a person can handle up to seven things at a time and, given sufficient clues, can recognize on the order of a hundred categories of information. Thus, when I is much larger than 100 and the project is very dynamic so that many problems can arise simultaneously, the manager has a very complex and perhaps unmanageable task. Figure 2.2 shows that whether you are dealing with a system of people or a system of inanimate objects, the number of interactions is very large for even relatively small numbers of elements. Furthermore, the number of interactions grows much faster than the number of elements. Two conclusions can be drawn.

1. It is essential to organize and design a system in such a way that no one manager has more elements than he or she can handle. (The most universal solution used is a hierarchical structure.)

2. For all but the smallest systems, interactions rather than people or program units dominate the manager's attention. Project controls are required to identify and monitor the system interactions in order to manage the system.

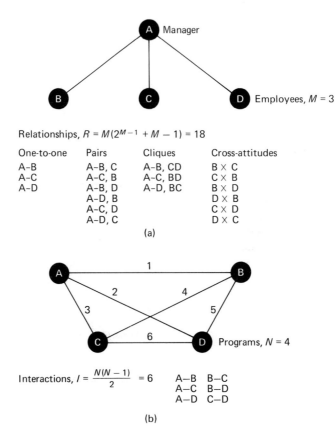

Relationships, $R = M(2^{M-1} + M - 1) = 18$

One-to-one	Pairs	Cliques	Cross-attitudes
A–B	A–B, C	A–B, CD	B × C
A–C	A–C, B	A–C, BD	C × B
A–D	A–B, D	A–D, BC	B × D
	A–D, B		D × B
	A–C, D		C × D
	A–D, C		D × C

(a)

Interactions, $I = \dfrac{N(N-1)}{2} = 6$ A—B B—C
A—C B—D
A—D C—D

(b)

People		Things	
M	*R*	*N*	*I*
1	1	3	3
2	6	9	36
4	44	27	351
8	1,080	81	3,240
16	524,528	243	29,403

(c)

Fig. 2.2 Complexity of systems: (a) a system of people, in which each employee's behavior is influenced by the presence of others and by the employee's attitude toward others; (b) a system of programs; (c) relative complexity.

A good, well-established, and proven design approach that suits large systems involves a tree structure with minimal cross-communication between units on different branches of the tree. In an organization of people, this structure is a hierarchy with a strong chain of command. In a program system, it is a top-down design of modular programs.

Referring again to the definition of *system,* note that the nature of the elements of a system is not spelled out. System managers will learn that anything that affects their plans and controls is an element of the system they are managing. They must deal with people as well as programs, support tools as well as deliverables, machine resources as well as office space, budgets as well as progress reports, subcontracts as well as in-house agreements, etc. The diversity of these elements multiplies the potential complexity of the system. System managers are always more likely to be surprised by the number of problems they face than bored by a lack of challenge. By stressing the "square law: I is proportional to N^2," one can keep reminding the manager that complexity is a major concern that deserves attention.

2.5 SOFTWARE VERSUS HARDWARE

Concept: One important way in which software differs from hardware is that all important design decisions occur early in the software development life cycle.

System development proceeds from project definition through design to implementation, test, production, operations, and maintenance. This obvious fact has led many people to assume that software development should follow the time-tested procedures used for hardware development. They have assumed that minor differences between software and hardware (such as a paper product instead of electronics or a single product instead of a manufacturing line) do not affect the development life cycle. In fact, these differences have a significant impact on the relative importance of decisions made at various points in the life cycle. Their effect is immediately evident in a chart of the project cost as a function of time (Fig. 2.3). Software projects incur their peak expenses during implementation and test.[3] Hardware projects peak during the production stage.

The most profitable hardware project is one which invests a reasonable amount of resource in building an engineering prototype and then exercises and reworks the prototype machine to find the least expensive way to manufacture copies. This *product engineering* phase occurs at the end of the

---

3. Some general-purpose operating systems incur much higher maintenance costs (as shown in Part 2) because of the need to respond to the requirements of many users. Total cost, however, is minimized by a good initial design.

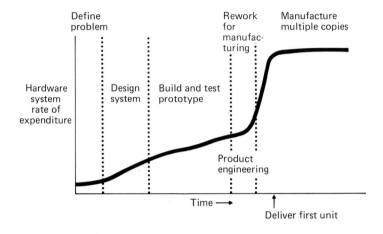

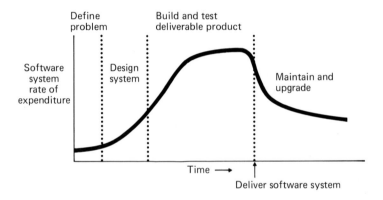

Fig. 2.3 Software versus hardware.

prototype development and test phase. If it is done well, the instructions to the plant will call for the fewest, lowest-cost parts and the simplest, least expensive production processes necessary to assemble a machine with all the required functions and features. In other words, the prototype is reworked to define the lowest *unit cost* of production. Then the manufacturing cost will be minimized and the total project cost will be minimized.

The same approach, when applied to software, results in maximum project cost, because there is no software "manufacturing" to compare with the production phase of a hardware project. In fact, the first complete software system (corresponding to the hardware prototype) is the only version of the software system required. One payroll program is enough for one payroll department. Even when the software system is a widely distributed operating system or compiler, to make copies by reproducing the master tape or disk is a simple matter. The production of copies of a computer program is a library control process, not a manufacturing and assembly process. What this means to software managers and designers is that they must do all their tradeoff analyses and try to make all the critical design decisions before the implementation phase starts. The end product of the implementation, when tested, is complete and deliverable. Changes during implementation are allowed when they are necessary to correct design errors or when they improve the design on the basis of information discovered during implementation. Changes after implementation and test are discouraged. After all, if the original design specified all the functions and features requested by the user, and if the tested system has all those functions and features, it is the least expensive version of the program that will ever exist. Any work done after test necessarily increases total project cost. The only justification for such expenditures is that requirements have changed. Thus, if the delivered program runs too slowly to satisfy the user, it may be cost-effective to spend some effort to improve its performance. The performance objective represents a new (or modified) requirement. It costs money to meet the new objective.

In summary, the minimum software project cost is achieved by doing the best possible design so that the first version of the system can be delivered. The development team must be constantly aware of the importance of getting the implementation plan right to start with, since there will be few opportunities to make it right after it has been built. The user, likewise, must be sure to include all requirements in the initial statement of work. A good software system contains only the necessary features. Gratuitous frills supplied by the system developer increase both system cost and system complexity.[4] Thus the best way to ensure mutual satisfaction between the user and the developer is to agree on a statement of work and deliver only what is required by that statement. Not that this is easy to accomplish. On the contrary, users tend to cram everything they can think of into their requirements, and they do not hesitate to request changes at any time. An optimum software plan is hard to achieve under these circumstances; however, strong management controls can moderate the consequences of user indecision.

2.6 DOCUMENTATION

Concept: A program system exists only in its documentation.

One of the factors distinguishing software from hardware is the intangible nature of computer programs. Programs cannot be touched and handled

---

4. Frills also increase the likelihood of error. They are often not part of the overall design, so the test plan does not take them into account.

the way hardware devices can. They cannot even be seen when stored in a computer-readable form. As a consequence, software developers have to learn many of the diagnostic and analytic techniques of doctors or detectives or, in some cases, archeologists. That is, they have to learn to understand the inner workings of software by studying its external manifestations. Like doctors, software developers must diagnose program troubles by observing a small set of symptoms, that is, output errors. Like detectives, they must develop a complete picture of the program system by piecing together a variety of descriptions prepared by individual programmers, each of whom has seen only a part of the action. Like archeologists, they must try to explain the behavior expected of a program by interpreting historical records. Only in exceptional cases does it do any good to examine the machine-readable form of the program. The physical form of the program—magnetic spots on tape or disk, flux patterns in magnetic cores—contains too few clues to the information carried by the program.

The only useful record of a program system, the program package, is a set of documents which include, as a minimum, the program listing and an explanation of the program's purpose, function, and environment. Ideally, the package contains a fully commented listing of the program code in a readable high-level language plus the following elements.

- The equivalent object program listing
- A narrative description of the program: specifications, user information, operator guides, behavioral characteristics, environment, adaptability, and other elements
- A high-level flowchart
- A sample test case and test loader
- A physical copy of the object program in machine-readable form

It is this package that is handed to the user when the program is delivered. Without this package, a copy of the program on magnetic tape may be useless.

2.7 CHANGE

Concept: Change is inevitable; therefore systems must be adaptable.

A review of the previous concepts suggests that software system development is immensely difficult. The logical management strategy, under the circumstances, would be to minimize the size and complexity of the system at the start. Then, with the system requirements and design specifications frozen, an orderly implementation plan could be laid out. Unfortunately, no one can afford the luxury of freezing the system requirements or the design specifications. A system of any size presents enough conceptual problems due to its complexity that no one can foresee all the implications of the initial system definition. This means that a rigidly defined system may be valueless when it is completed. The alternative approach is to anticipate changes to the environment, the system requirements, the details of the design, even the funding and schedule. It is harder to manage the alternative approach because special procedures are required for evaluating and incorporating changes to the system while it is in process. Nevertheless, an approach which adapts to change will produce a more useful end product.

The arithmetic of change is simple. Suppose a system has been proposed because it has a value to the user of $100 and an estimated cost of $50. The net value is $50. However, if the requirements change and the system does not, there is no benefit at the end of the project. The net value turns into a loss of as much as $50, depending on the salvage value of the completed programs. On the other hand, the same system could be built adaptively. A change-control procedure would be required at a cost, say, of $10. As the requirements change, the system components will have to be modified or replaced at the unit level. This may cost $20 over the original plan. The net value of the project is now only $20; however, it is achievable and is definitely profitable. In the words of the classic burlesque skit (in which the clever lawyer manages to escalate his friend's two-dollar traffic ticket into a life sentence), "Pay the two dollars!" Change control and adaptive system development represent a small cost for an assured profit.

Change affects a system as shown in Fig. 2.4. At the outset, the user, analysts, and developers all agree on precisely what the system should look like and how it should relate to the well-defined environment in which it will operate. Their agreement, however, takes place before any detailed design has occurred, so it is necessarily based on broad generalizations and assumptions. When the designers proceed to break the system into smaller pieces suitable for distribution to the implementers, everyone expects the smaller pieces to be perfect subelements of the large system. In machine-tool work, gage blocks are used to obtain precise measurement. The blocks are so well machined into flat, parallel surfaces that when two are wrung together, there is no room for air between them. They stick to each other as though they were a single block. That is the way designers expect programs to fit if they are built according to the design. Of course, a change to any part of the system will interfere with a proper fit. That is why the neat design blocks of Fig. 2.4 deteriorate into the misshapen end products of the development process. Furthermore, as the system is being built, the environment changes, so that not only do the system elements clash with one another, but they no longer fit the environment. When all these problems become

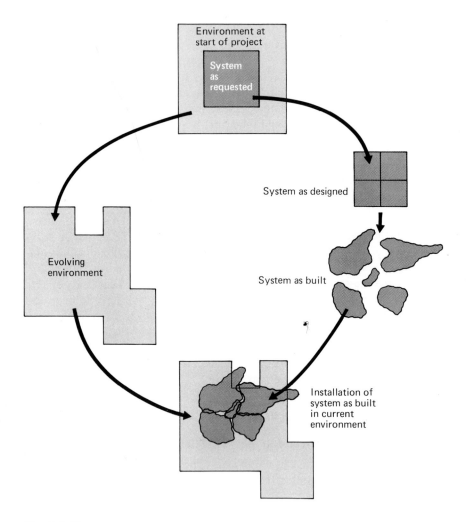

Fig. 2.4 Change.

evident during final system integration, there is an inevitable explosion as the system fails.

Consider some of the things that can happen to cause the programs as built to deviate from the design as planned. There is the unavoidable impact of ambiguity. The design is always stated in a language subject to misinterpretation. The most precise design language is mathematics. The notation is uniform and widely understood. But even an exact equation can be misinterpreted. For instance, in the statement of a function to calculate a logarithm, using the formula

$$\ln (1 + x) = x - \frac{x^2}{2} + \frac{x^3}{3} - \frac{x^4}{4} + \ldots + (-1)^{n-1}\frac{x^n}{n},$$

the designer has specified that a series approximation is to be used. The series is infinitely long, but for practical purposes, the implementer has to truncate it at a reasonable point. The actual result depends on the number of terms used. If the designer does not state the precision required, the implementer will pick an appropriate value. A four-term approximation may fit the word size of the computer and avoid computing double-precision values. However, for some values the logarithm will be in error by more than 0.00005. It requires an eight-term expansion to reduce the maximum error in the answer to about 0.00000003. All programs that use the logarithm routine will be affected by the precision of the result. If precision is critical to the application, it must be specified in the requirement for the logarithm. Its omission leaves too much room for interpretation.

Programming languages and natural language (English, etc.) also complicate the ambiguity problem. Not only do they permit the same errors of omission just illustrated, but they allow the use of words and phrases that have more than one legitimate meaning [5]. Thus the compound conditional statement "When the end-of-record flag is on and the channel is ready or the timer interrupt flag is on, transfer to A" can mean either of the following.

- ```
  IF (EOR AND CR) THEN CALL A;
  ELSE IF (TI) THEN CALL A;
        ELSE PROCEED;
  ```
- ```
  IF (EOR AND CR) THEN CALL A;
  ELSE IF (EOR AND TI) THEN CALL A;
        ELSE PROCEED;
  ```

Only one meaning can be correct. It is up to each individual in the project to use language carefully to avoid such statements or to supplement them with instructions for resolving ambiguity.

Despite the care taken to create an unambiguous statement of requirements, there will always be unavoidable differences in interpretation by the person receiving the statement. There is a parlor game that plays on this characteristic of human communication. The leader writes down a message and whispers it to a player. That player passes the message to another, and so on around the room. The last player reports the message out loud so it can be compared with the written copy. Invariably, the report is wildly off the mark. The players distort the message, a little at a time, by their choice of words or their failure to pay attention or their desire to improve the message (or the game). In the sea of little changes the original message is lost altogether. The same thing can happen in system development, where each message is created by an individual who states the message with nuances of meaning due to personal background and point of view. The message is read by someone else, who interprets it in the light of different personal biases. In the light of imperfect information transfer, therefore, changes must be made to bring the system as built back into line with the plan. Or alternatively, the plan must be changed to fit the situation.

Ambiguous statements are not the only source of system changes. Quite often the interplay of events will force the user or the designer to reevaluate a prior decision. Some examples of situations which lead to considerable rework during system development follow.

Throughput problem.   There is no precise way of predicting how fast a proposed program system will run on a particular machine configuration. As a result, when the system is ready for time trials it may be unsatisfactory. Redesign is required or a faster configuration must be ordered. The cause of the problem could be simply mistaken judgment. More often, however, the cause is a change in some detail of specification. For example, an information system may be supposed to respond to a query in one second on the average, given the assumption of four disk accesses to process the I/O queues, the file index, and the file itself. If the query results in an average of six accesses because of the way it references the files, responses could take 50 percent longer than expected.

A similar problem arises when the input characteristics change. Systems which handle variable-length records are affected by the statistical distribution of record lengths. Systems designed for a given number of items may have to move in-core tables to disk if the number of items grows. This slows up the system. Systems which allow priority multiprogramming may have unexpected workload distributions that prevent certain jobs from meeting their deadlines. In every case, discovery of the problem leads to a change in some aspect of the system.

Technical improvement.   During the lifetime of a program system development, the rest of the world keeps moving, producing newer and better ways of doing things. Conservative management will avoid disrupting the project with novelties. But when the new technique is a major improvement in cost or performance, it has to be considered carefully. Such improvements impacted a software system for the petroleum industry several times. The system was designed for a large scientific computer because the kernel computation was a time-consuming Fourier analysis (for reducing seismological data). Before the system was built, a hardware array processor was placed on the market that could do the kernel computation as a high-speed attachment to a smaller main computer. The cost advantage of the smaller computer justified redesigning the programs to delete the Fourier analysis. Then a new mathematical method for doing a fast Fourier transformation was published that would work on the smaller computer without the special array processor. So the programs had to be revised to include the new math; in fact, the final system had some of the math in the application program and some in a microcoded read-only store in the computer. Each change improved performance while reducing system cost.

Technical obstacle.   Sometimes the functions called for in the requirement cannot be provided, so a change to the system is called for. For example, a pattern recognition system was specified in about 1963 which relied on a high-resolution scanner to feed bits of picture data to a fairly simple matching program that would recognize letters formed by the bits. About six months into the project, it was clear that no vendor could deliver a scanner that would work at the resolution called for. Falling back to lower resolution required that a new method of recognizing the character be found. None was. At the end of a year, the project was terminated. This leads to a truism about software systems: *a system that requires an invention to succeed will never be completed on schedule.* Invention is fortuitous. It cannot be scheduled or produced on demand. Any manager who commits himself to providing an end product on a given schedule without knowing how to do it is using poor judgment. Yet there are many cases involving technical obstacles in which a solution was found by changing the system requirements and using some well-known but less advanced methods. In one, a plan to automatically distribute microfilm images to user viewing terminals via pneumatic tubes failed. The system was still built, initially with manual distribution and later with a TV transmission scheme. Note that technical obstacles are usually hardware problems. It is very difficult to conceive a program specification that cannot be implemented (see Section 4.3).

Unanticipated interactions.   Designers explicitly define all the interactions they intend to allow in their systems. They are less exhaustive when it comes to defining the remaining interactions—those that can exist but are either prohibited or immaterial. The result is that supposedly unimportant interactions can cause the system to fail. Such a problem occurred in a program system which controlled an automatic preflight test device for space rockets. The system consisted of a sequence of nine test programs which sampled various instruments and set them to the proper value for the next program. It was a simple program system that had been used successfully several times. Then one day a missile was launched after it had passed the tests, but it veered off its planned trajectory and had to be destroyed. In the investigation that followed, it was determined that the inertial guidance system had been aimed at the wrong target. After much more detective work, it was determined that the value in the guidance system could have been put there only by the automatic test system. The programmers found this hard to believe, so they set out to duplicate the problem. At no point in their programs did the test system generate the wrong value. To see if there was any peculiarity about the test run on the day of the accident, they went back to the prelaunch records. The search showed nothing unusual except that the tests were suspended temporarily after four programs had been run. The remaining five programs were run later. With this clue uncovered, a new study finally pinpointed the problem. The program system had been designed to run tests 1–9 from beginning to end without stopping or recycling. As a result, the instructions to the test operator showed how to initialize only test 1. On the day in question, the operator followed the same instructions when restarting the cycle at test 5. The wrong initialization values were thus fed to the system and left in the inertial guidance equipment in the missile. A simple change in the operator's instruction sheet corrected the problem temporarily. A program change that verified the initialization values fixed it permanently.

Environmental changes.   While the units within the system change to fit the situation, the environment surrounding the system changes in different ways. Thus, on a large project, when the pieces of the system are finally assembled, there is no guarantee that the result will be suitable. This is a risk, regardless of whether the system meets the original requirements or not. For example, the SAGE system was the classic masterpiece of large computer system development. But when it was completed and installed to defend against air-breathing weapons, it was already obsolete. Long-range missiles had become the new threat.

In another pioneering application, the U.S. Treasury designed a computerized check-reconciliation system to replace about 450 people sorting and collating some 1,300,000 checks each day. The computer design did not anticipate the changes in business practice which were tending to increase the total number of transactions paid by check. As a result, the system requirement of 1,300,000 checks a day laid down in 1954 was exceeded by 50 percent immediately after the system was installed in 1956. In this case, faster machines were obtained to handle the problem.

Interactive systems are frequent victims of environmental change because the user's behavior cannot be predicted. After the first-phase system is delivered, the user will really know for the first time how it will do the job. The odds are that this first test of human factors will generate a long list of changes to the external characteristics of the system.

At a much lower level of design, many systems incorporate actual values for supposed constants, such as the maximum size of core storage or the number of I/O device types that can be attached to a computer or the number of divisions in the corporate organization. Invariably, business conditions or other external pressures cause the environmental constants to turn into variables.

The management response to all types of change: Design the system so that it can adapt to change. Use flexible design techniques, such as those discussed in Chapter 4, to permit programs to be written before all specifications are frozen. Build in aids to modification. Build in tools for evaluating system performance. Deliver the job in separate phases so that useful results can be produced before the environment changes completely. Create a change-control mechanism that shows, at every stage of the job, what is required and how it will be provided.

Change is inevitable. It must be managed and it can be managed. Yet, of all the challenges facing software systems implementers, change is often the most difficult one to cope with.

REFERENCES

1. Aron, J. D., "Information Systems in Perspective." *Computing Surveys,* Vol. 1, No. 4, December 1969.
2. Miller, George A., "The Magical Number Seven, Plus or Minus Two: Some Limits On Our Capacity For Processing Information." *The Psychological Review,* Vol. 63, No. 2, March 1956.
3. Urwick, Lyndall F., "The Manager's Span of Control." *Harvard Business Review,* Vol. 34, No. 3, May–June 1956.
4. House, Robert J., and John B. Miner, "Merging Management and Behavioral Theory: The Interaction Between Span of Control and Group Size." *Administrative Science Quarterly,* Vol. 14, No. 3, September 1969.
5. Moyne, J. A., "Information Retrieval and Natural Language." *Proceedings of the American Society for Information Sciences,* 32d Annual Meeting. Westport, Conn.: Greenwood, 1969.

3
Problem Analysis and Planning

Programming is a comprehensive term. It includes the activities of analysis, planning, design, etc., as well as coding and debugging. Programmers, consequently, must have a broad understanding of the purpose of their programs. They must know why and how the program will be used in order to design it properly.

3.1 DEFINING THE PROBLEM

Programs are written to solve problems. The programmer's first act is to obtain a good definition of the problem. He must understand the problem thoroughly, even if the user must explain it several times. Often the user and the programmer, who have quite different working vocabularies, fail to take the time to clarify the problem in an unambiguous way. They may also leave out information. The programmer can cover the situation by obtaining answers to the following questions.

- What must the program do?
- What are the inputs for which the program must do its job?
- What outputs are required?
- What is the acceptable running time of the program?
- How much storage (in memory and in bulk storage devices) can be used?

- What other programs or operating systems must this program operate with?
- How does the program relate to the total environment—manual procedures, user needs?
- How much time and money are available to develop the program?
- What standards or conventions are to be followed?
- What machine configuration can be used (for development, for operations)?
- Is the program to be used once or many times?

Undoubtedly there are other relevant questions, but these cover the major decision points and allow the programmer to start design, coming back later for further clarification. For each of these questions it is helpful to ask not only what is allowed but also what is not allowed. For example, if one of the inputs contains proper names, a check on what is not allowed may turn up the fact that only names of fewer than twenty characters are permitted in the NAME field. This fact delimits the properties of NAME in a way that may simplify the portions of the program dealing with editing and storage management; yet the limit may complicate data retrieval.

When the user has no specific answer to a question, the programmer is free to design that element in any way. In such cases, however, it is best to show the initial design to the user to make certain it is acceptable. In most situations where the user has not arrived at a firm opinion of what he wants, he can pretty rapidly tell what he does not want. The programmer should tie up the loose ends as early in the programming cycle as he can, to avoid major revisions that may be necessary if his assumptions are rejected at delivery time.

The complete set of requirements and assumptions defines the *objectives* of the program.

3.2   EXAMPLE: DEFINING A SORT REQUIREMENT

For purposes of illustrating the process of problem definition, a single problem will be examined. The following statement of requirements will be used.

Sort a file of 80 character records into a sequence determined by the key number contained in the IDENT field.

The definition of the sort problem appears at first glance to be clean and completely stated. Nevertheless, the questions suggested earlier should still be asked.

- What must the program do?
  1. The program must sort a file of 80 character records.
  2. The sort sequence is determined by the value of the IDENT field.

Is this all the program must do? Consider the following additional questions, which are not explained in the requirements statement.

- How can the programmer locate the IDENT field?
- Are all the values of IDENT different for different records?
- Is the key a number, an alphabetic symbol, or a combination of alphabetic and numeric characters?
- Is the IDENT field a contiguous string of characters, or is it a name defining the string obtained by concatenating two or more subfields?
- Does this sort program stand alone, or is it to be a library subroutine called on by other programs?
- Is the sort sequence in ascending or descending order?

Before the programmer can know what the program must do, he should understand the answers to these supplementary questions, which are essentially ignored in the statement of requirements. Except for the fact that the input has 80 character records, there is next to no information in the data supplied. The programmer must find out the following.

- How many input records can there be? Is this number fixed or variable? If variable, what is the distribution of the number for all expected sorts, and what is the peak value?
- How are the input records supplied? As a list in computer core memory produced by another program? As a deck of punched cards? On tape? As a disk data set? If on disk, is the disk permanently available, or is it removable? Does the input file fill more than one physical storage device?
- Does the file have a name? Are there names for the records and fields within the records? Is there a system library definition for these names?
- Does any other program use these records? May the records be changed while they are in storage, or must they be left unaltered because some other program which uses them is operating in a multiprogrammed mode?
- When the file is sorted, where does it go? What is the output medium?
- Is the output formatted in any special way?
- Are there any error analyses required? Are there error output listings required?

- Is there a time limit on the sort?
- Is the available memory (for data plus program plus work areas) limited? Is the limit close to the file size?
- How many peripheral storage devices (and associated access arms or I/O channels) will be available?
- What operating system will be used when the sort is running?
- When is the program needed? How much is it worth? How much money has been budgeted to produce it?
- What sort programs are maintained in the facility library? Are funds available to procure a packaged sort routine, if applicable?
- Must the sort algorithm conform to a specific mathematical method?
- Is the documentation supposed to conform to a specific format standard?
- Is a sample file available for testing the program? If not, are there any statistics available to describe the nature of a suitable test file?
- What machine will be used for program development? Where is it? How is time obtained on it? Is it the same as the machine on which the sort program will be run? What is the accounting algorithm for the development machine?
- May the work in progress on the sort be stored in the development machine disk files for the duration of the project?
- How often will the sort be used?

3.2.1 Tradeoffs Influenced by the Problem Definition

Before going further, we note two points. The original requirements statement, though clear in the mind of the user, is inadequate to tell the programmer what is needed. The questions that the programmer must cope with are numerous and interdependent. The second point is embodied in the questions: "How often will the sort be used?" "Is the number of input records fixed or variable?" "What operating system will be used?" Obviously, if the sort will be run only once, the size of the input file is fixed. However, if the sort will be run often, the input file may be either fixed or variable. If it is variable, there will be additional housekeeping in the program to determine the file size and to adjust buffers and loop controls to fit the actual file. This, in turn, will affect the size and execution time of the sort. If the sort is to be used more than once, knowing the expected frequency of use is also valuable. A very frequently used program should be permanently available to the operating system and should be stored in an on-line device. If it is used only occasionally, it can be stored on tape or cards, to be loaded manually each time it is called for. By considering these three questions together, the programmer can make tradeoff decisions affecting program design and the design of operating procedures. The relative amount of sophistication in each aspect of the programming effort should depend on the value of that aspect to the overall objectives. Therefore, a sort that will be run only once should not be designed for automatic library loading by the operating system, nor should much time be spent looking for the optimum algorithm for sorting. In fact, such a situation probably calls for the use of a prepackaged program from a general-purpose library, even if the library program is known to be relatively slow. The added cost of running time should be more than offset by the savings in programmer and operator time. On the other hand, a frequently used sort may take an appreciable portion of the daily schedule of computer operations, and it therefore warrants careful optimization planning so as to minimize the computer time and operator expense [1].[1]

3.2.2   The Requirements Statement

Let us return to the original statement of requirements.

> Sort a file of 80 character records into a sequence determined by the key number contained in the IDENT field.

A simple discussion between the programmer and the requester could clarify the problem substantially. Consider the following revised statement of requirements, with relevant supporting data, that could result from a meeting between the programmer and the user.

Required: Sort a file of 80 character records in ascending order of the IDENT key field.

By whom: The user is responsible for analyzing computer usage for the financial office. The results of the analysis will affect computer configuration changes. The user is not a programmer.

Background: During normal computer operations, a record is kept of computer usage. This is done automatically by an existing system program that notes the start and stop times and the actual CPU usage for each job during a 24-hour period. It also records the resources assigned to the job. Disk and core storage are recorded in terms of the number of bytes used, rounded off to the nearest thousand bytes. Tapes, terminals, and other de-

---

1. These comments apply to all problems. Sorting is used as an example here because it is easy to understand. In modern practice, a sort utility program would always be preferred to original programming for file sorting.

vices are recorded in terms of the number of devices used. At the end of each job the usage data is summarized in an 80-column record, which is written on a disk. The records are accumulated for 24 hours, after which the file is dated and closed. A new storage file is opened for the next 24 hours. Every week the usage data for the seven-day period is to be sorted and merged for analysis by existing programs. This job is new. Only casual samples are analyzed at present using manual methods.

Why sort?   The computer is multiprogrammed with jobs of diverse charac-teristics. Long jobs are intermixed with short jobs. IDENT is the start time for each job. The analysis requires that all jobs be in sequence, according to the time of day they started. However, since the job summary records are placed on disk after they are complete, the disk file is sorted by job completion time, not by start time. Furthermore, since the jobs are all of different durations, there is no reason to expect the sequence of end times to be the same as the sequence of start times.

Format Data: The job summary record has the following format.

Job Name	8 AN
IDENT	14 N
END	14 N
Core	4 N
Disk (1)	3 N
Disk (2)	3 N
Disk (3)	3 N
Disk (4)	3 N
Disk (5)	3 N
Disk (6)	3 N
Disk (7)	3 N
Disk (8)	3 N
Tape	2 N
Data Cell	1 N
Reader	1 N
Printer	1 N
Punch	1 N
Console	1 N
Terminal (Keyboard)	2 N
Terminal (Display)	2 N
Control Data	5 AN
Total	80

Fields labeled N contain numeric characters, and those labeled AN contain alphabetic or numeric characters. The control data is supplied by the system program, and what it contains is not clear to the user. These records are

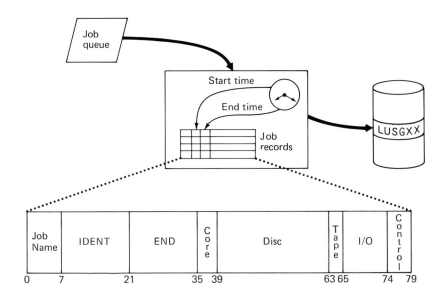

Fig. 3.1 Job record flow.

stored in a file named LUSGXX on a removable disk pack, which is placed in the disk library at the end of the third shift every day. This same disk pack contains other files used for cost accounting of computer usage and may contain miscellaneous job output for printing.

The times recorded in the IDENT and END fields are in the form YYDDDHHMMSSFFF. This data gives the time of day to the nearest thousandth of a second for a particular day of the year.

Volume: The installation has an average of 3000–4000 jobs a week. There have been peak periods due to very heavy engineering usage involving many short jobs, but even then, the daily workload has been less than 1000 jobs. Although there are times when the computer runs seven days a week, there has never been a week with more than 4000 job records.

Computer: The installation has an S/370-168 main processor fed by a 370-158 attached support processor (ASP); VS2 is the operating system used for most jobs. Program development is handled as normal batch input.

So far, the discussion has touched only on obvious characteristics of the problem to be solved and the environment in which it occurs (Fig. 3.1). Yet a great deal of useful information has emerged. The sort is a stand-alone job run once a week. The arrangement of the sort is known; it is a time sequence running from the earliest to the latest start time during a week. The IDENT field is a single 14-decimal-digit numeric field starting in the ninth position of the record. Quite a bit is now known about the physical characteristics of the records and the storage medium, and of course, the reason for sorting is now clear. (Although the programmer does not, strictly speaking, need to know why the sort is necessary, there is ample evidence that when he understands the purpose of the assignment, he performs better and more willingly.)

3.2.3   Analyzing the Problem

It should be noted that the information available to the programmer is still incomplete. Since his only source has been the user, his data reflects only the user's understanding of the system. The fact that the user is not a programmer is a flag suggesting that there may be characteristics of the problem the customer knows nothing about. In particular, the way in which the system program sets up the job record and the way in which the application programs process the job record are unclear. The user will not be able to clarify them; therefore the programmer must seek out the system and applications programmers, who know how they work. There are several new questions that may arise at this point.

- Do the interfaces described by the predecessor and successor programs correspond to the interface described by the user?
- Can the problem be simplified?
- Is this the right problem?

The programmer should not necessarily restrict his attention solely to the user's problem statement. By looking further, he may serve the user better. He may find a shortcut based on techniques available to all programmers but outside the scope of knowledge of the user. On the other hand, the programmer must avoid dilettantism. It is tempting to find an optimal solution or to generalize a problem to handle additional situations. It is fun to find a clever way to write a program that saves storage or runs faster, even though the method may be quite intricate. It is a source of competitive pleasure to be able to show a colleague an improvement to one of his programs. In general, programmers are stimulated by this type of mental gymnastics. However, much of this activity does not contribute directly to the solution of the user's problem. All it does is increase cost. Therefore, the programmer must accept reasonable constraints on his ability to innovate and polish. He must balance his approach so as to solve the customer's problem at the least cost.

In the sort problem, there is room for a variety of programmer creativity—some good, some bad. Given the problem statement so far, the programmer will undoubtedly talk to a systems programmer in the installation to find out what the CONTROL DATA is. He will learn that it actually consists of two fields:

| CPU TIME | 4 | B |
| OPERATING SYSTEM | 1 | A |

where B stands for *byte,* a string of eight bits.

The user apparently doesn't realize that the elapsed time between program start and end generally exceeds actual central processor usage. The difference represents operating system overhead, time used by other programs, and perhaps time spent waiting for mechanical input/output devices to process an I/O request. The application programmer presumably does know the difference and analyzes CPU use separately from job elapsed time.

CPU TIME is a binary field 32 bits long. It is recorded to the nearest millisecond and can register up to 2^{32} milliseconds. That is equal to 4,294,-967,296 milliseconds, or about 1200 hours, more than enough for the longest job that can be run in one day. The last field, OPERATING SYSTEM, contains a single letter code to show which of the four operating systems available in the installation the job was run under. The four allowable codes:

O   full operating system, VS2

D   small disk operating system

E   special emulator for programs carried over from an older installation

R   special real time system

This information discloses the fact that there must be four different system programs which produce job summary records, one per operating system. Further investigation discloses that they all use the same file LUSGXX, simply adding records at the end of the file. The operator's loading procedure has been modified to pass the next LUSGXX address from one operating system to another as he switches them in and out. From this much operational data, the analyst can see that changes to existing programs are to be avoided since there are at least four programs affected by any change.

A typical programmer, at this stage, will begin to wonder why the record format is set up so awkwardly. Why not eliminate redundancy and make the record length flexible so it won't use up too much disk space. For instance, the year and day are common to all records in the file, so why record them? A better file description might be as follows:

File:	LUSGXX	
Record type 1:	RECORD COUNT	5 N
	DATE—YYDDD	5 N
Record type 2:	JOB NAME	8 AN
	IDENT—HHMMSSFFF	9 N
	END—HHMMSSFFF	9 N
	CORE	4 N
	DISK QUANTITY	1 N
	(DISK)	(3 N)
	TAPE	2 N
	DATA CELL	1 N
	READER	1 N
	PRINTER	1 N
	PUNCH	1 N
	CONSOLE	1 N
	TERMINAL (KEYBOARD)	2 N
	TERMINAL (DISPLAY)	2 N
	CPU TIME	4 B
	OPERATING SYSTEM	1 A

Here the day and year are written only once in a header record. That saves 10 characters per job record. In addition, the disk resource is converted to a variable entry.[2] The number of disks used is always recorded; it may vary from 0 to 8. Then a subfield of 3 characters is entered for those disks actually used. This can save up to 23 characters per job record, although if all eight disks are used, the record length will be one character longer than before. A count of the number of records written in LUSGXX has been added as an additional control field and as an aid in selecting a fast sort algorithm.

The programmer has shown that compression can save space both in the disk and in memory. Making some simple assumptions, he can quantify the saving.

- Average number of jobs simultaneously active in computer   5

- Average number of job records per day in LUSGXX   700

---

2. The parentheses indicate that there may be multiple occurrences of the named field.

- Average number of disks used per job   2
- Core savings, bytes
   Original core requirement per job: 80
   Savings:
      Date reduced in IDENT and END: 10
      Disk data averaging two entries: 17
   New core requirement per job: 53
   Core saved for 5 job records: 5 × 27 =   135
- Disk savings, bytes
   Original disk requirement per job: 80
   New disk requirement per job: 53
   Disk saved for 700 job records: 700 × 27 =   18,900

The core saving seems nominal, but the disk saving can be several whole disk tracks.

Has the programmer's time been well spent? Probably not. The calculations don't address the sort directly—they are a diversion. After all, the disk format and core requirements of the job summary record were predetermined by the system program that accumulates the usage data. They are not within the scope of the sort problem. In a narrow sense, the programmer is spending his user's money on someone else's problem. More important, the calculation is very likely to lead to an invalid conclusion. Although it may be easy to modify the system programs to record the date once and to increase the record count every time a new record is placed on the disk, it is probably very difficult to modify all the system programs to handle variable fields for disk usage. In fact, the housekeeping necessary to vary the number of disk usage fields in core memory would probably use more bytes of program code than can be saved. Likewise, the analysis programs used at the end of the week would have to be revised to scan the record in order to locate each field. That is much harder than using a fixed address for every field. It is hard to justify reprogramming several jobs to achieve a saving of a few tracks of disk storage. This is particularly true when the disk involved is used primarily for accumulating one day's record, and in this problem it is clear that the disk is not packed full since there is room left for miscellaneous output files destined for printing, quite independent of the record-keeping task.

In summary, the programmer's effort to improve a program design based on his observation of one aspect of the problem can backfire. He may not only increase the cost of his own task but also cause unwarranted effort in programs impacted by his idea.

Nevertheless, the analytical effort was not totally wasted. Certain interface information was clarified, particularly between the various operating systems and recording programs. The contact between the analyst and the system programmers also has the advantage of cross-fertilization of ideas. The sort analyst learned something about the operational environment. The system programmers learned something about the ultimate purpose of LUSGXX. They may, for instance, mark down the record compression of YYDDD as a desirable design feature if and when they build a replacement data collection system for computer usage. They may also consider converting CPU TIME to a decimal format to make it more compatible with other data in the job record.

The sort analyst can ignore everything in the record except IDENT. His requirement is to order the LUSGXX file on the key field IDENT. The content of the rest of the record is irrelevant. On the other hand, he should know how the job records are generated because he may discover some natural sequences that will affect his choice of sort technique [2]. What he will learn is shown in Fig. 3.2 and below.

System program function

For each operating system there is a program XLOGR (X is the operating system code—O, D, E, or R) which is initialized when the operating system is initially located. XLOGR is called by the system reader program as soon as the header cards for an input program are encountered, and XLOGR extracts from the job control commands in the program deck all the job summary data except IDENT, END, and CPU TIME. It places this data, which identifies the resources to be allocated to the program during execution, in a memory area arranged like the job summary record. When the job is dispatched, XLOGR reads the time-of-day clock, converts to date, and stores in the space reserved for IDENT. When the job is terminated, XLOGR records END in the proper format. Then XLOGR requests CPU TIME from another system program which keeps track of resource utilization. XLOGR receives a 32-bit number, which it places in CPU TIME. The job summary record is then written on the LUSGXX file in the location designated by the XLOGR Address Counter. (This is initialized to the next LUSGXX address during the loading process.) The counter is advanced and XLOGR proceeds to the next summary record. The number of memory areas available to XLOGR for summary records is initialized by the operator, usually at 3, 4, or 5. XLOGR can expand this space up to 10 areas when space is available. When space is not available or more than 10 areas are needed, XLOGR notifies the operator by printing a message on the operator's console. XLOGR will simply ignore new program inputs until space is freed, either by operator action or because a completed summary is written to disk.

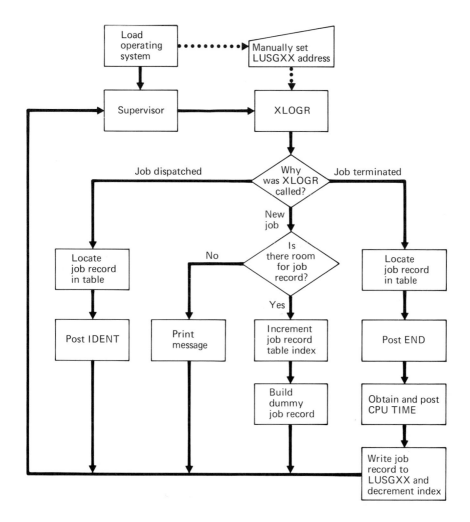

Fig. 3.2 Job record posting.

Hidden in this description is an interesting consideration that should make the analyst question the problem he is trying to solve. Each of the four system programs is designed to accept jobs as they arrive from the job queue, set up a summary record, complete three fields based on clock readings, and write the summary record on disk. The interesting point is that *at the beginning of the process the jobs are in sequence by IDENT.* Even though the machine is multiprogrammed, the jobs all enter the machine through a single queue. They are split off later when they are dispatched

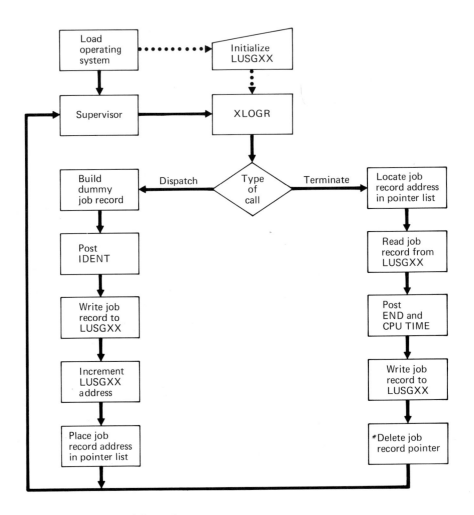

Fig. 3.3 Alternative job posting.

to a subqueue for execution. If it were possible to create the summary record on disk as the jobs were dispatched, they would already be in sequence by IDENT, and no sorting would be necessary. Of course, IDENT may have to be redefined slightly to correspond to dispatching time. But now that the user realizes that elapsed time and CPU TIME are different quantities, he will probably agree that the slight change in IDENT definition will not affect the results he is interested in. Elapsed time is a gross value used primarily for scheduling purposes. CPU TIME should be the number used for machine utilization and cost-accounting studies.

Now it is possible to postulate a redesign of the system programs. Instead of being written on disk after they are complete, the summary records will be written out as soon as XLOGR is called (Fig. 3.3). Then at the end of each job, the record will be updated by a random access to the disk. The operator's procedure will also be changed to permit him to retain one job summary file all week. All he has to do is initialize XLOGR daily the same way he does when he switches operating systems. This will string records for the first shift of day $(N + 1)$ consecutively after those for day N. Not only the daily sort but the weekly merge can be avoided. It will make no difference whether the weekly analyses involve five-day or seven-day weeks, whereas a five-disk merge may have been different from a seven-disk merge.

This type of analysis, which addresses the problem to be solved, is well worth the effort, in contrast to the earlier analysis that suboptimized relatively unimportant parameters. Although this analysis also forces reprogramming of the system programs, the effort is not unreasonable and may result in a net saving if no sort is needed. In addition, the data flow and operational duties for the user are improved by eliminating the sort with its contingent disk-handling and scheduling problems.

3.3 PLANNING THE JOB

The analysis of the problem brings the user and the designer/programmer to a decision point: Should the task be done or not? In order to make a decision, they should have an idea of the cost of the task. How is the scope of the effort determined at this stage?

In Chapter 2, the statement was made that, on the average, it takes 4–6 man-weeks to produce a program unit. This is clearly a generalization, but it is useful for estimating the aggregate production time of a system of many units. Any individual program unit, however, can take from a few hours to several months. Since there is no guide at this point to the number of instructions to be written, the job estimate can be based only on the programmer's experience and the external attributes of the problem. Such attributes as complexity, number of data types, language, etc., can be evaluated by various rules of thumb to construct an estimate. One way to make an estimate, given below, is based on reasonable but highly variable productivity factors, so it should be used cautiously. In particular, you should use your own experience to improve the factors shown in the tables.

3.3.1 Program Unit Development Activities

The time of one programmer developing one program unit is divided among detailed design, coding, debugging, and final documentation. As a start, the preliminary problem analysis gives a substantial amount of information about the problem environment. Each input and output has been described in enough detail to allow the programmer to lay out record formats down to the individual fields. The values in each field are bracketed within a permissible range, and editing criteria are given. A rough idea of the nature of the processing is provided. If the program unit is part of a larger system, all shared data and all control interfaces known at this time are provided. From this point until the completed program unit can be delivered, the programmer's time will be spent as shown in Table 3.1. In the average case, the schedule is split approximately three ways among design, coding (including documentation), and debugging [3,4]. Problems with particularly difficult logic require more than the usual design time. Particularly involved control flows require extra debugging. Proportionately less time is devoted to actual coding in such cases.

Literature references vary regarding the relative amount of work in each activity. Systems programmers and applications programmers in large projects tend to accept the figures in Table 3.1. The American Management Association assigns 30 percent to design, 40 percent to coding and docu-

TABLE 3.1.   PROGRAM DEVELOPMENT ACTIVITIES

Activity	Percent of schedule		
	Average	Complex logic	Complex control
Designing program logic	35	40	35
Program description Program flowcharts and/or decision tables Any corrections or changes to the above that may be necessitated by program or design changes			
Coding and developing test data	25	20	20
Coding computer program Developing test data Preparing run book			
Debugging	35	35	40
Desk checking Machine runs Analyzing test results			
Preparing final documentation	5	5	5
Final updating of previously prepared documentation			

mentation, and 30 percent to debugging [5]. In the extreme cases, a good analysis and a good library of report generators and utilities will reduce coding to only 10 percent of a 60-10-30 schedule [6]. The average in Table 3.1 is a 35-25-35-5 schedule, or with the assumption that documentation is done as code is written, a 35-30-35 schedule. It is a balanced schedule that recognizes that design and debugging are more significant to success than coding.

3.3.2 Program Unit Estimating

The number of days needed for development is a function of the problem attributes, the programmer attributes, and environment factors. By assigning weights to various attributes such that the weights are related to man-days under normal conditions, you can estimate the man-days to build the program unit. Tables 3.2 through 3.4 give a working set of weights (loosely adapted from [4]) which can be used in an estimating formula:

Program unit man-days =

(Sum of applicable weights) × (Know-how + Uniqueness)

This formula provides a raw estimate of the man-days required to do the activities shown in Table 3.1.

TABLE 3.2.   PROGRAM UNIT ESTIMATING WEIGHTS

Problem attributes	Weight
Input-Output	
Each record type, fixed format	1
Each record type, variable format	2
Each command, message, or inquiry type	1
Each special device type	1
Storage	
Each array generated by the program	1
Each file built and used	3
Each file with list structure and overflow built	5
Each multiple file relationship	2
Processing (according to difficulty)	
Real-time performance objectives	0–10
Data communications	0–5
Graphic displays	0–10
Language capability	see Table 3.3
Control	
Each shared data array or file	1
Each program control interface	2

TABLE 3.3.   LANGUAGE CAPABILITY WEIGHTS

Function	Weight							
	Assembly Language				Higher-level Language			
	Easy	Medium	Hard	Very hard	Easy	Medium	Hard	Very hard
Restructure data—combine, condense, rearrange, delete data	3	4	5	6	1	2	3	4
Monitor status—check controls, headers, trailers, labels, reasonableness of data, limits, errors	3	5	7	9	1	2	4	6
Retrieve and present data—file search, table lookup, address calculation, indexing	2	4	6	8	1	2	4	6
Calculate—all arithmetic computations	2	3	5	7	1	2	3	4
Link—overlay programs, checkpoint and restart procedures, interface linkages	2	3	4	5	1	2	3	4
Use program package								
Prepare control cards only					2	3	–	–
Add "own" code					2	4	8	16
Use utility program								
Prepare control cards only					1	–	–	–
Add "own" code					2	4	–	–
Use report program generator								
Prepare control cards only					1	–	–	–
Add "own" code					2	4	8	–

TABLE 3.4. ENVIRONMENT WEIGHTS

Know-how

Experience	Man-days per program weighting point
Senior Programmer. Has written and implemented many programs on different types of equipment. Very experienced with particular configuration and programming system.	0.5
Programmer. Has written and implemented programs of various complexities. Some experience with particular configuration and programming system.	1.0
Apprentice. Has written and implemented several programs. Limited experience with particular configuration and programming system.	1.5
Trainee. Has completed programming school and written training program.	3.0

Uniqueness

Job knowledge available	Job knowledge required		
	Much	Some	None
Detailed knowledge of this job	0	0	0
Good general knowledge of this job with fragmentary detailed knowledge	0.25	0	0
Fair general knowledge of this job but little or no detailed knowledge	0.50	0.25	0
No job knowledge but general knowledge of related subjects	0.75	0.50	0.25
No job knowledge and no general knowledge of related subjects	1.00	0.75	0.25

The estimating procedure involves reviewing the results of the problem analysis to determine (a) the quantitative information on records, files, and relationships, and (b) the degree of difficulty expected in processing. Table 3.2 shows that the planning, programming, debugging, and documentation associated with each separate record type will be about one man-day (which may be spread over a longer elapsed time). If the record has a variable length, it will probably take twice as long to deal with. Commands to the program and inquiries to files serviced by the program can be treated as though they were records. Output messages also fall in this category. The significant count is the number of *record types* not the number of records. Furthermore, no time need be allocated to records for which the processing is done by another program module and requires that you merely refer to named fields.

When the input or output uses a special device—i.e., a device not supported by the standard operating system—time must be allowed for adapting the I/O commands to the device interface.

Not all data arrives as input records. Many constants, intermediate results of computation, output images, and control indicators are created and/or used by the program unit. All such arrays of bits or characters must be laid out and named in the same manner as records, so they must be counted. Unfortunately, at the time the estimate is made, it may not be evident how many arrays will be specified during design. A minimum weight of 1 is recommended.

Records handled singly represent a certain amount of work. When records are organized into a file, additional work is required to build the file, plan an index scheme, provide an interface to an existing data access mechanism, coordinate file references with memory space and priorities, validate file references, etc. A weight of 3 is shown for this activity for each file owned by this program unit. Less effort is required for files (or data arrays) owned by other programs but used by this unit (see control weights). Relatively more effort is required when the file must be stored out of sequence, using lists and overflow mechanisms to keep track of where physical blocks are. That is, files that require special accessing methods in the program unit are weighted 5 rather than 3. Another source of programming complexity is a multiple file relationship, which permits one inquiry to cause a chain of searches through several files.

The degree of difficulty of the job also depends on the functions to be performed. Simple functions take less time than complex functions, but there are no simple rules for measuring complexity. The difference between *simple* and *complex* is a subjective judgment reflecting the programmer's personal experience and attitude. Although complexity is related to program size and the number of decision points and data elements involved, these quantities can only be guessed at when estimating a program unit.[3] Certain functional characteristics are known to cost effort. Real-time systems place constraints on the number of instructions permitted in the executable portion of a program unit in order to control execution time. Communications systems require additional control messages and error routines to manage the computer/communications interface. Graphic displays call for a reorganization of records into two-dimensional picture formats, which may have to be retained in memory as image data arrays in order to continually regenerate the output display. The relative difficulty of each of these is selected from a scale ranging from 0–10 for real-time requirements, 0–5 for communications, and 0–10 for graphics. The low values are selected for simple requirements or requirements that are so well known to the programmer that they are simple for him.

Language functions are also rated according to their complexity—again, on a subjective scale. The top of Table 3.3 shows the productivity advantage attributed to higher-level language compared with assembly language. For each type of function present in the program unit, the appropriate weight is selected from the table. Higher-level language is about twice as productive as assembly language, but this advantage applies only during coding and portions of debugging and documentation. In the lower part of the table, several special types of higher-level language capabilities are listed. Program packages (such as commercially available data base management systems) do a lot, but it takes some time to apply them under the best of circumstances. Most such packages provide hooks to let the user attach his own code to do things unique to his application. Simple "own" code is easy to attach. Very complex "own" code is hard to write, even though it may take advantage of some of the services of the package. It is unrealistic to attach very complex "own" code to limited-ability packages, such as sorts, disk-to-print utilities, and simple report program generators.

The last category of weights in Table 3.2 allows for the work required within a program unit because it is part of a larger system. Control of shared data and interface specifications must be rigid to protect the system; consequently, the unit programmer must pay special attention to them.

For each item in Tables 3.2 and 3.3 that applies to the program unit, a weight is obtained. The sum of the weights is then multiplied by the sum of the two main factors in Table 3.4. The first is *know-how,* a measure of programmer experience relative to programming in general and to the particular hardware/software system involved. The second is *uniqueness,* used here to describe the programmer's knowledge of this particular job subject

---

3. A more detailed discussion of complexity as it relates to larger systems will be given in Part 2.

area relative to the degree of job knowledge required. *Job knowledge* required is defined as follows:

Much: Detailed knowledge is required and subject is complex and difficult to understand, and/or job requires knowledge of complex mathematical or statistical formulas, and/or job requires application of special program concepts not in common use.

Some: Detailed job knowledge is required but subject either is not complex or is complex but can be easily explained, and/or job requires knowledge of standard mathematical or statistical formulas.

None: Job can be understood with little or no background on the part of the programmer (a job similar to a classroom problem).

Comparing the most experienced programmer (know-how = 0.5) who has detailed job knowledge (uniqueness = 0) with the least qualified programmer (3.0, 1.00) shows that the estimating formula ranges from

$$0.50 \times \text{(Total weight)}$$

to

$$4.00 \times \text{(Total weight)},$$

according to the situation. An approximation useful for rough estimates is based on an experienced programmer with fair job knowledge (1.0, 0.25):

$$\text{Man-days} = 1.25 \times \text{(Total weight)}$$

A department manager might want to approximate the work load before assigning the job to an implementer. The rough estimate will give an idea of the level of skill required to complete the unit by a certain date.

Note that the estimating procedure gives the net number of man-days for one person to develop and deliver one properly documented program unit. No provision has been made for lost time, machine unavailability, or systems overhead (for units in large systems). The weights are not precise even though, for convenience in scaling, some of them are shown to two decimal places. Results should always be rounded up to the nearest full day. Interpolation is permitted in all the tables.

Please realize that this method—or any method of estimating—is highly subjective. The guidelines and weights are arbitrary. The attributes of interest vary from one organization to another. For any single attribute, people will differ on the value to assign. Some use weights twice as large as these. Others, more optimistic, use much smaller weights. The best guidelines are local guidelines derived from experience and personal knowledge. Other people's methods may apply in your organization, but be very cautious about using their quantitative guidelines. When in doubt, be conservative.

It is less painful to finish early with money left over than to consistently miss objectives.

3.3.2.1 Example: sort program unit, assembly language

The sort requirement described in Section 3.2.2 involves *one record type,* the Job Summary Record, which has a fixed format. *One file,* LUSGXX, must be *shared* with other programs. No files must be built (the sorted output is simply the output stream of records). At least *two data control arrays* will probably be needed: one to hold pointers to keys during the sort and one to hold information regarding the progress of the sort. Since the sort is run as a stand-alone program, there is *one interface* with the operating system. Sorting *restructures* data to place records in sequence. This activity is the heart of the sort but is only of *medium* difficulty. No significant requirements have been stated for *status monitoring* or error checking. There will be a lot of *data retrieval,* intricate enough to be *hard.* There is *simple calculation:* comparison of keys. No *linkages* have been requested.

If assembly language is used, the sort can be estimated as follows:

Record types, fixed	1
Data arrays generated	2
Assembly language	
Restructure	4
Retrieve	6
Calculate	2
Shared file	1
Interface	2
Total weight	18

For a programmer with fair general knowledge of the job, the estimate is

$$\text{Man-days} = 1.25\,(18) = 23.$$

3.3.2.2 Example: sort program unit, higher-level language, without built-in sort functions

Record types, fixed	1
Data arrays generated	2
Higher-level language	
Restructure	2
Retrieve	4
Calculate	1
Shared file	1
Interface	2
Total weight	13

$$\text{Man-days} = 1.25\,(13) = 17$$

3.3.2.3 Example: sort program unit, sort utility program or higher-level language with built-in sort function

In this case all the internal processing is done by the utility program. All the programmer does is prepare control cards from the data in the requirements statement. The estimate is

$$\text{Man-days} = 1.25 \, (1) = 1 \text{ or } 2,$$

depending on the amount of documentation desired.

3.3.2.4 Comment

In these three examples, a wide range of estimates was obtained. Each estimate depends on the estimator's background and the tools available.

Use of a sort utility leads to an estimate that seems reasonable to both system programmers and applications programmers. The estimates above for assembly language or higher-level language seem too large to applications programmers although they are considered reasonable by system programmers. This assumes that the estimates account for all the work necessary to deliver a working end product meeting usual standards of quality as expected in the software contracting business. Business managers concerned with minimizing risk are inclined to think these estimates are low.

The estimating weights shown in the tables are generally lower than those in [4], as are the know-how and uniqueness factors. The reduction is compensated for by additional attributes dealing with processing and control requirements. System programming is more sensitive to these attributes than is the commercial application programming for which [4] was intended.

Under certain circumstances the estimate can be reduced. If the task involves rework of an existing program, recoding an existing program in a new language, or coding from an existing design specification, the existing work does not have to be completely redone. The percentage of programmer activity devoted to each task in Table 3.1 is the guide to the savings achievable.

- A completed design specification may save up to 35 percent of the effort.
- A line-for-line language conversion may save up to 50 percent—35 percent because a design exists, 15 percent because the logic has been tested. That still leaves time to write and debug the new source code.
- Up to 90 percent of the time can be saved if there is a complete program that can be transferred to this job. In essence, this is what happens when a program package is used. For the sort example, the sort utility estimate was only about 10 percent of the full programming estimates.

Another reason for reducing the estimate would be that the programmer is using a tool, such as interactive debugging, which increases productivity for coding and debugging.[4]

The procedure described here applies to program unit development and not to maintenance. Most maintenance tasks are very short—hours or days—because the trouble report is restricted to a very specific part of the existing program. The author knows no reliable methods of estimating a single maintenance task. In most organizations the question seldom arises because the amount of maintenance done is a function of the number of maintenance hours budgeted. It is almost always smaller than the amount of maintenance requested.

3.3.3   Scheduling the Program Unit

Given the estimate of man-days required, a schedule can be prepared showing the *elapsed time* planned for the assigned task. Elapsed time is the calendar time from start to end of the job. It exceeds the man-day estimate since it includes weekends, vacations and holidays, time spent on other assignments, and the usual time lost in coffee breaks, etc. It may also be inflated by unusually poor machine turnaround.

A schedule is produced by adding the explicit number of unproductive days (weekends, planned vacations and holidays) to the estimate and multiplying the result by an adjustment factor. An adjustment of 5–10 percent would cover unplanned absences (sickness), rest periods, lost time due to coordination problems. A larger factor, say 20 percent, could be selected if the machine service is poor, providing less than one run a day. Applying these factors to the sort problem shows a range of schedules: two days using a program package, 25 days using POL, and 33 days with assembly language. (The longer schedules include weekends but no vacations; the adjustment factor is 10 percent.) This result was obtained for a simple task involving only one record and one file. Both of the larger estimates fit the generalization that a unit requires 4–6 weeks on the average. What this means is that a program unit should be designed to deal with a very small number of record types and files. It should have few interfaces. Otherwise the expected time to complete the unit could extend for several months.

3.3.4   Control and Coordination of the Plan

Very few programmers wait until their designs are complete before they start coding. Neither do they postpone debugging until all the code is writ-

---

4. Interactive coding and debugging speed up the process only when the programmer is experienced in the use of the tool (see Chapter 7).

ten. There is a great deal of overlap of coding, documentation, and debugging. A programmer who implements "top-down," as described in Chapter 5, loses all distinctions between the various activities. Nevertheless, it is convenient to schedule and set checkpoints at which progress can be evaluated. The design should be well in hand at about the 35 percent point. If it is not, there are serious logic problems that require the attention of the manager. When 60 percent of the time is gone, the problem should be completely coded except for selected easy sections that have been set aside. In the top-down method, 60–75 percent of the problem, representing the main structure of the program, should be coded and debugged at the 60 percent point. A wide deviation from these objectives must be corrected. To be effective, action has to be taken at these interim checkpoints. Once 95 percent of the time is gone, it is too late.

The checkpoints represent convenient points at which to review the progress of the task with the manager and the user. The checkpoint dates should be included in the project plan so that the interested parties can be available at the right time. A critical checkpoint occurs as soon as the key design decisions are made regarding which language or package will be used. At this point, the designer/programmer must coordinate support requirements with the computer manager and any other support managers whose help is required.

An estimate of machine time needed for debugging is required so that time can be budgeted and allocated. Debug runs are usually short; however, as the program unit progresses, it uses more and more resources for debugging. In the sort example, early debugging runs will require only the normal assembler/compiler support provided by the machine room. Later, runs will have to have a file of records to sort. Eventually, that file should be a copy of LUSGXX (or a similar file generated by the programmer). Arrangements must be made with the machine operators to set up the test data file. Care must be taken to avoid confusing the test data with the real LUSGXX.

The amount of machine time required can be approximated. The figure of two hours per programmer man-month has been used by many systems programmers. This figure seems to be suitable for machines of any size (except real-time, sensor-based computers, which require more time). Apparently, the number of debug runs is the determining factor rather than machine speed. Good turnaround and enhanced debugging aids in checkout compilers should reduce the average utilization, but in the absence of personal experience to the contrary, programmers can estimate two hours per man-month. Note that this estimate refers to CPU time, as opposed to job elapsed time (in the sense of the sort example). Since each installation has its own accounting and billing formula, the two-hour rule-of-thumb may have to be restated to fit local usage.[5]

Documentation requirements should be planned in conjunction with (a) the people who control documentation standards for the library to which your program will be delivered, and (b) the people who will assist you with typing and artwork. Arrangements have to be made for keypunch assistance, or if you plan to use an interactive system, a terminal must be made available. The estimating procedures assume that all these things will be done in plenty of time to get the type of support normally available in your organization. It is your own fault if you miss a schedule because you delayed getting a commitment for support from a support group, and when you finally asked for help, they were unable to come through.

REFERENCES

1. Lorin, H., "A Guided Bibliography to Sorting." *IBM Systems Journal,* Vol. 10, No. 3, 1971.
2. Lorin, H., *Sorting and Sort Systems.* Reading, Mass.: Addison-Wesley, in press.
3. Watson, D. A., "Some Factors Involved in the Establishment of Programmer Performance Standards." *The Computer Bulletin,* Vol. 13, No. 6, June 1969.
4. *Management Planning Guide for a Manual of Data Processing Standards.* Form GC20-1670-2. White Plains, N.Y.: IBM Corporation, February 1971.
5. Lecht, C. P., *The Management of Computer Programming Projects.* New York: American Management Association, 1967.
6. Orlicky, J., *The Successful Computer System.* New York: McGraw-Hill, 1969.

---

5. More detail on machine time estimating will be given in Part 2.

4
Program Design

Once the problem is thoroughly defined, program design can begin. Actually, the line between definition and design is not sharp. Both activities are processes of *discovery and resolution.* As they proceed, the analyst/designer discovers new requirements, anomalies in the system structure, errors in work done so far, and opportunities for tradeoffs in cost, performance, and other objective criteria. Each of the discoveries is resolved when it is encountered. As the problem is defined and the major tradeoffs are made, the objectives document is created. The definition phase is nominally completed when the objectives document is complete and has been agreed to by the user and the developer. Up to that point most of the analyst's energy has gone into understanding the problem. Beyond that point most of his energy goes into specifying how he will solve it.

The design phase is complete when the *specification* is finished. This is a document describing how the program will be built. It is necessary to document the specification in order to record the many details of design that are lost because they cannot be committed to memory. Equally important, the document serves as the basis for discussion with the user and the operators. It is also the only tangible backup mechanism if, for any reason, the programmer must be replaced by a substitute during the job. Finally, the specification is the baseline against which the final program should be tested to verify that it does the things it is supposed to do. The specification, then, is a document explaining how the programmer intends to accomplish the objectives set out in the definition of the problem.

4.1   WHO IS THE DESIGNER?

Note that no careful distinction has been made among *analysts, designers,* and *programmers* up to this point. In most situations where the problems can be handled by one person, the same individual can do all three tasks: define the problem, specify the solution, build and test the solution. The author believes that experienced programmers should be qualified to do all these tasks.[1] As will become apparent in later chapters, however, large organizations may enforce specialization of certain employees in order to simplify resource management. Thus an applications programming department may differentiate between systems analysts, who interface with the users, and applications programmers, who interface with the analysts. In very large systems-programming shops, there may be designers, who are the architects of new systems, as distinct from systems programmers, who build and maintain the specified systems.

The management philosophy regarding the division of labor has changed over the years and may even be cyclic. One of the main sponsors of specialization was Charles Babbage. He is more familiar to most people as the inventor of an "analytical engine," the precursor of modern stored-program computers. His interests were much broader than computation, though. He had a major influence on such diverse subjects as operations research, actuarial theory, codes and ciphers, railroad improvements, and standard interchangeable machine parts [1]. Others, such as the economic theorist Adam Smith, had promoted similar ideas, but Babbage added the precision of quantitative analysis [2]. The trend toward such scientific management reached widespread acceptance early in the twentieth century with the work of Taylor, Gantt, Gilbreth, and others. More recently, though, the pendulum has started to swing the other way. Time-study and piece-work measures are being supplemented by motivational research. The results have convinced some students of management that job enrichment—i.e., the reintegration and generalization of tasks—contributes so much to employee performance that it offsets the efficiency of the assembly line [3]. In systems programming, total job involvement can be achieved on small jobs. On large jobs, there is a point at which the problem gets too big and forces some degree of specialization.

One advantage of having the same person carry an assignment through from start to finish is that it avoids confusion. For instance, a fact stated

---

1. The programmer should not be expected to perform supporting tasks, such as keypunching, typing, and machine operation. Programmer skills are poorly employed in such activities, and much better support can be provided by regular operators.

by the user during problem definition remains a fact during the design phase. It does not get distorted or lost, as it might if the problem changed hands.

4.2 WHAT DATA IS AVAILABLE?

The data available to the designer includes the data in the objectives document, all data in documents referenced in the objectives document or supporting analysis reports, and all data obtained by direct contact with users, operators, experienced programmers, or others. The quality of the data can be accurate and reliable, but it can also be incorrect and misleading. All inputs must be tested in some way to establish their validity.

4.2.1 Facts and Other Data

The best data input is a directly verifiable statement of fact. In the sort example in Chapter 3 "the job summary record is an 80-character record" can be checked by listing the contents of LUSGXX. The computer configuration can be verified by a visit to the computer room. The number of jobs run each day can be determined by sampling techniques. Of these three directly verifiable statements, however, only the first is a statement of fact. The second describes the maximum computer configuration and must be treated as a boundary condition that may not actually be achievable. Some boxes in the system may be down for maintenance. Some boxes may be attached to the M168 when the sort program is running on the M158. Some boxes may be reserved for a higher-priority use. It is necessary to learn the operating policies and procedures of the computer facility to find out what the most likely feasible configuration for the sort program will be. The third statement deals with a statistical estimate. The job volume for any single day would be an unacceptable estimate of the average volume to be expected. A sample of volumes over a one-month period would be better, but it would not necessarily be accurate. Suppose that all the short engineering jobs were suspended during the month so that the year-end accounting could be done for the user's firm. A sample for this period could be unrealistically low compared with other months. The sampling method must be selected to fit the situation. If usage is cyclic, the sampling period should at least span the cycle. Unusual biases must be recognized and accounted for. The results must be fully qualified, giving enough information about statistical methods, mean values, and standard deviations to describe the probable variation to be expected in future periods.

So far, we have identified *facts, bounds,* and *statistical estimates.* At a lower level of reliability are *personal experience, conventional wisdom,* and *educated guesses.* All the latter methods of establishing data have some merit when more reliable methods are inapplicable. Personal experience means that, in the absence of other data, the attributes of a similar previous problem will be assumed to apply to the present problem. When the designer has no similar previous experience but the problem is well known to others and has perhaps been written up in trade journals, textbooks, or manuals, the characteristics of the problem everyone else refers to can be adopted for the present problem. This is conventional wisdom. The information obtained from people in the user's shop falls in this category. As a last resort, the designer can fix a needed item of data by making an educated guess. The accuracy of these three methods is generally unpredictable and may be very poor. Nevertheless, they provide a starting point for the design. As the design proceeds, its inherent discovery/resolution process will improve the data. It is better to get started, conscious that the available data contains some questionable items, than to tread water interminably, waiting for unavailable facts to somehow appear.

4.2.2 Algorithms and Other Processes

Facts, bounds, and estimates describe the way things *are* in the problem environment. Algorithms and other processes describe the way things *work*.

An *algorithm* is a step-by-step procedure for solving a problem. *Communications of the ACM* publishes algorithms submitted by its readers because of their general interest to other readers. Many of these are mathematical procedures, such as matrix operations, internal sorts, and statistical routines in the form of ALGOL programs (or FORTRAN or PL/I). Well-documented algorithms are an excellent source of design data when they describe the problem at hand. Thus, if the user can state his problem in algorithmic form, the design process will be shortened. Likewise, if an algorithm in the literature fits the problem, it can be adopted by the designer. Algorithms can often be proved correct. They are known to terminate; i.e., they will not loop eternally for some data values. Most algorithms can be represented by flowcharts or algebraic equations. This makes it fairly easy to trace the flow and calculate the execution time of the program [4].

Other computer programs or procedures may be referenced in the data provided with the objectives document. These may not have the same strengths as algorithms—they may not have been tested; their functions may not be readily apparent; they may not even behave the same way for all inputs. Included in this list of processes are all the existing installation programs related to the problem at hand. In the sort example, the XLOGR programs, the operating system, the operator's procedures guide, and all the relevant library programs fall into this category. Experience indicates that the information value of such processes is related to the quality of the process and its documentation. The reliability of the process documentation is often a function of the time and effort that went into its preparation. This tends to mean that general-purpose vendor products are most reliable; widely distributed and widely used programs from other sources are next best; local products are least reliable.

A key characteristic of algorithms and other processes that distinguishes them from the quantitative statements of Section 4.2.1 is that their meaning depends on variable factors. An algorithm or computer program is defined for only a certain range of data. Its behavior for data outside the range may be unpredictable. The dynamic behavior of these step-by-step processes is subject to error due to machine failure or, in the case of manual steps, operator mistake. It is also possible for the algorithm to cause errors in other processes if it is poorly designed or incorrectly used. An example of the last type of problem occurred in an early vendor operating system that had a procedure for handling tape and disk labels. The process read the label when a new file was opened. It checked the label against the OPEN request to see that the correct file was being processed. It then decremented the GENERATION field in the label to indicate that the next time this file was used it would be the OLD file instead of the CURRENT file. This procedure worked fine as long as the program using the file ran to completion. However, if the program crashed and had to be restarted, the procedure would fail. When the OPEN was reached the second time, there would be no CURRENT file in the facility. This procedure caused a lot of tapes to be "lost" because of program crashes. A simple change to the procedure postponed decrementing the GENERATION field until after normal completion of the requesting program.

The gist of this example is that existing algorithms and other processes can provide useful data to a cautious designer. It is best to assume that the process does *exactly* what its documentation says it does. Then ask whether that particular sequence of steps is applicable to the problem at hand. Never assume that a procedure which is valid under one set of circumstances will remain valid when the circumstances change.

4.2.3 Assumptions, Constraints, Safety Factors

After all the factual, quantitative, and procedural data has been assembled and examined there will still be some unanswered questions regarding the requirements. In order for the design to proceed, these gaps must be filled, as indicated above. Three additional classes of data may be needed to fill the gaps.

Assumptions are made regarding the outcome of deferred decisions. For example, the designer knows that the facility manager plans to add disks to a tape system, but no decision has been made as to what type of disk will be ordered or when installation will be scheduled. The designer must make assumptions about these items in order to decide whether to design for tape or disk or whether to plan a device-independent design which can be quickly tailored to either. Assumptions are not guesses. All the possible outcomes of the deferred decision can be determined when the assumption is made. The assumption is simply the selection of what appears to be the most likely or, for safety, the most conservative outcome.

Constraints are imposed by the user or the environment. Typical constraints force the designer to use a particular programming language or restrict the design to a limited portion of machine memory. These constraints are often in the form of programming and operating standards that are intended to enhance efficiency and compatibility while reducing maintenance and training costs. Other common constraints limit the time and budget available for a job. These are based on the relation this job has to others; either it is a necessary link in a chain of events or it is the best investment opportunity among a set of proposed jobs. As noted above, the constraints as well as the job requirements belong in the objectives document.

Safety factors are the designer's (or manager's) margin for error. Since the items of data available for design vary in reliability and precision, decisions based on the data will be subject to error. The safety factor reflects the designer's confidence in the data. The main items that influence the size of the safety factor are the quality of the objectives document compared with what the designer is used to, the designer's self-confidence regarding the assignment, the availability of good computer service, and the designer's opinion as to the stability of the requirements. The last item is a reflection of the user's knowledge of the problem and the thoroughness of the statement of the problem. A user who doesn't know his own applications or a wishy-washy user will ask for many changes to the requirements while the job is under way. Such changes increase the complexity of the task and the workload for the designer/programmer.

4.2.4   Relationships and Intuition

All the kinds of data described above can be documented with varying degrees of precision. Once the list is assembled, an attempt should be made to organize the data. By structuring the items in tables or hierarchies or diagrams, the designer can begin to recognize relationships among the data elements that were never stated explicitly. The process of looking for relationships is itself a useful design aid. Decision tables and activity networks have been developed to support this process. The relationships, when found, are a useful input to design because they provide guidance on which functions belong together in the program, which ones are exceptions or append-ages, what the file and record formats should be, and what conditions represent computational errors. The relationships may be the only aid the designer/programmer has for resolving design decisions.

The list of data and relationships describes and delimits the problem but does not provide a solution. The designer must study the data and relationships, integrate them into a picture of the problem, and concentrate on the integrated picture to discover a solution. Polanyi describes the dis-covery process as straining the imagination until the solution appears vir-tually spontaneously [5]. Poincaré called the second stage "illumination." Polanyi calls it "intuition." Intuition integrates the clues and other material the imagination has dug up. It happens by tacit means that are impossible to explain. The same process, Polanyi explains, allows a person to recognize a friend or ride a bicycle. There is no explicit rule for integrating facial details. There is no book that teaches balance and timing. The individual tacitly knows how to do it. Similarly, there is no rule that explains how to integrate all the data and relationships in a problem to provide an under-standing of how to solve the problem. Fortunately, the person who strains his imagination to understand the problem will intuitively find a path to a solution. The published principles of design are merely signposts to keep him from wandering too far from the direct route.

4.3 SELECTING AN APPROACH

Any programming task that can be completely defined can be programmed.[2] This is true because the statement of the problem, if complete, contains all the equations and logic necessary for solution. Another truism is that any problem can be programmed in many ways. The wide variation in pro-grammer productivity that is so evident in classroom situations where all the students are given the same problem demonstrates the second statement [6]. The conclusions to be drawn from these two statements include the following.

---

2. This is "Aron's axiom." The somewhat facetious label was applied by the author to draw attention to the fact that few projects get into trouble because the programs cannot be written. Many projects get into trouble because of poor problem defini-tion or weak management. Aron's axiom is a recommendation to emphasize man-agement education and project control. It was important to make this recom-mendation in the author's organization in 1966 when third-generation technology made it necessary to decide where to spend education and investment dollars—on project management or programming technology training.

Orchard-Hays stated the converse principle at the 1960 Western Joint Computer Conference: "Nothing can be mechanized which cannot be precisely defined."

- Thorough problem definition ensures feasibility of the end product.
- For every problem there is a large set of feasible programs, one of which is better than all the others (according to some set of criteria).
- Good program design is a search for the best program.

The crudest brute-force methods should lead to one of the feasible programs. The difference between just any design and a good design is the degree of judgment exercised by the designer in making tradeoffs among alternative feasible programs to come up with the best one. The designer will not be able to investigate all possible alternatives but should always consider at least two or three.

The tradeoffs that are important in a given situation depend on the circumstances. The factors affected by the design tradeoffs can include any or all of the following [7].

Project cost

Project schedule

Skill required to implement

Computer requirements for implementation

Operating costs after delivery

Maintainability, modifiability of delivered program

Effect on designer/programmer satisfaction and career growth

Effect on future opportunities for user's (or designer's) organization

A decision based on one of these factors affects all the others. When there are clear criteria for ranking the factors, the side effects may be unimportant. Without clear criteria, the designer's judgment will favor decisions which protect him against failure and enhance his image. That means that he will design a program that fits his skills and experience. It may lack innovation except in those areas where the design particularly interests him. This approach is probably optimal when the programmer has a lot of experience in the problem area. It may yield inefficient programs or overruns when he is less familiar with the subject.

4.3.1   Cost and Schedule are Most Important

The use of existing programs, library packages, or libraries of macroinstructions is recommended when it is important to do a job rapidly and at low cost. When existing programs fit the job, the development time is sharply reduced. The weakness of this recommendation is that unless the existing program is an obvious and suitable solution to the problem, the designer may spend so much time studying it or modifying it that nothing is saved.

Macroinstructions are not so risky. They are usually prepared within organizations which have many jobs of the same general type. For such organizations it is cost-effective to identify the common functions that occur in most of their jobs and develop macros (or subroutines) to handle them. Each macro has a small functional scope which can be very clearly described. It is easy for a programmer who knows the macros to use them as building blocks for any job in the same class. To facilitate this, the designer should lay out the program so that all of the functions that correspond to macros are readily identifiable. The language of the design and the language of the macro library catalog should be identical where possible.

Certainly cost and schedule targets are easier to make if the design is kept as simple as possible. This guideline is not unique to a low-cost environment. As noted in Chapter 2, unnecessary frills should always be avoided because they increase complexity and cost without any offsetting advantage. Programming in a higher-level language is also appropriate in all contexts. It is particularly important when development cost and schedule are more critical than program execution time since the higher-level language can increase programmer productivity.

4.3.2 Computer Time is Scarce

Many installations are so fully loaded that time is not immediately available for program checkout. It may take one or more days to get the results of a run. When this type of turnaround is expected, the designer should plan the job so as to reduce dependence on the computer. This can be accomplished by careful modularization of the design and by increased emphasis on desk checking. Modularization breaks the program and the work plan into relatively independent pieces so that when one module is sent to the computer, there is always another available to work on. Each section of the program must be separately processible for this approach to work. Consequently, the modules may have to be embedded in a simulated environment, which provides the data and driving commands that would normally be provided by the neighbor modules. The simulated environment creates extra work at both ends of the implementation. It represents additional code that must be added to each module for checkout purposes and later removed when the completed program is reassembled. Nevertheless, it permits implementation to proceed on several modules in parallel.

Thorough desk checking reduces the number of runs required to debug each module. The programmer who studies his unit carefully before he submits it to the computer looks at the entire program unit. He sees its global logic, as well as the small details of code. Consequently, if there are basic design errors, he can catch them. He can also find all, or at least several, of the errors in the lines of code. Good turnaround often interferes with good desk checking habits. The programmer finds it too easy to let the computer find the bugs, one· at a time. This is a poor use of both the programmer's time and the computer. Even when interactive debugging from a terminal is possible, debugging line by line can overlook logical errors (see Chapter 7). Thorough desk checking is *always* good programming technique; when computer time is scarce, it may be essential.

4.3.3 Program Execution Time is Critical

Program execution time is a direct cost that the user wants to minimize. In the 1950s, computers were so expensive that every job was hand-tailored for fast execution. By the 1970s, computer costs had shrunk to such an extent that it would sometimes be better to waste machine cycles than to pay the tailoring cost. Therefore a tradeoff is necessary between the cost of execution and the cost of development. As a general rule, optimization is justified only for programs run repetitively for long periods of time. Within this class of programs, three situations most commonly require optimization.

1. Real-time systems, in which response requirements limit the running time permitted the program [8].
2. Production data processing where the running time is measured in hours, the program uses a lot of computing resources, and the program is run frequently.
3. Production data processing where several long-running programs must be run sequentially and the last must be finished by a deadline [9].

Critical kernels of large systems programs are a special case of real-time systems. A dispatching algorithm, an allocation routine, or a protection interlock may be shared by all other programs in the machine. The time-shared function is a bottleneck. It is common to set a maximum service response time for such a program to prevent the bottleneck from being troublesome. Regression tests of large systems programs and programming support library operations are examples of frequently run production jobs. Deadline schedules for production usually apply to cyclic business applications. They usually affect systems programmers only when one machine supports both activities.

Given a performance objective, many designer/programmers automatically assume that the program will have to be written in assembly language. They do not believe that a higher-level language will provide the ability to get at specific machine facilities; therefore the object program compiled from a higher-level language will be inefficient. This belief is not always valid, but even if it were valid, it is irrelevant. The important issue regarding performance is to make the design optimal. Once the shortest execution path is designed, the implementation language is arbitrary. If a higher-level language is selected for its ease of use and readability, and the design in this language executes fast enough, the problem is solved. If the object program is too slow, it can be hand-tailored to improve its speed. But if the design is clumsy, no language will compensate.

The guidelines for design of fast object programs include the following.

- Use top-down stepwise programming refinement (see Section 4.4.1) to minimize program steps.

- Use large core space to minimize memory overlays.

- Establish the main loop and place all other steps outside that loop.

- Organize the data to minimize search and access time.

- Minimize overhead by using as few operating-system services and as few execution-time linkages as possible.

- Organize the program functions and hardware devices to maximize the number of simultaneous I/O and compute activities that can logically proceed.

The guidelines for fast execution tend to undercut the principle that small modules represent good design. A balance must be struck between the length of straight line code resulting from elimination of linkages and the maintainability of the end product. The situations where performance is important also place a high premium on reliability and maintainability.

4.3.4 Maintainability and Modifiability are Important

Maintainability is the ability to repair bugs in operating programs. *Modifiability* is the ability to make functional changes to operating programs. Developers of software systems who make multiple releases of their products spend upwards of a third of the total product cost maintaining and modifying the current release. For a long-lived system, such as OS/360, the cost of maintenance and upgrade was substantially larger than the cost of building OS/360-Version 1. In addition, every user of such a system must install the fixes; this requires a system support group in each location. Such a large investment justifies considerable design effort to make maintenance and modification easier.

The primary design objective is to eliminate the need for maintenance and modification by making the program perfect. No one knows how to accomplish this goal. Instead, designers plan with maintenance and modification in mind. They follow such guidelines as these:

- *Protect the program.* Build in defensive mechanisms, such as data controls, checkpoint/restart, reasonableness tests, privileged or protected modes, diagnostic aids.

- *Prove the correctness of the program.* Apply one of the techniques for showing that the program terminates with the correct result [10].
- *Simplify the change process.* Break the program into small, logically isolated modules so that a change can be plugged in with minimal side effects; provide a generator to reconstruct the program with the change properly included.

The decision to protect increases development cost and execution time. The decision to prove correctness increases development cost and may be too hard or even impossible. The decision to modularize conforms to the general rules of good design, but it may increase execution time. A system generator will increase development cost. (In each case, it is assumed that the program documentation is thorough and useful to a maintenance programmer.) All these problems are to be expected in a tradeoff analysis. Every situation has some pluses and some minuses. The designer is forced to weigh them— objectively if possible, subjectively if necessary and make a decision.

4.3.5   Effect on Peripheral Issues is Important

Situations arise in which none of the previous factors are as important as peripheral issues. Employee satisfaction and career growth constitute such an issue. Consider the following two examples.

Example 1.   An experienced employee has been working very hard on her last job and expects to have a respite to catch up on the technical literature. Instead, she has been called on to do an urgent but straightforward program unit. During design, she notes that a standard approach is available, but there is a chance that a new technique can have a significant effect on the running time of the end product. She estimates that the standard approach will take four weeks. The novel approach will require two weeks of study and two to four weeks of work, with a possibility that it will not succeed. In this situation, many managers will let her proceed with the novel approach because (a) she wants to and her job satisfaction will improve, (b) she may come up with a substantially better result, (c) the risk can be absorbed, and (d) she has earned some reward for her prior performance.

Example 2.   A manager has several junior employees who have been through basic programmer training and have been writing simple programs for several months. A new job request calls for one programmer, but it is much more sophisticated than any of the juniors have tackled. The manager has several options. He can do the whole job personally. He can do the design personally and let a junior code and debug it. Or he can let a junior do the whole job. If the junior can handle it, the manager should let him go it alone. What if it is too hard for the junior? The manager can still leave him alone and hope he will learn from his mistakes. But this decision will not necessarily get the job done, and it will probably annoy the user. The middle ground is to give full responsibility to the junior but arrange to review his work frequently—say twice as often as usual.

Some additional investment in cost or schedule is warranted when training is the most important objective. This mode of operation has been very successful in training departments when the managers were told they must qualify their employees for promotion to the next level. Nontraining managers were not given this explicit objective. After one year, the programmers in the training department were the most sought-after programmers in the organization. They had developed better work traits and programming technique than their peers. This mode of operation was expected to cost extra because of the time spent on progress reviews and education discussions, but in fact, no cost differential was found.[3]

The decision to invest extra resources in a program can also be made to build a base for future opportunities. Thus, where the normal approach is to design only to the limit of the objectives document, it may pay to broaden the specifications to cover other functions that logically relate to the current objectives. The most common and most simple such design assigns a name to any multivalue entity. Changes to the number of values the entity can have will not affect the program logic. Table-driven programs are extensions of the symbolic name approach. They store information in tables which are free to expand and contract while the program that refers to them stays fixed. The tables can contain data, definitions, subroutines, pointers, etc.

If the user has not asked for such extra facilities, the odds are pretty good that he does not want them and will not pay for them. Therefore this type of tradeoff is usually made by a developer who sees a future value to his own operations and is willing to bear the expense.

4.3.6 Summary of Tradeoffs

Considering only the factors discussed above, one can identify design techniques which are recommended all the time plus some which are favored under certain circumstances (Fig. 4.1). The list at this point is gross and incomplete. It is given to emphasize the need for tradeoff analysis in the design phase. Additional tradeoff decisions must be made throughout the course of the project [11]. As problems arise, as conditions evolve, it is

---

3. The author had such training departments as well as nontraining departments in his area of responsibility in 1962–1963 and again in 1967–1969. The results were as stated above.

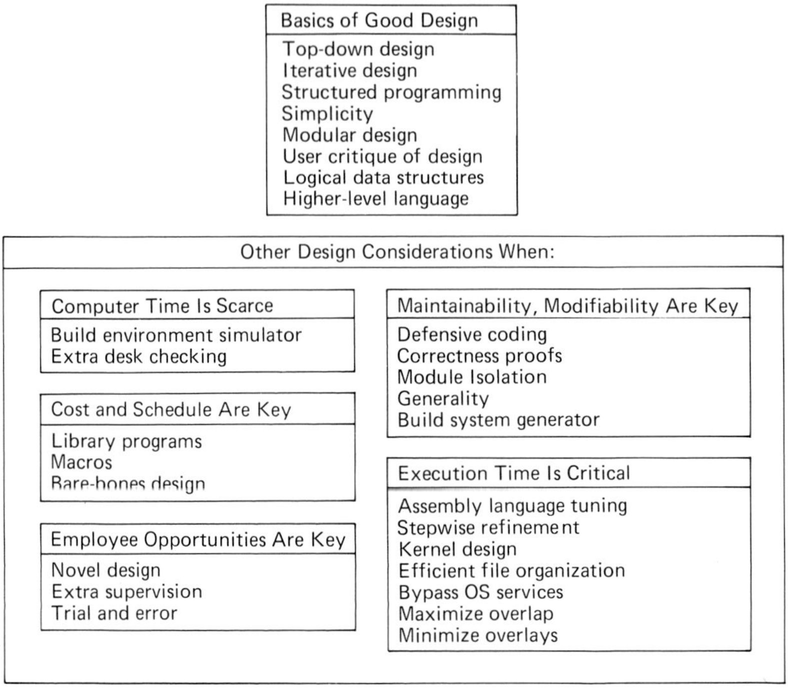

Basics of Good Design
Top-down design Iterative design Structured programming Simplicity Modular design User critique of design Logical data structures Higher-level language

Other Design Considerations When:	
Computer Time Is Scarce Build environment simulator Extra desk checking	**Maintainability, Modifiability Are Key** Defensive coding Correctness proofs Module Isolation Generality Build system generator
Cost and Schedule Are Key Library programs Macros Bare-bones design	**Execution Time Is Critical** Assembly language tuning Stepwise refinement Kernel design Efficient file organization Bypass OS services Maximize overlap Minimize overlays
Employee Opportunities Are Key Novel design Extra supervision Trial and error	

Fig. 4.1 Design tradeoff considerations.

necessary to reevaluate the design specifications and make new decisions. The discovery/resolution process is continuous and iterative. Frequently, the process will back up to modify a previous decision and start again from that point. A good design will allow such iterations and contain the rework within the affected area. The integrity of other sections of the program will be preserved, and the work done on the other sections will not be wasted.

4.4   TOP-DOWN DESIGN

Top-down is the natural way to design a program unit. As long as the unit is conceptually manageable, most designers will approach it in the same way. They will decide (a) what the inputs are, (b) how the data should be represented, (c) what the outputs must be, and (d) what processes will transform the input into the output.

By completely defining the inputs, the data sets, the outputs, and the transforms, the designer has structured a solution to the problem. The details of how the transform processes work need not be spelled out in order to demonstrate that the data flow is correct. Thus, on one page, the designer can show the logic of the entire program at a top (or gross) level of design.[4] The important facet of top-down design is that it establishes the logical *structure* of the solution before it decides on the detailed *elements* of the solution. The approach lends itself to controlled, verifiable, economical development of a design that satisfies the tradeoff criteria. When top-down design is combined with top-down implementation, as described in the next chapter, program development approaches optimum performance.

4.4.1   Stepwise Refinement

After the top-level design has been evaluated and verified, the designer begins to expand each of the process blocks in more detail. At this point, discovery/resolution comes into play. A particular process will turn out to be more complex than expected. In order to simplify it, the designer will return to the top-level design and reconsider the original decisions regarding data specifications, control, and data flow. The process will continue to iterate, with each new decision refining the design to meet the criteria selected for the project. Wirth in an excellent tutorial paper [12] uses the Eight-Queens Problem to illustrate *stepwise refinement*. The problem involves arranging eight queens on an 8 × 8 chessboard so that no queen can take any other; i.e., every row, column, and diagonal must contain at most one queen. The problem is simple, but the most direct solution to it—testing all possible board layouts—requires the evaluation of 2^{32} possible answers. Stepwise refinement of the obvious solution leads to equally valid solutions which take far fewer steps. The general idea is to find a method of rejecting all moves that do not lead to a solution and to try to avoid reexamining any rejected moves. To accomplish this, Wirth must readjust his data specifications as well as his procedural logic. He ends up with a program that finds 92 solutions to the Eight-Queens Problem in 15,720 tests. For this problem the improvement in performance is on the order of 25,000 to 1—from an estimated seven hours to an actual run time of less than a second.

The experienced designer learns to look for certain fundamental opportunities for refinement, but unfortunately, there are no simple guidelines that apply to all situations. Some of the more common refinements include the following.

Formatting data to simplify data references

Ordering data to shorten search paths

---

4. Although the term *top-down* is widely used to describe logical design, it would be equally effective to think of the process as *outside-in*. In either case, the procedure grows progressively more detailed.

Using indexes to shorten search paths

Encoding data to reduce space requirements

Omitting data that can be calculated

Employing flags to record information learned during execution

Scheduling processes so that they execute faster

Batching transactions to make processing more efficient

Saving intermediate results or status indicators to avoid recalculation

Postponing processes that may become unnecessary if certain events occur

Placing programmed decisions as high in the design structure as possible so that they will be executed the smallest number of times

Examining the input as it arrives and adjusting the program so that it is optimal for the actual data

All the decisions create problems as well as solve them. The time required to encode data may offset the time saved in moving shorter records. The decision to treat certain processes on an exception basis may backfire if the frequency of the exceptions is underestimated. Placing programmed decisions at the top level of the design may interfere with later modifications to the program. Nevertheless, each of these refinements is decidable. Reasons can be found to explain the advantages and disadvantages of each decision. Once made and documented, the decision can be reevaluated, if necessary, when the design process turns up new information.

Much harder to cope with are situations that are undecidable or very difficult to analyze. A disk access queuing strategy may depend not only on the inherent order of retrieval requests but also on whether other, unrelated system programs have access to the same disk. A strategy which assumes that the disk access arm has not moved since the last retrieval may fail if several programs can move the arm in between retrieval requests. In such a case, the designer lacks the knowledge necessary to assess the impact of the operating environment on the design. A useful guideline in this situation is to adopt weak assumptions because the environment is not under your control. A weak assumption regarding disk queues is that the requests arrive randomly and the access arm is in an arbitrary position. The design strategy can take its chances that, on the average, requests will be serviced in the average access time for the device. A strong assumption might be that queries arrive randomly and the access arm is positioned over the last requested track. This assumption suggests batching and sorting the requests by disk location so that the arm makes minimum-length moves between fetches. If the assumption holds, fetch time will be much better than average disk access time. But if the assumption fails, access time may be worse. The damage done when a strong assumption is wrong can be fatal. The effects of weak assumptions can generally be repaired as operating experience is gained with the program. In the absence of certainty, totally safe assumptions should be made.

4.4.2   Modularity

Modular design isolates the functions of each program block from all others. Communication between programs is permitted only through well-defined interfaces. As a result, the inner workings of a module need not be known to other modules. Design changes can often be restricted to a single module with no side effects propagating to neighbor modules. These features of a modular design parallel the features of human organizations where each group of people can function independently of all others as long as the chain of command is effective. Just as human organizations depend on the personality of the person in charge, program designs depend on the style of the designer. At least three approaches to modularization can be recognized.

1. Modularization of program function [13]
2. Modularization by sequence of execution [14]
3. Modularization by hierarchy of program control flow [15]

Each approach can solve the problems of function and change isolation, which are important to the manageability of the project [16].

Modularization of program function is based on identifying all the things the program must do. Some designers favoring this approach tend to segregate manipulative functions that are used more than once during program execution. The functions could be character string readers, string modifiers, file search, status or value tests, ordering routines, output writers, etc. As far as possible, they are defined to be content-independent so that they will work even when their input specifications change. This approach is particularly attractive to those organizations which build macro or subroutine libraries for reuse on subsequent jobs. In use the functional modules provide service on request to application-oriented processing routines. The modules are defined in terms of the input they need and the output they will generate. Their method of operation is often not disclosed. Modularization by activity appears in some data communications systems; each incoming transaction type is associated with a set of program modules that completely process it. Data-based systems are sometimes organized in such a way that all processing associated with a single file is placed in a single module. Both of these approaches are less common than segregating manipulative functions.

Modularization by sequence of execution breaks the problem into the major activities to be performed sequentially from the start of the job. This is the most common approach to design since it matches problem flow with program functions. Its disadvantage is that, although it isolates modules, it permits modules to share common data; therefore a single data change can affect multiple modules. A combination of this approach with modularization of function can offset this disadvantage.

The third method of modularization can be used in combination with either or both of the others. Hierarchical design assigns superior and subordinate roles to the modules. The relationships established in the hierarchy determine the permissible module interactions. Isolation of noninteracting modules is complete; isolation of interacting modules is partial. Changes to modules are not allowed to propagate upward, but they can affect subordinate modules.

The choice of an approach to modularization depends on which method is easiest to visualize. Flowcharts and diagrams are more useful in the latter two methods than in the first. Many people find it easier to explain what they are doing when they key the design to flow rather than (or in addition to) function. Top-down implementation also benefits from a flow-oriented design since meaningful simulative tests can be run at any stage of the implementation. On the other hand, a function-oriented design may be easier and more economical to maintain. It may also reduce the gross cost of multiple implementations of similar problems.

4.4.3 Working Within a Large System

Top-down design presents no problems on a one-person job which is completely independent of other programs. The designer can get the whole problem straight in his head. He has considerable latitude in his choice of the top-level functions and need not force his design into a mold dictated by others. The designer whose assignment has been carved out of a large project is not so fortunate. By definition, if the large project is being designed from the top, many critical decisions will have been made before the program units are assigned. Data sets used by more than one unit will have been specified and formatted. Control flows and program-to-program communications will have been specified. Language conventions, naming conventions, and even document forms may have been established as project standards. Under these circumstances, program unit design can still proceed from the top down, but the designer has less freedom of action.

In the extreme cases, large projects cannot be subdivided into 100 percent logically coherent program units. The natural breakdown of the job will result in the definition of some units that are too big for one person.

When this situation is recognized, the large unit can be assigned to a team. The team can then carry the design further and generate subunits which, although they are not logically coherent by themselves, can be understood by each team member in the context of the larger unit. It is necessary for the team to work together on the design breakout in order for each person to get the whole picture. If the task is subdivided arbitrarily prior to assignment, the individual designers may not be able to find a logical thread around which to do stepwise refinement. They will be able to design a solution by brute force, but there is little chance that their results will be optimal.

4.4.4   Maintenance

The role of a maintenance programmer is to modify existing program units in order to fix errors or improve the unit. In either case, the same kind of analysis and design is required as for a new program unit. Maintenance should require less analysis since, after all, the program exists. Nevertheless, unless the maintenance programmer is already familiar with the program, he must make a thorough analysis of what it does and how. The effort needed for analysis depends almost entirely on the quality of the program documentation. A program package that contains current specifications as well as a fully commented listing in structured programming format is easy to understand. If only the program listing is available, analysis may be harder than writing a brand new program.

Design should be done so as to localize and minimize the extent of the program change. If the change is in response to an error report, the first step is to verify that the reported error in fact exists. Next, verify that the error is a program error, not (a) an input data error, (b) an operator error, (c) a result of machine malfunction, (d) a job control language error, (e) a mistake in a test program, or (f) any other trouble that does not require a program change. Next, determine whether the error is due to an error in the program or an ambiguous or poorly worded specification. If the trouble is due to a faulty specification (as often occurs when a program is improved or changed and the specification is not brought into agreement with the program), decide whether to change the specification—in which case the program is correct—or to change the program. Finally, using the design specification, isolate the portion of the program that is in error and fix it. Prepare new tests to verify the correction, and go through the program package thoroughly, updating all references to this portion of the program so that the listings will be compatible with the other documents.

If the change has been authorized to add a new function or improve performance, the justification procedure need not be repeated. Here the emphasis should be placed on isolating the change so that it has minimum impact on the rest of the program, which is known to work. The easiest way to isolate the change is to make it an appendage to a convenient break-point in the existing program. This can be accomplished by inserting a new block between existing blocks or by extending a transfer vector or case table to include the new block of code. Each of these methods has a single entry and a single exit from the new code, but each uses some linkage code that may degrade performance. That may call for hand-tuning of the entire program to meet the performance objective. As before, the new design features must be shown in every applicable document. Only when all program documentation reflects the change is the maintenance task complete.

4.5 DESIGN SPECIFICATION

The output of the design process is a *specification*. The specification document serves two purposes in development. It conveys the design to the implementer, and it establishes the criteria for testing the end product. If the designer intends to implement his own design, there is a tendency to slight the specification document and carry some of the design in the head. This is unwise. Not only will some of the logic get lost along the way, but an important communication device will be lost. The design specification should be the basis for communication with the user. Only by reviewing the written specification with the user can the designer be sure he is doing the right job. Later, the user will be able to relate acceptance test results to the spec. And after delivery, the spec can serve as the functional description portion of the user's program package. The document includes the following kinds of data when applicable.

Title and identifier of program

Description of program function and performance

    Inputs

    Outputs

    Interfaces

    Method—how the program works

Usage information—how the program is run

    Initialization procedures

    Interactive user sign-on procedures

    Operator messages

    Interactive user messages

    Cross-reference list of data sets used

    Cross-reference list of programs referred to

Programming language
Equipment configuration
    Development support
    Operational system
Support software required
Test specification
Documentation specification
Standards, conventions, linkages, constraints
Reference documents
Responsible individuals
    Designer programmer
    User
Management and control data
    Reporting requirements
    Schedules and estimates
    Justification and evaluation criteria
    Graphic summary of program
        Flowchart
        Tables
        Record formats
        Core and bulk storage layouts

It is useful to the user and to maintenance personnel to have the designer's reasons for critical design decisions recorded with "Method." If any of this data is unavailable when the designer and the user get together to agree that the spec is acceptable, it can be filled in later unless it is critical to further progress.

The form of the specification need not be rigid as long as it communicates effectively. Most programming managers have local standards for documentation, which dictate the form they will accept; however, there is no proof that one form is superior to all others. The author prefers a combination of narrative, structured, and graphic techniques. The narrative serves as an abstract that anyone can understand, whether knowledgeable about programming or not. The structured portions—tables, lists, shorthand, specialized design language—provide precision, economy of expression, and convenience for the designer/programmer. Graphics—flowcharts, layouts, configurations—clarify complex interactions or time-dependent flows. No one technique is entirely satisfactory for all purposes. A few important ones deserve special mention.

4.5.1   Specification Language

Chapter 1 suggested that higher-level languages could be used for specifying program designs. Formal specification languages, such as APL, do not appear to have wide appeal to systems programmers even though the language is rigorous enough for the purpose. More and more programmers, however, are using informal techniques to the same end. The purpose of a specification language is to provide an expressive, precise, unambiguous, readable notation that is easy to use. The language should be machine-readable, so that on-line specification libraries can be maintained. The informal languages that can be used in this way include pidgin versions of PL/I, ALGOL, and similar higher-level programming languages. Existing programming languages make an attractive base because they permit the specification to grow into the program with a minimum of rework. The difference between the specification and the source program is that the spec may contain illegal statements, including ordinary natural language, interspersed with the allowable statements of the language. The designer uses the syntax of the programming language where it is convenient, and he lapses into a loose descriptive form elsewhere. Thus, the pidgin specification cannot be compiled. It can, however, be read by a programmer. It will flow the same way the program should flow. It will provide hints as to how to proceed with the details of coding. It will explicitly provide the language for program interfaces and external references. It may provide all the necessary data declarations and file structuring statements.

The deficiency of a specification language is that some people find it hard to visualize the program structure by reading a programlike listing. They prefer a more graphic spec. Yet the listing may be more complete than a flowchart because there are no such limits on expression as those imposed by flowchart box dimensions. Structure can be emphasized to a degree by indenting blocks of the listing. But the choice of technique is largely a matter of taste (and local standards).[5]

4.5.2   Flowcharts

A *flowchart* is a graphic representation of a process that uses a variety of symbols for the different kinds of activities in the process. Its primary purpose is to clarify complicated process flows. It shows structural information

---

5. R. E. Sprague in "A Western View of Computer History" (*CACM,* Vol. 15, No. 7, July 1972) recalls that graphic-oriented and equation-oriented tastes are not restricted to programmers. Pioneer computer engineers also split into two schools: East Coast (logic diagrams) and West Coast (Boolean equations).

explicitly: precedence relationships, transfers of control, loops, decision points, block structures. It can be as detailed as desired and can be organized just like a program. A top-level flowchart can refer to separate lower-level flowcharts. References to substructures such as subroutines or library programs can be included. At each level, a well-drawn flowchart is as clear and easy to read as the top-level chart. But as noted above, the use of small area symbols limits the amount of explanatory data that can be placed on the chart. A flowchart must almost always be accompanied by a narrative or specification language description of its operation.

The widespread use of flowcharts early in the history of program development encouraged standardization of flowchart symbols [17]. People wanted to be able to recognize at a glance which sections of the chart referred to processes, which to data, which to decisions. They also wanted to be able to automate flowcharting so that a programmer could store a flowchart in the computer and make changes in it without redrawing the whole thing. The computer could then produce a nice, neat, printed version for the program documentation. Vendors cooperated by supplying flowcharting templates, automated flowcharting forms, and computer input sheets. By 1970, the ANSI (American National Standards Institute, Inc.) and ISO (International Organization for Standardization) flowchart standards were compatible worldwide. It was relatively easy to get agreement on the flowchart standards because the symbols were simple and placed no constraints on the design process [18]. Designers do things with flowcharts which are hard to do with specification languages. Hardware and software configurations can both be shown with flowchart symbols. In program flowcharts, manual inputs or operator actions can be shown graphically, and specific hardware storage devices can be pictured. These things can be done in a spec language using comments, but they are not immediately recognizable as in a flowchart. Within limits a flowchart can show several concurrent parallel operations. A sequential specification language can not achieve this visibility. Finally, the flowchart can expand beyond the confines of the program. The same flowcharting techniques can be used to describe systems comprising manual activities, machine processes, programs, files, what-have-you. In fact, flowcharts were commonly used by systems analysts to describe applications long before computers were available. The most common of these charts showed inputs on the left of the sheet, outputs on the right, and in-between a box containing an abbreviated list of the functions in the process. Complicated processes were broken into several hierarchical charts, in which explanatory notes under the hierarchical input/process/output boxes clarified each chart.[6]

---

6. In IBM, this method supplanted detailed flowcharts; it is referred to as HIPO.

Some organizations require not only that a flowchart be provided in the design specification but that a very detailed instruction-level flowchart be provided in the deliverable program documentation. The benefits of such detailed ex post facto flowcharts are questionable. They are intended to help users and maintenance programmers diagnose errors, but they do not. When an error has been isolated in a section of code, the most helpful data is in the program listing itself. A modular program with thoroughly commented code can be read directly by the diagnostician. It need not be accompanied by an equivalent flowchart.

4.5.3   Tables and Decision Tables

A table shows the value of one or more arguments. It is a compact way to record a large number of conditional or dependent items. Properly used, tables are aids to clarity and completeness, and they have the added advantage of suggesting implementation techniques to programmers.

The simplest type of table is an index which shows the values of Y for each value of X. For example, a computer interrupt is identified by a number, X, which is also the argument of a table containing Y, the address of the program that responds to interrupt X. This simple one-dimensional table format can be used to list error conditions and operator messages. A two-dimensional table containing binary entries can be used to show that program X refers to program Y. This is a basic cross-reference table. The same format can be used for multivalued entries. More complex tables can be constructed, but they tend to be too hard to use, and therefore it is common to tabulate relationships between many dimensions in multiple two-dimensional arrays.

The entry in a tabular display can be anything from a single mark or character to a long expression. This means that tables can be used to show the layout of data records, files, and other items with internal structure. A variety of such tables is shown in Figs. 4.2 and 4.3. The tables in Fig. 4.2 are one-argument lists; they are read

IF X THEN Y ELSE UNDEFINED;

where X is the input argument and Y is the entry in the table. Figure 4.3 contains two-argument lists; they are read

IF (X AND Y) THEN Z ELSE UNDEFINED;

where Z is the entry in the table. When a one-argument table, such as Fig. 4.2(d), contains an entry with internal structure, a programmer may treat it like a two-argument table. A reference to Job Summary would apply to

Input	Address
3	1234
5	3725
8	9046

(a)

Message Number	Message
Condition 11	Task queue space full
Condition 12	Task execution time exceeded — Abend 12
Operator action 1	Mount file (K) on unit (M)

(b)

Word	Definition
RECSIZE	Logical record length
BLKSIZE	Physical record length
UNIT	Direct access device type

(c)

Record Name	Field Name, Length
Job Summary	Job Name (8AN), IDENT (14N), END (14N), Core (4N), Disk ((3N)), Tape (2N), Data Cell (1N), Reader (1N), Punch (1N), Console (1N), Terminal Key (2N), Terminal Display (2N), Control Data (5AN)

(d)

Fig. 4.2 One-argument tables: (a) index (transfer vector, case table); (b) message list, including items to be completed at execution time; (c) dictionary of symbols, names, data elements; (d) record format.

the entire record. Job Summary (3) would apply only to the field END. Thus the designer's table suggests a hierarchical indexing scheme to the programmer.

All tables are inherently complete. For every valid argument, there is an entry. For any input value that cannot be found in the argument list,

Program ID \ External References	XIUNC	REFCBIC	REFCDPT	REHALLOC	GETMAIN
QMBEDIT	x				x
REFCDSUB					x
REFCNTRL		x	x		x
REHTAPCP	x				
REHTEOF		x		x	x

(a)

User \ Data Set	Log in Codes	Application A	Application B	Job queue	Library Directory
Smith, Systems Support	3	4	1	3	3
Jones, Dept A	4	3	1	2	1
Brown, Dept B	4	4	3	2	1
Johnson, Dept C	4	4	4	2	1
Roberts, Operations	1	4	1	3	

1 Read
2 Write
3 Read/Write
4 No access

(b)

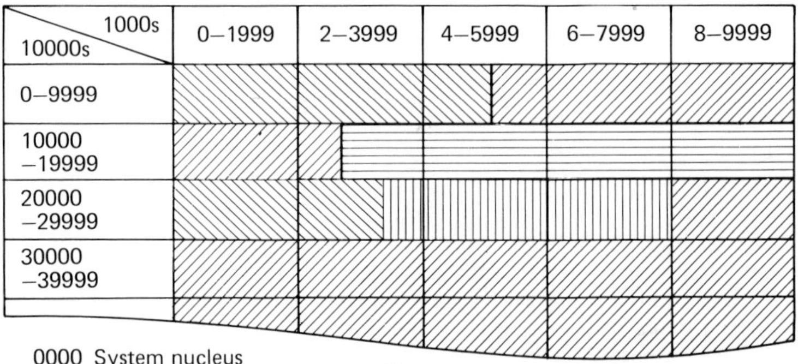

(c)

0000 System nucleus
5000 I/O buffer space
12750 PL/I
20000 Real region I
23250 Real region II
28000 Virtual storage region

Fig. 4.3 Two-argument tables: (a) single-valued cross-reference; (b) multivalued authorization table; (c) semigraphic storage map.

Decision Table A.3.2 Output Printer Control	Rules							
Conditions	1	2	3	4	5	6	7	ELSE
First line	Y	N	—	—	N	N	—	
Line buffer full	Y	Y	N	—	Y	Y	Y	
Printer Ready	Y	Y	—	N	Y	Y	Y	
Carriage control	—	1	—	—	2	3	—	

1 = Single space
   2 = Skip two spaces
   3 = Skip to new page								

Line Count < 50	—	Y	—	—	—	—	N	
Actions								
Skip to new page	x					x	x	
Print heading	x					x	x	
Skip two spaces	x				x	x	x	
Space		x						
Print line buffer	x	x			x	x	x	
Print check	x	x			x	x	x	
Release line buffer	x	x			x	x	x	
Wait loop			x	x				
Go to Flowchart A.3.7								x
Return	x	x			x	x	x	

Stub   Entry

Fig. 4.4 Decision table.

there is no defined entry. The designer must provide instructions for the use of the table covering what to do when an input value is not accounted for in the table, for example:

- Call an error routine.
- Interpolate between the two nearest argument values (or extrapolate) if the table entries are related by an equation.
- Design an explicit entry for the input.

A special kind of table, called a *decision table,* has unique value to the designer. It is a device for itemizing very complex decision procedures with assurance that all possible conditions have been accounted for. It is a problem-oriented tool in that it organizes information about the problem, but it does not necessarily do so in a way that is efficient to program [19]. Decision tables are constructed as in Fig. 4.4 to show the action to be taken for each possible set of conditions. There are four sections to the decision table.

1. *Condition stub:* a list of the conditions relevant to the choice of action. Conditions are determined during problem analysis. In general, only conditions that can exist simultaneously are relevant in the decision table technique. Other conditions can be handled separately in flowcharts or listings. A condition can be either a statement or an expression.

2. *Condition entry:* a list of the possible states of the environment, i.e., all combinations of all possible states of the conditions. The entries are constructed one condition at a time. First, all allowable states of the first condition are written down. Second, all allowable states of the second condition are written down for each possible state of the first condition. This step requires the first condition entry to be repeated once for every state of the second entry. Any condition can be multivalued; e.g., "Operating System" can be O, D, E, R in the example of the previous chapter.

In Table 4.1, the process is illustrated for a set of condition statements which can have two states, represented by Y (yes) or N (no). When all conditions statements are Boolean (i.e., the condition entry is yes/no or true/false), the decision table has *limited* entries and the number of entries (columns) is 2^c, where c is the number of condition statements. The number of entries can be reduced by using DON'T CARE entries. For instance, if a parity error always leads to an error routine, it may be immaterial that interrupts were enabled and an I/O interrupt had occurred. Table 4.1 could be shortened to Table 4.2.

When the statement in the condition stub can have more complex states, such as multiple values (O, D, E, R) or ranges ($20 \leq a \leq 40$, $40 \leq b \leq 60$), it adds a new block of the table for every possible value or partition of the range. A table with 3 Boolean conditions, one 4-valued condition, one 9-valued condition, one "greater than" condition, and one 4-part range condition will have a maximum of

$$2 \cdot 2 \cdot 2 \cdot 4 \cdot 9 \cdot 2 \cdot 4 = 2304 \text{ columns.}$$

This is obviously too large to manipulate. Fortunately, practical problems can be partitioned by using DON'T CAREs and by lumping exceptions into a single category ELSE, which leads to an error routine or another table. [A multivalued statement (Operating Systems: O/D/E/R) can be converted to a set of limited entry expressions (Operating System = 0: Y/N, etc.). This tends to increase the potential size of the table since a 4-valued condition will become four 2-valued conditions, but it may also increase the number of DON'T CAREs for a net reduction in table size.] In any case, it is possible to account for all possible entries; this makes the decision table a disciplinary aid to design completeness.

TABLE 4.1. BUILDING LIMITED ENTRY DECISION TABLE

	Condition stub	Condition entry
Step 1	Interrupt enabled	Y N
Step 2	Interrupt enabled I/O interrupt	Y N Y N Y Y N N
Step 3	Interrupt enabled I/O interrupt Parity error	Y N Y N Y N Y N Y Y N N Y Y N N Y Y Y Y N N N N

TABLE 4.2. CONDENSED DECISION TABLE

Stub	Entry
Interrupt enabled	– Y N Y N
I/O interrupt	– Y Y N N
Parity error	Y N N N N

3. *Action stub:* a list of all actions that can be specified in the problem solution as a consequence of the conditions in the condition stub. The action portion of the decision table is its unique feature. Ordinary tables provide only data. Decision tables show what to do, given certain data.

4. *Action entry:* a list of indicators showing which actions should be executed for each state of the environment. A state is described by the condition entry in one column. The state plus the action entry in the same column is a *rule.* If the action is self-explanatory in the stub, the action entry is simply a check mark. Otherwise, the action entry can be a statement, a computation, or a reference to another specification (listing, flowchart, table, etc.). It is convenient to list the actions in the sequence of execution when possible.

A complete decision table has all four sections. It contains $(n + 1)$ rules. The first n rules are based on the explicit, relevant states of the problem. The $n + 1$st rule, ELSE, is a pointer to another portion of the specification that takes care of all other conditional states. In practical decision tables, n is less than 20. Larger problems should be partitioned into several small tables.

Using a decision table consists of determining the current state of the environment, looking up the corresponding rule, and carrying out the specified actions. The table is read "IF the conditions of Rule i are met THEN

DO the actions of Rule *i*, ELSE GO TO the location indicated by the pointer in Rule *n* + 1." In other words, each rule is tested until either an applicable rule is found or the ELSE rule terminates the search. Programming from a decision table is not so simple since the method of searching the table depends on the probability that a particular rule will apply. Converting a decision table to a program is very much like solving the Eight-Queens problem. Several basic approaches are mentioned in the next chapter.

4.5.4 Combined Techniques

Since each design technique has some pluses and minuses, it makes sense to use a combination of techniques. The attributes of the different techniques suggest their use.

1. *Narrative* is user-oriented. It is easy to read, highly descriptive, often evocative of related facts and concepts. But it is bulky and ambiguous. Narrative should be used for abstracts, comments and descriptions of method, references, and scenarios of planned console activities for operators or interactive users.

2. *Specification language* is terse, precise, machine-readable, and sometimes machine-processible. It is highly effective for expressing sequential processes economically. It can be used for the program summary and for displaying algorithms used in the program.

3. *Flowcharts* are terse, hierarchically structured, graphic representations of a program and its environment. They are highly effective for displaying structure and control flow economically. They can be used for the program summary, operator guide, time dependencies, equipment and support software configurations.

4. *Tables* are arrays of data that are easily referenced by one or more keys or arguments. They are concise means of showing all possible conditions or actions for various situations. Decision tables also incorporate limited procedural and control information. Decision tables can be used to display complex conditional procedures and verify that the design is exhaustive. Other tables can be used to list data formats, storage layouts, cross-references, languages used for programming, error conditions, operator messages, etc. Boehm uses a matrix of system requirements versus properties (such as reliability, response time, storage size, etc.) to guide his analysis and design. He finds this technique effective in reducing redundancies, finding contradictions, and shaping tests. It also helps him maintain control of a complex system which is constantly changing [20]. Aids of this type are discussed further in Part 2 since they have substantial value in large projects.

5. In combination, narratives are used for an overview of the whole design and for elaboration of difficult sections of the detailed design. Flowcharts are used to create the upper levels of the program structure and to show the system flow. Specification language is used to expand the lower-level flowcharts, particularly the process blocks. Tables are used to organize multidimensional data referred to elsewhere in the design and to ensure that no data has been omitted.

There is no fixed rule for deciding how much information to document with one technique.[7] The designer's guideline is that the resulting design specification should be complete and clear. Furthermore, it should be clear to everyone who must use it, not just to the designer.

4.5.5   Example: Subtask Detach Processor

To illustrate one form of design specification, a small program unit from a medium-sized on-line system is shown in Fig. 4.5 and Table 4.3. The system runs on a general-purpose computer to which both standard and special input/output devices can be attached. The vendor's disk operating system (DOS) is used as a base, but a substantial amount of new design is required to process the on-line devices which include variable numbers of the following.

1. I/O typewriters (TYPE)
2. Input keyboards (KEY)
3. TV displays (DTV)

Inputs arrive randomly from these devices. Some messages are search queries processed by a data management subsystem. Others are associated with editing and page composition. The ultimate purpose of the system is to assist in the editing, layout, and composition of newspapers and other publications.

The on-line system is designed to run asynchronously. Each input is processed by a series of programs which are "attached" to DOS and run as soon as resources can be assigned to them. Programs requested by different inputs are interleaved so as to make maximum use of the computer

---

7. Advocates of top-down structured programming (Chapter 5) lean toward the rule that the only suitable form of documentation is source language plus the corresponding object code listing. All other forms of documentation, they say, become obsolete when program changes are made. They base this opinion on the generally poor enforcement of procedures for maintaining compatibility between the spec and the program. The author is sympathetic with their point of view but cannot advocate such a rigid approach for all situations, since many users cannot or will not read source statements.

OLS Program Specification   ID 3.2.44   Rev 0
System Control Program   Shipston
OLSC44 — Subtask Detach Processor   Mgr: France

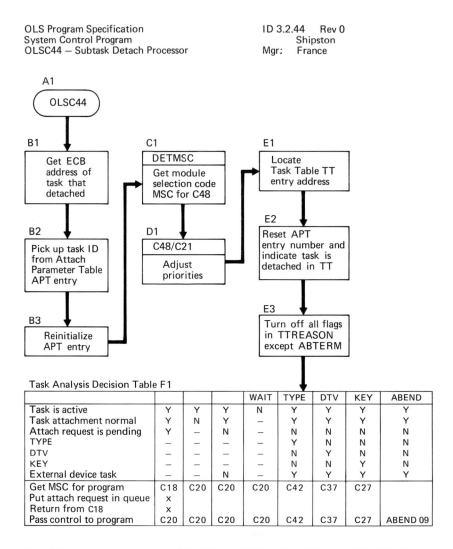

Fig. 4.5 Graphic description of OLSC44—SUBTASK DETACH PROCESSOR.

Task Analysis Decision Table F1

				WAIT	TYPE	DTV	KEY	ABEND
Task is active	Y	Y	Y	N	Y	Y	Y	Y
Task attachment normal	Y	N	Y	–	Y	Y	Y	Y
Attach request is pending	Y	–	N	–	N	N	N	N
TYPE	–	–	–	–	Y	N	N	N
DTV	–	–	–	–	N	Y	N	N
KEY	–	–	–	–	N	N	Y	N
External device task	–	–	N	–	Y	Y	Y	Y
Get MSC for program	C18	C20	C20	C20	C42	C37	C27	
Put attach request in queue	x							
Return from C18	x							
Pass control to program	C20	C20	C20	C20	C42	C37	C27	ABEND 09

resources. For each type of input there is a list of the programs to be executed. This list is stored in a Task Table. The parameters used when each
task is attached are in an Attach Parameter Table. When programs run to
completion (or terminate abnormally—ABEND) they are "detached" by
DOS. The interface between the on-line system and DOS is program C20.
Neither C20 nor any other on-line program can be directly addressed.
Whenever control is passed, the identifier of the module receiving control

TABLE 4.3. PROGRAM SPECIFICATION

Identification		
On-Line System Program Specification		ID 3.2.44
System Control Program	Page 1	Revision: 0
Subtask Detach Processor		4/1/72
OLS C44		Programmer: Shipston
	Mgr.: France	Monitor: Pierce

1. Description of Program Function and Performance

Brief statement of purpose

OLS C44 performs processing which is required whenever a subtask detaches from DOS normally or abnormally.

Input description

a. Inputs—The entry point of C44 is OLS C44. When entered from C20 (via C21), C44 receives:

1) the address of the Task Table entry in register 12
2) the address of the Attach Parameter Table entry in register 13
3) the address of the detaching task execution control block in register 9

See the specifications for C48 and C18 for inputs received when returning from these routines.

Output description using concise summary table

b. Outputs—When passing control to other programs, C44 leaves registers 12 and 13 unchanged. C44 places the module selection code for the module receiving control in register 10 and passes control via the branching routine C21. Output register settings are shown in the table below. TT = Task Table entry address of detaching task. ID = task identification of detaching task.

Pass control to	C20	C48	C18	C42	C37	C27
R1 = 0			x			
R1 = 1		x				
R7 = TT		x				
R9 = ID				x	x	x
R10 = MSC	x	x	x	x	x	x
R12 = R12	x	x	x	x	x	x
R13 = R13	x	x	x	x	x	x
R14 = 0	x					
R14 = Return		x	x			

TABLE 4.3 (continued)

Interface description

c. Interfaces—C44 interfaces with the following (* means C44 can pass control to the indicated program).

Programs	Mode	Cross-reference
C20	invokes C44,*	2.1.20
C21	module interface	2.1.21
C18	provides services to C44,*	3.2.18
C48	provides services to C44,*	3.2.48
C42	*	1.0.42
C37	*	1.0.37
C27	*	1.0.27

Data	Mode	Cross-reference
Task Table	C44 reads and modifies	401
Attach Parameter Table	C44 reads and modifies	402

Macros	Mode	Cross-reference
OLS/ABEND	C44 uses macro	7.6
OLS/AUTOSS	C44 uses macro	21.5
OLS/DETMSC	C44 uses macro	21.6

Detailed narrative description of design

d. Method—C44 is entered whenever C20 detects the detachment of an OLS task as a DOS subtask. The address of the execution control block (which was passed to DOS when the detaching subtask was attached) is available to C44 in register 9.

C44 uses the ECB address to determine the identity of the detaching subtask. It then clears all but the permanent portion (see Specification 402) of the Attach Parameter Table entry being used by the detaching task.

C44 then calls C48, which adjusts priorities to reflect the detached status of the given task.

Next, C44 locates the Task Table entry associated with the detaching task. C44 sets the current entry number in the Task Table to all ones. It sets the field TTREASON to zero (except for the abnormal termination indicator, which, if on, is left on). Then all the flags in the status byte, TTST, are adjusted to show that the task is detached.

At this point, the task is available for attachment again. C44 checks outstanding requests for this task. If any internal requests are pending, C44 passes control to C18, which places the task in the Attach Request Queue. If the task is related to a 2740, DTV, or 1017, external requests may be pending. If so, C18 is used as before. If not, control is passed to C42 (TYPE), C37 (DTV), or C27 (KEY) to enable external interrupts. In all other cases and after C18 returns control, C44 completes its work by passing control to the Main Wait Procedure, C20.

e. Attributes—The program is serially reusable. It is written in Basic Assembly Language to operate in the enabled state. If C44 terminates abnormally, it provides a 9 ABEND code to the ABEND macro.

User information

C44 conforms to the standards and conventions of both OLS and DOS.

Additional external device types may be added to the configuration by inserting the device routine at point F1 in the flowchart prior to the ABEND call. This change requires reassembly. Other configuration changes do not affect C44 since it is shielded from them by the Task Table and Attach Parameter Table.

2. Test Specification

Description of tests

Test cases must be executed both in stand-alone and multitasking modes. The ability to receive and pass control among all valid programs is to be tested by a sequence of program requests that (a) attach a mix of tasks in random order, (b) attach a series of requests to the same internally requested task, (c) attach a series of requests from the same external device (for each device type). Invocation from some source other than C20 and failure to return from C18 and C48 will be simulated to test ABEND operation.

3. Graphic description

Flowcharts and decision tables

See Figure 4.5.

is placed in module C21 to effect the transfer. The Subtask Detach Processor, C44, is called whenever DOS detaches a subtask. C44 resets the on-line system so that the detached function identified in an event control block (ECB) can be called again. The specification of the Subtask Detach Processor program unit C44 consists of a narrative (Table 4.3 is incomplete since it omits such control data as Standards and Management Data) with some tables plus a flowchart incorporating a decision table (Fig. 4.5). (The format is arbitrary and needs to be consistent only within the project.)

4.6   DESIGN COMPLETION

The design process is not complete when the design specification is complete. There remains a final step—design verification. During the designing stage, the algorithms should have been analyzed to ensure that they do what the design calls for. Design verification goes further to ensure that the design does what the objectives document calls for. The designer is not always capable of evaluating his own design. For this reason, he is well advised to ask others to help him. The user is the best source of help at this point since he understands the objectives and he will be realistically critical in his own best interest. If he reviews the design and agrees that it satisfies his objectives, no additional work is needed unless, of course, he decides to change his objectives. A nonconcurrence from the user means that the design does not meet the objectives. No matter how clean or logical the design, it is not satisfactory as a solution to the given problem.

The user can verify the suitability of the design but not its accuracy, efficiency, or technical quality. A fellow designer/programmer should be asked to review the design specification to critique these features. A complete program unit specification should be clear enough to be reviewed in less than an hour. It is not much of an imposition on an associate to ask for help, particularly if you are prepared to return the favor later. The types of things to be examined during the review of a program unit are logic flow, modularization, sequence timing, data structures—in other words, the things which required design decisions in the first place.[8] Thus, while the user might not notice the order in which C44 resets the on-line system tables, another designer would. The reviewer would look to see that the very last reset step released the detached program for reuse (as indeed is true in Fig. 4.5, Block E3). He would know that otherwise an interruption of the C44 program could dispatch the detached program before it was completely prepared for reuse.

---

8. A more comprehensive list of review topics is presented in Part 2.

Successful reviews by the user and by a technical associate are the signal to proceed to the next step—implementation. Unsuccessful reviews permit corrections to be made before any significant amount of coding has been done. In this way, reviews contribute to successful problem solution at low cost.

REFERENCES

1. Bowden, B. V., *Faster Than Thought.* New York: Pitman, 1953.
2. Babbage, C., *On the Economy of Machinery and Manufactures.* Philadelphia: Carey and Lea, 1832. Reprinted in H. F. Merrill (ed.), *Classics in Management.* New York: American Management Association, 1960.
3. Likert, R., *New Patterns of Management.* New York: McGraw-Hill, 1961.
4. Knuth, D. E., *The Art of Computer Programming, Volume 1: Fundamental Algorithms.* Reading, Mass.: Addison-Wesley, 1968.
5. Polanyi, M., *Knowing and Being.* Chicago: University of Chicago Press, 1969.
6. Weinberg, G. M., *The Psychology of Computer Programming.* New York: Van Nostrand Reinhold, 1971.
7. Sammet, J. E., "Perspective on Methods of Improving Software Development." *Software Engineering,* Vol. 1, 1970.
8. Aron, J. D., "Real-Time Systems in Perspective." *IBM Systems Journal,* Vol. 6, No. 1, 1967.
9. Ditri, A. E., J. C. Shaw, and W. Atkins, *Managing the EDP Function.* New York: McGraw-Hill, 1971.
10. Elspas, B., K. N. Levitt, R. J. Waldinger, and A. Waksman, "An Assessment of Techniques for Proving Program Correctness." *ACM Computing Surveys,* Vol. 4, No. 2, June 1972.
11. Weinberg, G. M. "The Psychology of Improved Programming Performance." *Datamation,* Vol. 14, No. 4, April 1971.
12. Wirth, N., "Program Development by Stepwise Refinement." *Communications of the ACM,* Vol. 14, No. 4, April 1971.
13. Parnas, D. L., "On the Criteria To Be Used in Decomposing Systems into Modules." *Communications of the ACM,* Vol. 15, No. 12, December 1972.
14. Gauthier, R., and S. Pont, *Designing Systems Programs.* Englewood Cliffs, N.J.: Prentice-Hall, 1970.
15. Dijkstra, E. W., "The Structure of 'THE'-Multiprogramming System." *Communications of the ACM,* Vol. 11, No. 5, May 1968.
16. Constantine, L. I., "Integral Hardware/Software Design, Part 2—Software Status and Direction." *Modern Data,* May 1968. This material is expanded at length in "Course Notes for Course 2100, IBM Systems Research Institute."
17. Chapin, N., "Flowcharting with the ANSI Standard: A Tutorial." *Computing Surveys,* Vol. 2, No. 2, June 1970.

18. Chapin, N., *Flowcharts.* Princeton, N.J.: Auerbach, 1970.

19. Pollack, S. L., H. T. Hicks, Jr., and W. J. Harrison, *Decision Tables, Theory and Practice.* New York: Wiley-Interscience, 1971.

20. Boehm, B. W., "Some Steps Toward Formal and Automated Aids to Software Requirements Analysis and Design." IFIP Congress 74. In press.

5
Coding

An individual program unit, as the smallest defined unit of a program system, is usually the responsibility of one person. It is his job to design and implement the unit and deliver it to the user without bugs. (*Bugs* are errors in the individual's program unit due to mistakes in logic, incorrect code, or other failure to meet the specifications.) The program unit design specification he prepares is the most detailed level of specification of the system and, as such, contains much more information about how the program works than would a higher-level subsystem specification. It is the detailed record of how the designer/programmer intends to solve the problem, and with minor modification, it should serve as the deliverable program unit documentation showing how the program works. A system designer does not go to this level of detail when describing the functions of each program unit in the system. Such an effort on his part would be counterproductive for two reasons.

1. The time required for detailed design would leave too little time for him to validate the system as a whole.
2. The programmers receiving such detailed instructions would have no flexibility to be creative in coming up with the best implementation of the units.

Therefore system designers allow a great deal of latitude regarding how a function is to be provided. They expect the implementer of each unit to do the unit design, as indicated in Chapter 4, and then proceed to write the program. They expect the implementer to do this job according to professionally accepted guidelines for quality programming. That is, the programmer is charged with selecting the best solution (within the given constraints on space, time, money, etc.) and presenting the solution in the most suitable form for the intended use.

The hallmark of style in computer programming is *simplicity*. This contrasts with the extreme *elegance* of mathematical proofs and the elaborately complex *sophistication* of much technical writing.[1] A beautiful program does its job correctly (the primary criterion) with the minimum amount of code, and it can be easily understood and maintained by the user. Its logical paths are straight and clean. Its language is as close as is practicable to the everyday working language of the user. Its structure is modular, and changes can therefore be made easily. Its documentation is thorough and straightforward. Such a program may not be the shortest program that will solve the problem, and it may not use the most advanced technological innovations, but it will serve the user well.

In this chapter, some guidelines for producing programs will be presented. The emphasis will be on those features that are important to reviewers and users. The rules for writing specific programs will not be covered. Other sources should be consulted for such programming techniques [1,2,3].

5.1   SOURCE LANGUAGE

The language used for writing a program unit is either (a) imposed by the user (or the designer of the system incorporating the unit) or (b) selected by the designer/programmer of the unit.

When the language is imposed, the programmer should become familiar not only with the capabilities of the language but with the features of the compilers to be used. It is possible for an individual programmer to improve the efficiency of a program unit substantially by taking advantage of built-in features of the language and its compiler. Estimates of 3:1 improvement in object program execution have been made for PL/I programmers who use all the features of the language rather than a limited subset. A further 3:1 improvement may be achieved by taking advantage of the compiler's ability to control the computer. (Taking advantage of special features of

---

1. George H. Mealy, a computer consultant, disturbed attendees at the 1968 National Symposium on Modular Programming when he reminded them that the *sophisticated* systems they were so proud of were sophisticated only in the dictionary sense of "unnecessarily complex." They were not "intellectually perceptive" or "advanced."

a compiler may cause compatibility problems when a different compiler or, less often, a new version of the original compiler must be used, but the risk is tolerably small in many installations.) Although working programs can be written without expert knowledge of the source language and its implementation, the potential order-of-magnitude improvement in the end result warrants thorough preparation [4]. In a more pragmatic vein, it is essential to learn the specifics of the imposed language to avoid mistakes. ANSI Standard FORTRAN is not identical to all versions of FORTRAN IV. The compilers for FORTRAN IV produced by various vendors are not all compatible. Within one vendor's catalog of FORTRAN IV compilers for different-sized machines, there is no assurance that all programs compiled by the largest version can also be compiled by the smaller versions. The number of programming languages and the variety of implementations make it necessary to learn specifically which version has been imposed.

Given the freedom to select a language, the designer/programmer should pick the highest-level language that is suitable. Recognizing this, some facility managers not only standardize on a high-level language but limit the complexity of the language to a subset their people can handle. The criteria that could be used include the following.

5.1.1 Expressiveness

The language must be able to express the functions of the problem in terms which lead to efficient machine execution of the program. In addition, the language must be natural for the programmer to use. Programmers develop preferences among languages—usually they prefer the language they learned first—that may lead them to use a favorite language where it is not particularly efficient. Others tend to use languages because of some novel feature. Aside from matters of taste, languages can be rated in terms of expressiveness.

The highest-level source languages tend not to be languages in the ordinary sense. They are more properly commands to problem-solving systems. Sort generators, report program generators, mathematical subroutine packages fall into this class. So do an increasing number of simple but broadly useful program generators for small business applications. Typically, such systems are very efficient, machine-oriented, problem-oriented program packages, whose input is a simple parametric description of the problem and whose output is either a program or the problem solution.

Among the procedure-oriented languages (POL), wide usage has established FORTRAN and ALGOL as the most expressive languages for numerical scientific work; COBOL as most expressive for business data processing; LISP, COMIT, and SNOBOL for string and list processing; and PL/I for multi-purpose use [5]. Each of these has been used for other purposes, but only PL/I (and JOVIAL in U.S. government circles) sets out to be a language for all applications. These languages are machine- and problem-independent to a degree. Each is designed for a class of procedures, such as evaluating algebraic expressions, and can express any procedure in the class effectively. Other procedures have to be described, albeit in a clumsy way, in terms of defined procedures in order to be processed.

Within well-established problem areas, macro libraries have often been developed. When used with intermixed assembly language, the macros can provide the expressive power of POLs without sacrificing the manipulative ability of assembly languages. The result, however, is machine-oriented and may be difficult to transport from one machine to another.

Basic assembly language (BAL) tends to be the most expressive way to manipulate hardware. The fact that BAL is machine-oriented makes it the only programming language that can be used to write precisely timed routines. BAL is therefore applicable to real-time programs and other programs in which execution time is critical.

Microprograms are hard to write, but they permit optimization of the machine's ability to execute specific instructions on machines which can be microprogrammed. When the value of an optimized routine is very high, it justifies the cost of expert microprogrammers and the potential loss of compatibility with other program packages.

5.1.2 Usability

A suitable programming language is easy for the programmer to use. Some languages are attractive to programmers but not to their clients. To be really suitable, the selected language and its implementation must be acceptable to the end user as well as the programmer [6]. It must be easy to learn, easy to read, easy to write, easy to debug. Compilers must exist for each machine used for developing or maintaining programs written in the language. The language must have a long anticipated lifetime, so that programs written today will still be supported years from now.

You can see where the programmer and the user could differ in their evaluation of a language. The programmer feels at home with machine-oriented languages; the user does not. Although both are concerned with program performance, the programmer is willing to sacrifice modularity to achieve performance; the user wants to preserve modularity to simplify maintenance. The programmer may prefer a language supported only by the vendor for whom he works. The user may own several competitive machines, and he wants to be able to run the program on any one of them. The programmer may plan to use an on-line, interactive language; the user may not have the equivalent on-line facilities. All these differences can be resolved by negotiation prior to writing code.

It is generally considered advantageous for the selected language to use the same vocabulary or application jargon used by workers in the subject areas. Thus, English-like languages are preferred to mathematical languages in English-speaking business organizations. Special-purpose vocabularies occur in languages used in various engineering applications. The trend is evident in some systems languages, where special notations have been introduced for describing languages, arrays, and sequence controls [7,8,9]. The key to usability of such specialized languages lies in the degree to which the language represents the vocabulary and concepts of the people who must work with it. Thus a language which permits MILL, REAM, and TOLERANCE operators may be natural in a machine-tool control environment but not in a systems programming house. More relevant to systems programmers are languages which treat data structures as arrays or lists, but even these languages may be unsuitable if the programmers have not been taught to look at data structures as abstract entities instead of collections of named fields. Care must be exercised to match the language to the known capabilities of the programmer and the users, not to choose it for some theoretical goals that can be achieved only by computer scientists. It is fair to expect some extension of the programmer's capabilities through appropriate training, although not much training time is available in an immediate assignment of 4–6 weeks' duration.

5.1.3 Efficiency

Efficiency with respect to languages can be measured several ways. The expressiveness of the language itself may make it possible to write programs that require fewer execution steps. An example of this is the implicit ability of APL to handle rows and columns of arrays compared with the need for explicit DO loops in FORTRAN for the same procedures. APL might not only result in a shorter source program but the resulting object program may run faster. As is true in determining usability, the total environment must be considered in evaluating efficiency. Four factors are relevant.

1. Program development time
2. Source program compilation time
3. Object program execution time
4. Program modification time

Program development time is the time required to write and debug the source program. Although individual programmers vary widely in their performance, it is generally accepted that higher-level languages shorten program development time by at least a factor of two [10, 11]. The improvement is attributed to the ease of writing in a more convenient language, coupled with the generally good debugging aids built into many language processors.

Source program compilation time may be of no consequence when it represents only an hour or so of machine time to complete a program unit. It does become significant when optimization is required and the only optimizing compiler available takes four times as long to run as the regular compiler and machine time was budgeted for the lower figure. Compilation time may also be a problem in an interactive system, where long compilations may destroy the programmer's continuity of thought. Finally, source program compilation time is significant whenever the object program is to be used only once. In such a case, the compilation cost may exceed execution cost and cannot be ignored.

Compilation is a preprocessing step which is supposed to produce the most efficient object program. Some languages are interpreted as they are executed. This avoids the preprocessing, but it increases the execution time. Compilers must have all the data defined ahead of time in order to set up storage assignments, indexes, etc. A major advantage of interpreters is that they can adjust to data as it arrives. Therefore many programmers prefer interpreters during implementation when they are trying out different ideas. An ideal situation would be to have access to an interpretive, interactive system for program development plus a compiler for the same language to generate an efficient, deliverable version of the debugged end product. Some languages are available with both types of translation in a compatible form.

The factors affecting program modification time are the source language debugging aids, the quality of program documentation, the stability of the language and its processors, and the compile time. All of these affect the time required to identify an error, fix the source program, regenerate an object program, update the documentation, and get back into operation.

5.1.4 Balanced Selection

Since there are many factors affecting the choice of a language, some judgment must be used to select the best one in a given situation. Sammet [12] suggests a weighted scoring system for selecting the best member of a class of languages. The method can be used to pick the highest-level language suitable for an assignment.

If the language has been imposed, the selection process can be bypassed unless there is an obvious and overwhelming reason to reject the specified language.

If the language has not been imposed, the first step in selection is to look for a problem-solving package that completely fits the situation. There are two important considerations: (a) the package must fit the problem completely, and (b) the time to find and evaluate the package must be modest. If these conditions do not apply, the cost of selecting the problem-solving package will exceed the cost of writing a new program. The risk of choosing unwisely is reduced when the search is restricted to those well-known commercial packages which are already supported within your organization.

Suppose that no complete package exists in the form of either a program generator or a special-purpose macro system. The next most attractive language will be a POL. There are many POLs, so the field must be narrowed to those that are supposed to fit the class of procedures that dominates your problem. This set is further narrowed down to those that are readily available. Then one of the remaining candidates is selected on the basis of its comparative advantages in the current situation. The relative language and compiler features are compared, weighted, and scored. The language candidate with the highest total score is picked. Among the criteria that can be taken into account are the following.

- *Technical factors*

  Syntactic elements, such as reserved words, built-in functions, labels
  Consistency
  Generality
  Machine and operating system independence

- *Human factors*

  Ease of learning
  Ease of reading, writing, debugging
  Naturalness
  Relevance to problem area
  Simplicity
  Self-documentation
  Interactive capability

- *Efficiency*

  Ease of writing succinct programs
  Compile time
  Object code optimization
  Maintainability

- *Compatibility*

  History of support and expectation of future support
  Growth potential
  Transportability across machine types
  Ease of conversion

- *Cost*

  Cost of acquisition and retention
  Cost of operation
  Cost of training
  Cost of implementation (new equipment, procedures)

If several languages have equal scores, select the one you have had the most successful experience with. Only if all POLs fail some test, such as the efficiency test, according to quantitative criteria should it be necessary to drop down to BAL. (Microprogramming, on the other hand, may be a meaningful adjunct to any level of language when a particular repeated kernel of the program requires faster execution than can be achieved by using the built-in machine instruction set. The use of microprogramming is a last resort, however, because it actually modifies the computer and may interfere with normal operations and maintenance.)

The overall process of selection consists of seeking a high-level language that is suitable, available, and cost-justifiable for this programming task. The decisions required in selecting a language are the same for program systems at all levels of complexity; however, different conclusions may be reached for subsystems and even program units within a system according to their unique requirements.

5.2   TOP-DOWN VERSUS BOTTOM-UP PROGRAMMING

Top-down design simultaneously provides complete design control and logical modularity. These advantages can be carried over into implementation by *top-down programming*, that is, writing the code for each level of the design as the design is developed. The alternative method of implementation delays coding until most or all of the lowest-level modules have been designed. The separate modules are then integrated from the bottom up.

5.2.1   Top-Down Programming

Programmers who implement from the top down tend to dispense with flowcharts or, at most, use them as working sketches of overall program flow. For program descriptions they use a specification language or work directly in programming language. At each stage of top-down design, they write down the interface specifications, data descriptions, and module functions. The design and, in fact, the documentation are completely defined by the source statements of the program. Procedurally, the programmers start by asking themselves, "What must this program do?" What are the inputs?" What are the outputs?" Next, they probably decide how the inputs will be handled and what data structures will be required to accommodate the

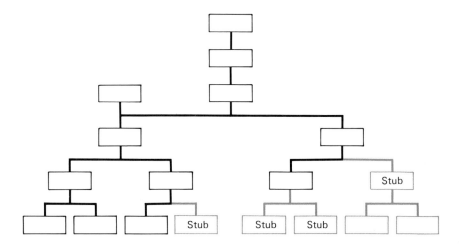

Fig. 5.1 Top-down implementation.

inputs. They will proceed to add detail in program execution sequence, imposing some degree of hierarchical order on the subroutine [13]. At each stage, all higher-level modules exist before a lower-level module is implemented. For convenience, *stubs* naming lower-level modules are included in the program, to be replaced by actual code when it is developed (Fig. 5.1).

The Subtask Detach Processor of Chapter 4 might be handled in the following way.

5.2.1.1   First version

The program definition explains the relation of the Subtask Detach Processor to other parts of the existing On-Line System (OLS). When program C20 invokes the detach processor, C44, some of the data needed by C44 has been used by OLS and DOS and should still be available. The event control block (ECB) of the detaching task, the Attach Parameter Table, and the Task Table are examples of items which have already been defined, containing such fields as APT ENTRY and TTREASON. By copying the appropriate declarations into the program unit, the C44 programmer can avoid some effort while ensuring compatibility. The definition of data structures at a high level makes it possible for the low-level C44 unit to communicate with the rest of the system at no risk to the integrity of the system design. In a similar way, the control interfaces are given and the method of control (via a common switch, C21) shields the system from illegal transfers out of C44.

```
A1.1    SUBTASK_DETACH_PROCESSOR:
        PROCEDURE;
        %INCLUDE OLSDCL;        /* Include OLS declarations */
        %INCLUDE SDPDCL;        /* Include internal declarations */
        %INCLUDE APTCOD;        /* Fetch and reinitialize APT entry */
        %INCLUDE PRCOD;         /* Adjust priorities */
        %INCLUDE TTCOD;         /* Fetch and reset Task Table */
        %INCLUDE TACOD;         /* Analyze type of task and routine */
            CALL OUT;           /* Transfer to next routine */
        END SUBTASK_DETACH_PROCESSOR;

A2.1    SDPDCL:
        DECLARE
            OUT CHARACTER (3) INITIAL ('C2L'); /* Symbolic exit */
```

Fig. 5.2 SUBTASK DETACH PROCESSOR: first version, top-down program.

With this background, a first pass at C44 design and implementation (in a PL/I-like form) can be made (Fig. 5.2).

In this pass the major activities are laid out. The variables C44 will need for its own use are declared; On-Line System variables are copied from the library. The command % INCLUDE is used to place statements in line; CALL is used to incorporate closed subroutines. (This notation permits each segment of the program to be written on a separate sheet, stored separately in a library, tested separately if possible, and linked to other segments as desired. The use of INCLUDEs presumes the availability of a linking loader.)

5.2.1.2   Second version

The next step depends on the programmer's style. Each INCLUDEd module can be handled in sequence or the most important one can be expanded first. Another approach is to expand the program by deciding what must happen to a single detach request as it passes through C44. In Fig. 5.3, the latter approach is used to expand TACOD. It adds detail to the control structure and identifies the need for some test variables—ACTIVE, NORMAL, REQ, EXT—and a parameter on the exit OUT. All the test variables can be expected to be set by the On-Line System except for NORMAL, the internal name for the result of combining several APT and TT bits, including ABTERM. NORMAL must be added to the declaration list for C44. Likewise, the parameter which tells C21 where to pass control must be declared.

Indentation is used to make the program easier to read. The program is thoroughly commented so that someone other than the programmer can figure out what is going on. The comments are particularly dense at this level; they will become sparser at more detailed levels. It is possible to replace INCLUDEs by their expansion up to the page length allowed for a program (usually 30–50 lines). Alternatively, and perhaps better, the expansions are placed in separate blocks. The advantage of blocking in this way is that each level of the program design remains clean and uncluttered by lower-level detail. This can be a time saver when reading or debugging the program.

5.2.1.3   Third version

Continuing to concentrate on control structure and interfaces, the programmer finds it appropriate to develop DEVCOD next. This subunit has more decision points and sets up some additional exits. At the same time, the register settings necessary for passing control can be taken care of. For instance, after the declarations, registers 12 and 13, known to the On-Line

```
A1.2  SUBTASK_DETACH_PROCESSOR:
      PROCEDURE;
      %INCLUDE OLSDCL;                  /* Include OLS declarations */
      %INCLUDE SDPDCL;                  /* Include internal declarations */
      %INCLUDE APTCOD;                  /* Fetch and reinitialize APT entry */
      %INCLUDE PRCOD;                   /* Adjust priorities */
      %INCLUDE TTCOD;                   /* Fetch and reset Task Table */
      IF ACTIVE = '1'B THEN             /* Is task active? */
         IF NORMAL = '1'B THEN          /* Can task be attached normally? */
            IF REQ = '1'B THEN          /* Is attach request pending? */
               %INCLUDE QCOD;           /* Queue next attach request */
            ELSE
               IF EXT = '1'B THEN       /* Is this an external device task? */
                  %INCLUDE DEVCOD;
               ELSE;
         ELSE;
      ELSE
         CALL OUT (MSC20);              /* Return to C20 */
      END SUBTASK_DETACH_PROCESSOR;

A2.2  SDPDCL:
      DECLARE
      OUT      CHARACTER (3) INITIAL ('C21'),  /* Symbolic exit */
      NORMAL   BIT (1),                        /* Normal attachment indicator */
      MSC20    CHARACTER (3) INITIAL ('C20');  /* MSC for C20 */
```

Fig. 5.3 SUBTASK DETACH PROCESSOR: second version, top-down program.

System as R12 and R13, should be saved so that they can be restored just before each CALL OUT (MSCXX). The programmer introduces % INCLUDE SAVCOD for this purpose. Other register settings can also be made prior to the exit. With reference to the output description in the description of the problem, it appears that C21 always expects to find a Module Selection Code in register 10. This suggests that all exits should be to OUT (R10), with R10 being set to the MSC just prior to the call. Here is a case where the detail suggests a change to the higher-level design (Fig. 5.4).

As the third iteration proceeds, it will again be necessary to extend the declaration list. At all stages of the top-down process, both the control structure and the data definitions should exist before the detail is developed. Note that the procedure being followed is a hierarchical execution sequence. The functional blocks, such as APTCOD and TTCOD, are essentially being treated as black boxes. Their inner workings need not be known in order to trace the flow of action in C44. The only function used by lower levels which must be programmed in order for the program to be exercised is NORMAL.

After the control flow is complete and debugged, the remaining functional blocks can be completed in arbitrary order. Of course, it is possible that as they are programmed, new problems will turn up that affect what has already been done. This is a normal aspect of discovery/resolution. Fortunately, the logical strength of top-down implementation minimizes the impact of such discoveries.

5.2.2   Bottom-up Programming

The only difference between top-down and bottom-up programming at the program unit level is in the amount of detail in the control logic at the time the functional blocks are coded. The bottom-up approach typically starts with a flowchart outlining the completed design of the program unit. Each block in the flowchart is programmed without much regard to the other blocks. The blocks can be done in any order, although most programmers will attack the kernel computation first, or if there is no dominant kernel, they will proceed in execution sequence. Depending on computer service, they may start several blocks in parallel so that there is one to work on while another is being run.

By taking this approach, the programmer does not have all the block dependencies and structures defined at the start. In order to complete a block of code, it is necessary to create a temporary *driver* which defines the data and the control interface the block needs for execution. The definition of the driver is built up from the local needs of the block. It has no relation

```
A1.3    SUBTASK_DETACH_PROCESSOR:
        PROCEDURE;
        %INCLUDE OLSDCL;                        /* Include OLS declarations */
        %INCLUDE SDPDCL;                        /* Include internal declarations */
        %INCLUDE SAVCOD;                        /* Save Registers */
        %INCLUDE APTCOD;                        /* Fetch and reinitialize APT entry */
        %INCLUDE PRCOD;                         /* Adjust priorities */
        %INCLUDE TTCOD;                         /* Fetch and reset Task Table */
        IF ACTIVE = '1'B THEN                   /* Is task active? */
          NORMAL = FLAG3|TTERR|ABTERM;
          IF NORMAL = '1'B THEN                 /* Can task be attached normally? */
            IF REQ = '1'B THEN                  /* Is attach request pending? */
              %INCLUDE QCOD;                    /* Queue next attach request */
          ELSE
              IF EXT = '1'B THEN                /* Is this an external device task? */
                %INCLUDE DEVCOD;
              ELSE;

          ELSE;
        ELSE DO;
          R10 = 'C20';                          /* Prepare to return to C20 */
          R12 = AR12;
          R13 = AR13;
          R14 = 0;
          CALL OUT (R10);                       /* Return to C20 */
          END;
        END SUBTASK_DETACH_PROCESSOR;

A2.3    SDPDCL:
        DECLARE
        OUT       CHARACTER (3) INITIAL ('C21'),    /* Symbolic exit */
```

Fig. 5.4 SUBTASK DETACH PROCESSOR: third version, top-down program.

```
          NORMAL BIT (1),              /* Normal attachment indicator */
          AR12  FIXED (31),            /* Temporary storage for R12 */
          AR13  FIXED (31);            /* Temporary storage for R13 */

A3.3    DEVCOD:
        IF DEVICE = TYPE THEN          /* External device analysis */
          R10 = 'C42';                 /* Determine type of external device */
        ELSE;                          /* Prepare to transfer to device routine */
        IF DEVICE = DTV THEN
          R10 = 'C37';
        ELSE;
        IF DEVICE = KEY THEN
          R10 = 'C27';
        ELSE;
          % INCLUDE ABEND09;           /* Error in task type codes */
        R7 = AR12;
        R9 = APT.ID;
        R12 = AR12;                    /* Restore registers */
        R13 = AR13;
        CALL OUT (R10);                /* Transfer to device routine */

A4.3    PRCOD:
        R1 = 1;                        /* Priority processing */
        R9 = APT.ID;
        R10 = 'C48';                   /* Task ID to register 9 */
        R12 = AR12;                    /* MSC48 to register 10 */
        R13 = AR13;
        R14 = 'C44';                   /* Set return address */
        CALL OUT (R10);                /* Adjust priorities */
```

Fig. 5.4   (continued).

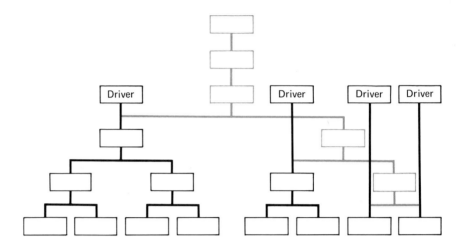

Fig. 5.5 Bottom-up implementation.

to the rest of the program environment (Fig. 5.5). Gradually, as several blocks are coded, it will become clear that some of the support provided by the drivers is common to several blocks. Data structures and improved interfaces can be constructed with this knowledge. The major risk is that some data needed by several blocks is unrecognized by any block; therefore it never gets defined. A thorough top-down design with detailed interface, data, and test specifications is supposed to prevent the possibility of things slipping through the cracks in a bottom-up implementation. Nevertheless, the probability of error is higher when implementing a top-down design from the bottom up instead of from the top down.

5.2.3 Scheduling

The estimate that 35% of the program unit schedule is used for design, 25% for coding, 35% for debugging, and 5% for final documentation applies to bottom-up programming. In top-down programming, design and coding proceed together. The last line of code written is the last step of the design. No standard estimate is available for this approach since the activities are all wrapped up together. A rule of thumb is that a top-down implementation will take less time than a bottom-up one—anywhere from 0% to 50% less, depending on the programmer. From 10% to 25% of the program unit schedule should be reserved for running test cases and cleaning up the documentation. The rest of the time is devoted to concurrent design, coding, and debugging.

5.3 CODING TECHNIQUES

The top-down example in Section 5.2.1 illustrates several techniques that
lead to more useful programs. The program is structured so that it can be
read from beginning to end without a lot of intricate threaded references
to other code. It is explained in the comments so that the programmer's
intent is clear and the abbreviations can be understood. Names are selected
that convey some sense of the object they refer to.

All declarations are placed at the head of the block they serve in order
to simplify data control and facilitate debugging. Housekeeping, such as
register saving or switch setting, precedes other processing. Tests of conditions affecting program decisions or branch settings are performed prior to
the decision (where the language allows). This last technique essentially
divides the program into partitions that are executed only if the test at their
entry point is successful.

Each program can be written on a single sheet of paper. As is done
with flowcharts, long programs are broken into one-page subunits, which
are cross-referenced. The one-page rule, when applied to top-down programming, requires that the high-level description of the complete program
appear on one page. Each INCLUDE or CALL on the first page refers to
one other page. The collection of these pages represents the second level
of the program. Each of these pages may contain references to further pages,
in effect forming nested INCLUDEs reaching down to the lowest level of
the program. In Fig. 5.4, the labeled sections would be pages. The code
in block A1.3 plus the declarations in block A2.3 constitute the top-level
program. Blocks A3.3, A4.3, and other expansions of A1.3 references are
the second level. An expansion of the ABEND in A3.3 would be a third
level. Bottom-up programs can also be written one per page, but there is
no corresponding hierarchical pyramid of programs. The bottom-up subunits may be all at the same design level although they may refer to each
other by INCLUDEs and CALLs.

5.3.1 Structured Programs

A structured program is written in execution sequence so that there is a
visible relationship between the program listing and the dynamic execution
of the program [14]. A decisionless structured program would be a simple
string of declarations and executable statements. Decisions are incorporated,
using IF p THEN DO f ELSE DO g, WHILE p DO f, FOR CASE p DO
$f(p)$ constructions (or their equivalent in the programming language selected
for the project). Each of these constructions involves testing a control variable and then following the path determined by the test. There are no
unconditional branches allowed; therefore, some people refer to structured

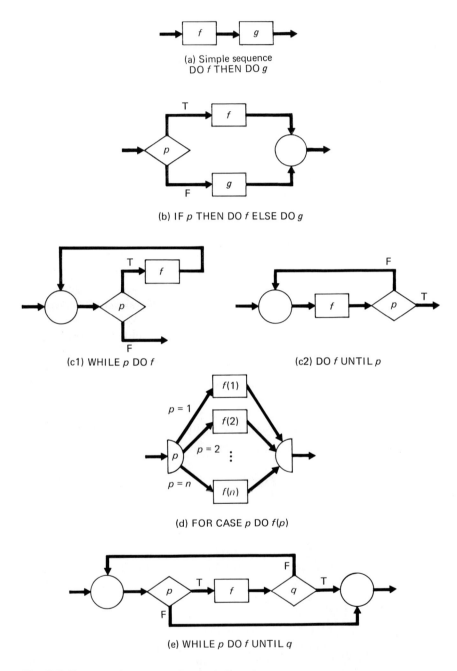

(a) Simple sequence
DO f THEN DO g

(b) IF p THEN DO f ELSE DO g

(c1) WHILE p DO f   (c2) DO f UNTIL p

(d) FOR CASE p DO f(p)

(e) WHILE p DO f UNTIL q

Fig. 5.6 Structured programming logic flowcharts.

programs as GO TO–free programs. GO TO statements are not excluded
from structured programs; in fact, in some languages GO TOs are the only
mechanism for implementing such conditional branches as the CASE statement. The concept of design excludes unconditional branches from the design, not from the implementation. In essence, this rule requires the programmer to think through the problem thoroughly before coding it. He
cannot leap right into coding, hoping that, if he leaves something out, he
can insert it later with a GO TO patch.

Figure 5.6 shows the basic control logic flowcharts, from which any
structured program can be written. Included is a variant of WHILE p DO
f, which says DO f UNTIL p has a specified value. A further variant, WHILE
p DO f UNTIL q, is also allowed (Fig. 5.6e). In every case, the logic flowcharts have one entry point and one exit point, and for every node in the
chart, there is a path from the entry to the exit. It is this characteristic which
permits programs written in these figures to be read from top to bottom.
If such a one entry–one exit figure is called a *proper flowchart*, any sequence
of proper flowcharts is also proper. Thus any program which can be rear-
ranged into a sequence of proper flowcharts can be read from top to bottom.
Figure 5.4 is a structured program; the equivalent proper flowchart is Fig.
5.7. If this flowchart strikes you as obvious, compare it with the unstructured
flowchart in Fig. 5.8. Here the flow of control is interrupted, and the paths
permit side effects. Structured code avoids potential problems that can occur
in unstructured code for even such a simple case as the Subtask Detach
Processor.

Structured code arranges processes into logical blocks. Asynchronous
interruptions occurring during execution of a program cannot be represented by any of the structures available. The actions taken at these points
can be coded in structured form, but the asynchronous events are best
covered in narrative and graphic form, the best graphic being a flowchart
modified to show the relative duration of each activity. Timing diagrams,
such as Fig. 1.4, also help to clarify asynchronous events.

In programs written using top-down structured programming, the correctness of a particular subunit depends only on its higher-level predeces-
sors. Formal proofs of correctness are easier to apply to structured programs
because the proper flowcharts constitute clean segments about which prov-
able assertions can be made. Even debugging is easier because the structured
program contains no loose ends. Programmers who use structured techniques may have some initial reluctance to follow such rigid rules, but very
soon they find the benefits irresistible.

- Structured programs contain fewer coding errors.
- Structured programs are easy to read.

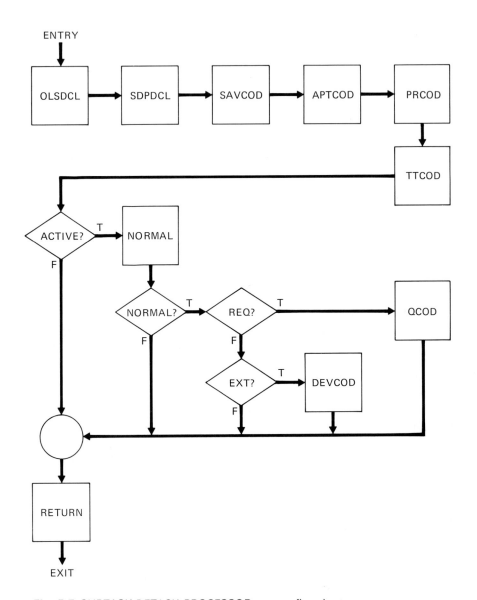

Fig. 5.7 SUBTASK DETACH PROCESSOR: proper flowchart.

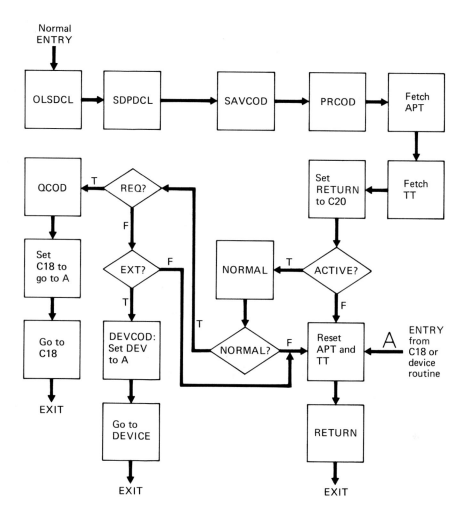

Fig. 5.8 SUBTASK DETACH PROCESSOR: "improper" flowchart.

- Structured programs are easy to debug.
- Structured programs are easy to maintain and modify.

In one large organization, a key programming executive doubted these benefits. He was concerned about introducing a requirement for structured programming in his area of responsibility, which involved several hundred programmers working on a real-time system. Of particular interest was the fear that, even if benefits were obtained in program development, an unacceptable price would be paid in program execution time. To prove his negative point, he decided to code up some sample problems using the unstructured approach and then recode the same problems following the rules for structured programs. As he expected, the structured programs were far slower. When he asked his associates to review the results, they said the test was unrealistic because the sample problems never came up in their environment. They suggested a more appropriate set of samples, and the executive tried the test again. But he ran into trouble immediately. It turned out that, after having learned structured techniques, he couldn't program any other way. The logic and the facility inherent in the structures made such good sense that they drove other techniques out of his mind. His organization proceeded to introduce the techniques, and by 1972 they were in wide use. The predicted benefits were achieved, and no significant real-time problems arose.

5.3.2 Readability

Structured code, page-length program subunits, indented blocks, and extensive comments contribute to readability. Identifiers which are both easy to remember and suggestive of the object identified are always helpful. R10 may be a perfectly adequate identifier for register 10, particularly if all registers are referred to by the same convention. TYPE as the name of the flag identifying an external typewriter device is less adequate. There are so many uses of the word "type" that it could easily be misinterpreted as "type of device" rather than as "DEVICE = TYPEwriter." Long names have merit when they clarify meaning without leading to errors. NORMAL is better than NO as the name of the normal attachment indicator. NORMAL-ATTACHMENT-INDICATOR carries more information, but a 27-character name is likely to be written down incorrectly. The proper compromise is to use the shortest unambiguous identifier you can think of and explain it fully in a comment.

When working in a large system, avoid using identifiers that are used elsewhere, even though your local reference is supposedly unknown to the rest of the system. Distinctions between global and local names are usually observed by compilers and operating systems, but test teams are less perfect. They may mistake a local reference for a global reference and embark on a wild goose chase as a result.

Names that can be pronounced are more likely to be written correctly. Arbitrary strings offer no protection against transpositions, particularly if they exceed 4–5 characters. ARAARA1A is a poor symbol. IOCHKSUM is better. It is often convenient to use a prefix to identify members of a group. The notation R10 uses "R" as a prefix to identify symbols naming registers. In AR10 the "A" is a local prefix for data saved in temporary storage. The notations 10R and 10AR are better symbols because they emphasize the unique data without concealing the fact that this is a register. In some organizations, each programmer uses his initials as a prefix for all the programs he stores in the computer room. When the completed development work is released for general use, the prefix can be erased. In this case, prefixes are used to separate work in process from library programs.

Above all, readability is based on simple, clear, logical programming. Resist the urge to be clever. Don't present puzzles or riddles by using obscure techniques or by using hardware gimmicks in an unusual way. If you must be unorthodox in order to meet performance objectives, be very thorough in your explanation of how the program works. The use of mixed media (listing, flowcharts, tables, narrative) was discussed in Chapter 4 as an aid to the readability of design specifications. The same comments apply to program documentation, which is, after all, an elaboration of the design spec. However, additional care is required to ensure that the components of the mixed-media package are all properly labeled and cross-referenced so that the reader can use them as a compatible package.

5.3.3 Libraries of Reusable Programs

Years ago, the driver starting a car had to manually adjust the ignition timing and then turn over the engine with a hand crank. No one but an antique collector would think of buying a car of that type anymore. It is taken for granted that automatic ignition systems and electric starters will be provided. By analogy, it is taken for granted that a loader program will be provided with every operating system, so programmers and operators do not have to write their own to get their computer started. The loader is but one of many good programs available in every installation library. Over the years, programming managers have created very large libraries of checked-out programs which could be reused in developing new programs. The success of public program libraries depends on their character. Those that provide thoroughly tested, general-purpose, algorithmic program packages at no charge have been the most successful. Their success is due to low cost and ease of use.

The oldest libraries were collections of unedited contributions of programs by people with related interests. In fact, one of the main user groups called itself SHARE, reflecting the importance of the library of contributed programs shared by the members. Initially, the user groups were identified with only one computer, but as time passed, the groups tended more to represent major application areas. Thus SHARE grew from a set of IBM 704 users into an affinity group interested primarily in scientific and engineering computation. GUIDE focused on business applications. As the number of installed computers grew and users exhausted the free library, a market began to develop for programs on their own merit. Users began to buy program packages from software houses, whose executives had speculated that they could sell enough copies of a program to make its development a profitable venture. This market required that programs offered for a price be protected against free dissemination by the user. Contract terms and conditions, licenses, copyrights, and patents (where allowed) have provided such protection. The result is that current libraries contain some free programs and some priced programs, with restrictions on the use of the latter.

To take advantage of existing programs, describe your requirements clearly in broad generic terms, such as "airline reservations system," as well as in specific terms, such as "poll up to 1000 dial-up terminals of type x every five minutes." List the system constraints: type of CPU, memory available, peripheral devices, special features. Since the cost of modifying an existing program is relatively high for anyone but the originator, a library program which deviates too far from the system at hand has little value. An estimate should be made of the cost of developing and maintaining a new program. This cost should be compared with the cost of procuring and maintaining the library program. Since each library program is unique with respect to its quality and its assured maintenance, the latter point is worth some study, including contacts with other users. The language of the library program must be one that can be translated to run on the user's machine. The flexibility of the library program relative to the requirements is important. Select an existing program that allows you to change such variables as table sizes, names, number of devices. Only if the existing program will save a great deal of money should you accept it as is and rearrange your problem to fit it.

As this list of caveats grows, it is obvious that it is easy to find reasons why a particular library package is unsuitable. There is a gray area between true unsuitability and arbitrary rejection. The NIH ("not invented here"), syndrome is typical of the thinking of programmers (and many others) who prefer to develop their own solutions to interesting problems. NIH alone will lead programmers to reject all library packages as unsuitable. The manager who is concerned with cost effectiveness must combat NIH by showing his people that a library package may free them to tackle more interesting parts of the job. If he can achieve this result, the programmers will examine the library candidates on their merits.

5.4   PERFORMANCE

A number of suggestions related to logic design have been made previously. Given a good design, there remain many opportunities for programming decisions that can further improve performance and reliability.

5.4.1 Optimization

Fast execution is achieved by minimizing the number of machine cycles
required. The most significant savings can be made during design by arranging execution blocks so that each one is entered the minimum number
of times. Additional improvements can be made while coding.

Some savings are usually achieved by using in-line INCLUDEs instead
of subroutine CALLs. The difference is in the linkage and housekeeping
code required by the CALL. Program loops have similar overhead associated with condition testing; i.e., in a WHILE p DO f loop, p must be
evaluated once for *every* execution of f plus a final time to terminate the
loop. A nest of DOs, such as

```
1. DO I = 1 TO a;
2.    DO J = 1 TO b;
3.       DO K = 1 TO c;
4.          A (K,J) = B + X*Y + C (I,K) * D (K,J);
```

requires a loop initialization once for statement 1, a times for 2, and $a \times b$
times for 3. At the end of each execution of 4, tests are made to see if
the loops can be closed. There are $a \times b \times c$ tests of K, $a \times b$ tests of
J, and a tests of I. The total number of loop control steps is

$$(a \times b \times c) + 2 (a \times b) + 2a + 1.$$

In those cases where it makes no difference which subscript comes first, the
DOs should be arranged so that $a \leq b \leq c$. This minimizes the number of
instructions executed.

A further saving can be made by removing (B + X*Y) from statement
4. Since it does not vary as the subscripts vary, it can be calculated once
and stored.

```
TEMP = B + X*Y;
DO I = 1 TO 5;
    DO J = 1 TO 10;
        DO K = 1 TO 20;
            A (I,J) = TEMP + C (I,K) * D (K,J);
```

The number of loop control instructions can also be reduced by unrolling
the loop. This uses more instruction space.

```
DO I 1 TO 10;    ────────▶   DO I 1 TO 10 BY 2;
    A(I) = B(I) + C;             A(I) = B(I) + C;
                                 A(I+1) = B(I+1) + C;
```

Some optimizing compilers automatically unroll loops or jam together two loops that use the same execution controls.

Allen and Cocke [15] discuss a number of program optimizing techniques, including the loop operations and the movement of invariant code out of inner loops. They also point out the advantages and disadvantages of each technique. For instance, it is generally desirable to calculate a value only once, if possible, and save it in a register or temporary storage location. To accomplish this, though, you must be able to (a) recognize that the calculation is used in several places, (b) supply a spare register, and (c) ensure that there are no unplanned side effects. Although the opportunity to reduce redundant calculations is apparent in the DO loop above, not all opportunities are obvious; for example, the identity of C and E in:

1. C = A * B;
   ...
10. D = A;
11. E = D * B;

Also hard to spot are areas of dead code which have been bypassed by various optimizations or program modifications. The dead code should be deleted.[2] Somewhat easier to recognize are situations in which a variable has been assigned a constant value: A = 5, B = 2 , . . . , I = (A*B) , ... Here, the variable I can be replaced by its value, 10, wherever it appears, and the calculation of A*B will be avoided.

The savings so far have been relatively independent of machine type. Some, such as loop unrolling, are attractive for parallel processors because they result in multiple, independent expressions that can be simultaneously evaluated. Additional machine-dependent savings, such as storing data in the number base of the machine to avoid conversions, tend to complicate program maintenance and are recommended only for projects in which optimization has great value. An exception to the rule is that a program should be packaged so as to run efficiently on a machine with virtual storage or base-offset addressing.

5.4.2 Packaging Subroutines

The physical organization of the program can have a significant effect on performance since bulk storage devices are so slow compared with the computer. When a program is too large to fit in main memory, the time required

---

2. Dead code should be deleted by the individual responsible for the program unit. After the unit is integrated into a system, an attempt to delete dead code may introduce errors; therefore dead code is sometimes ignored in large systems.

to bring in the overlay segments is large compared with the execution time. Sometimes the overlays can be completely overlapped with useful execution so that the only cost is the elapsed time to complete the program. If the overlays are not overlapped, both time and money are lost. The problem is aggravated when there are multiple overlay segments (normal in virtual memory systems) and there are numerous references back and forth among segments. The ideal program would load segment 1, execute it and go to 2, then step sequentially through the remaining segments. This ideal is seldom achievable. The compromise objective is to group routines that talk to one another in a single segment. A careful analysis of the program flow is required to accomplish this, and the solution may actually store copies of some routines in several segments. Consider the following paths through the Subtask Detach Processor.

(80%) SAVCOD $\rightarrow$ APTCOD $\rightarrow$ PRCOD $\rightarrow$ TTCOD $\xrightarrow{\text{T}}$ NORMAL $\xrightarrow{\text{TTT}}$ DEVCOD $\rightarrow$ RETURN

(10%) SAVCOD $\rightarrow$ APTCOD $\rightarrow$ PRCOD $\rightarrow$ TTCOD $\xrightarrow{\text{T}}$ NORMAL $\xrightarrow{\text{TT}}$ QCOD $\rightarrow$ RETURN

(5%)   SAVCOD $\rightarrow$ APTCOD $\rightarrow$ PRCOD $\rightarrow$ TTCOD $\xrightarrow{\text{T}}$ NORMAL $\xrightarrow{\text{TTT}}$ RETURN

(3%)   SAVCOD $\rightarrow$ APTCOD $\rightarrow$ PRCOD $\rightarrow$ TTCOD $\xrightarrow{\text{T}}$ NORMAL $\xrightarrow{\text{T}}$ RETURN

(2%)   SAVCOD $\rightarrow$ APTCOD $\rightarrow$ PRCOD $\rightarrow$ TTCOD $\xrightarrow{\text{T}}$ RETURN

(Each T represents a small block of test code. The percentages are an estimate of the likelihood that a given path will be followed.) There are seven modules and four tests in the most likely path. In addition, the data described by OLSDCL and SDPDCL must be available to some or all of the modules. All of this could be placed in memory in one operation if there were room. A worst-case overlay arrangement, with each block of code and each data region in a separate segment, would require 13 read operations. Fortunately, there is no backtracking, so a segment need never be read twice. All paths use SAVCOD, APTCOD, PRCOD, TTCOD, and RETURN; 98% of the paths also include NORMAL; and 80% use DEVCOD. Only 10% use QCOD. Using this data, the programmer can alter his packaging to fit the situation.

The natural package is a single segment which fits in memory. In a virtual storage machine it will appear to the programmer that available memory is much larger than his program [16]. Actually, the virtual storage machine may use a small memory and, without bothering the programmer, divide each program into fixed-length pages, which it reads into memory only as they are needed. If the virtual machine uses pages 1000 bytes long, the program will be executed in 1000-byte chunks, regardless of the programmer's intended segmentation. Thus a routine which starts on one page and ends on another may be read in two separate operations. If the routine contains a loop which spans the page boundary, the virtual control program

Module Name	Module Size	Page or Segment Size									
		1000						2000			8000
		1	2	3	4	5	6	1	2	3	1
SAVCOD	200	200						200			200
APTCOD	500	500						500			500
PRCOD	400		400					400			400
TTCOD	1800	200	600	1000					1800		1800
Test ACTIVE	20	20							20		20
NORMAL	40	40							40		40
Test NORMAL	20	20							20		20
Test REQ	20				20				20		20
QCOD	1300				900	400				1300	1300
Test EXT	20				20				20		20
DEVCOD	1100					100	1000	500		600	1100
RETURN	20	20*			20*	20*		20*	20*	20*	20
TOTALS	5440	1000	1000	1000	960	520	1000	1620	1940	1920	5440

*   Multiple copies
- - ➤   Sequence of module placement

Fig. 5.9 Packaging routines in fixed-size pages.

may be forced to overlay the pages every time the loop is executed. (A similar problem occurs in machines which can address only part of their main memory. Many small process controllers are designed with short words. An instruction may have only enough room for, say, 10-bit addresses covering 1024 memory locations; yet it may have 32,768 words of memory. One instruction is used to select a 1024-word block. All subsequent instructions refer to the selected block. If routines cannot be squeezed into a single block, the Select instruction must be used every time a block boundary is crossed. The cost of such base-offset addressing is small compared with the cost of overlaying virtual storage from a drum or disk.)

The programmer's goal is to maximize the likelihood that each instruction will be followed by an instruction currently in memory. This is done by packing related routines and/or data into the same page [17]. In Fig. 5.9, pages are filled with sequential modules. (Data storage is not considered in Fig. 5.9.) If a module break is unavoidable, the overflow is placed in the nearest adjacent page that will hold it; otherwise a new page is started. The RETURN routine is repeated in each page that could reasonably call

Path: 80% likelihood
SAVCOD→APTCOD→PRCOD→TTCOD→Test ACTIVE→NORMAL
→Test NORMAL→Test REQ→Test EXT→DEVCOD→RETURN
Replacement: least recently used page replaced

Page Size = 1000	
One Real Page	Three Real Pages
-Read 1	Read 1
Read 2 over 1	Read 2
Read 3 over 2	Read 3
Read 1 over 3	Read 4 over 2
Read 4 over 1	Read 6 over 3
Read 6 over 4	Read 5 over 1
Read 5 over 6	
7 pages read	6 pages read

Page Size = 2000	
One Real Page	Two Real Pages
-Read 1	Read 1
Read 2	Read 2
Read 3	Read 3 over 1
Read 1	Read 1 over 2
4 pages read	4 pages read

Fig. 5.10 Effect of packaging on performance.

on it. (Replicated routines must never be modified during execution.) This saves a page overlay without much cost in space. After all modules are laid out, the results should be reexamined to see if a rearrangement can save a page. In Fig. 5.9, six 1000-unit pages are required to hold 5480 units of code.[3] This includes 40 units of duplicate code. Clearly, no pages can be saved unless the capacity of the pages used exceeds the unduplicated amount of code by the size of one page.

Figure 5.10 shows the savings available for various real memory availabilities. The tables show that the sequential nature of the program requires

---

3. The Subtask Detach Processor as described up to this point should not be a large program. The sizes in Fig. 5.9 are not representative.

that every page be used at least once. With a page size of 1000 units, at least three real pages are needed to achieve the minimum number of page reads. The same is true with 2000-unit pages; however, a repackaging that places TTCOD in pages 1 and 2 and DEVCOD in 2 and 3 allows the program to run with only three page reads in a real space of two pages. Since the amount of real memory available is a function of total work load at any given time (as well as replacement strategy), the number of pages available to your program may vary from run to run. It is best to shape the program design and layout to fit a paging environment and take advantage of whatever real space is allocated. The general rule is to group together those portions of the program that are executed together, replicating commonly used modules as required. This rule, regardless of machine page size or real memory allocations, should improve performance by reducing the working set size [18]. It may force a complete redesign of some existing programs whose segments span and loop across many pages. (In general, measurements of actual program behavior are necessary in order to assess the benefits of redesigning such a program.)

5.4.3   Converting Decision Tables

Decision tables are compact, complete descriptions of involved relationships. Evaluating them in program code can take a lot of source statements. Basically the tables are IF p THEN DO f ELSE DO g structures. One obvious way to code the logic is by a sequence of proper flowcharts. Two ways of doing this were introduced by Montalbano [19] in 1962. His methods applied to any decision table, covering limited entries, extended entries, DON'T CARE conditions, and ELSE rules. Since any extended-entry table can be restructured as a limited-entry table, subsequent literature tends to discuss only limited-entry tables [20, 21, 22]. Special problems can arise when a table contains ambiguities. Methods for dealing with ambiguities using rule masks—individual tests of every condition against every rule by comparison of bit strings—are also available [23], but they are generally poorer performers than the condition trees based on Montalbano's methods.

Both decision tree methods convert the decision table into a tree of IFTHENELSE tests. One method arranges the tests so that they take minimum storage. The other method arranges the tests so as to optimize execution time. The first, or "quick rule," method searches out the conditions that are immediately decidable and tests them first. In a limited-entry table the first decidable condition is the one with the fewest DON'T CARE conditions and the greatest disparity between Yes and No entries in its row. Testing this condition splits the table into two parts, the smaller of which is often the single rule invoked by that condition. The second, or "delayed rule," method defers final decisions as long as possible on the assumption that the average length of any path will be less in this tree than in the quick rule tree. The delayed rule is further improved by weighting decision criteria to represent the probability that each rule will be invoked.

The steps in the two methods are comparable for limited-entry tables.

Step	Delayed rule	Step	Quick rule
1.	Compress table until each rule has unique action.	1.	Same
2.	For each column, calculate $\left(\dfrac{\text{COLUMN}}{\text{COUNT}}\right)$ by adding up dashes in column (r) and setting $\left(\dfrac{\text{COLUMN}}{\text{COUNT}}\right) = 2^r$.	2.	Same
3.	For each row, calculate $\left(\dfrac{\text{DASH}}{\text{COUNT}}\right)$ by adding up $\left(\dfrac{\text{COLUMN}}{\text{COUNT}}\right)$ for all dashes in row.	3.	Same
4.	For each row, calculate Δ. $\Delta = \text{YCOUNT} - \text{NCOUNT}$, where $\text{YCOUNT} = $ sum of $\left(\dfrac{\text{COLUMN}}{\text{COUNT}}\right)$ for all Ys in row, $\text{NCOUNT} = $ sum of $\left(\dfrac{\text{COLUMN}}{\text{COUNT}}\right)$ for all Ns in row.	4.	Same
		5.	Label each column with expected frequency of occurrence of that rule.
		6.	For each row, calculate Weighted Dash Count (WDC) by adding up $\left(\dfrac{\text{COLUMN}}{\text{COUNT}}\right) \times \text{FREQ}$ for all dashes in row.
5.	Select row with lowest $\left(\dfrac{\text{DASH}}{\text{COUNT}}\right)$ as first condition to be tested.	7.	Select row with lowest WDC as first condition to be tested.
6.	Resolve ties by selecting row with *highest* Δ.	8.	Resolve ties by selecting row with *lowest* Δ.
		9.	Resolve further ties by selecting row with lowest $\left(\dfrac{\text{DASH}}{\text{COUNT}}\right)$.

Step	Delayed rule	Step	Quick rule
7.	Resolve remaining ties by selecting any row in group.	10.	Same
8.	Generate two new tables: one for all Ys and dashes in selected row, one for all Ns and dashes. Row selected in previous step is deleted from new table.	11.	Same
9.	Repeat from Step 2 until only one rule remains after each test. Test remaining Y, N conditions to isolate each selected rule and identify ELSE results.	12.	Same

If all frequencies are the same or unknown, steps 5, 6, and 9 fall out of the delayed rule. The only remaining difference is in the treatment of Δ. Quick rule looks for the highest Δ, delayed rule for the lowest. The two rules produce identical programs if, at every stage, there is one row with no dashes or several rows with the same values for all counts. These conditions apply to the Subtask Detach Processor decision table. As a consequence, the flowchart shown in Fig. 5.11 will be produced by either method. It gives the decision table from Fig. 4.5 and shows the flowchart segment obtained after each reduction of the decision table according to the quick rule procedure.

The program produced in Fig. 5.11 is different from the one in Fig. 5.5 in that ELSE conditions have been generated after the device tests. Something must have been omitted from the original decision table. As a check, determine how many rules there must be for a seven-condition limited-entry table. That number is $2^7 = 128$. There are only eight rules shown. Where are the others? Remember that DON'T CARE stands for both Yes and No; thus each rule with a dash in it represents two rules. Each rule with r dashes represents 2^r rules. Column counts under each rule show what they represent. Summing the column counts for the original table yields

$$16 + 32 + 8 + 64 + 1 + 1 + 1 + 1 = 124.$$

Thus there are four rules unaccounted for which must be encompassed by an ELSE. Investigation shows that the missing rules cover situations in which two or three devices have Yes codes at the same time—an illegal situation.

For illustrative purposes, a table which will generate different programs for quick rule and delayed rule is shown in Fig. 5.12. The execution time

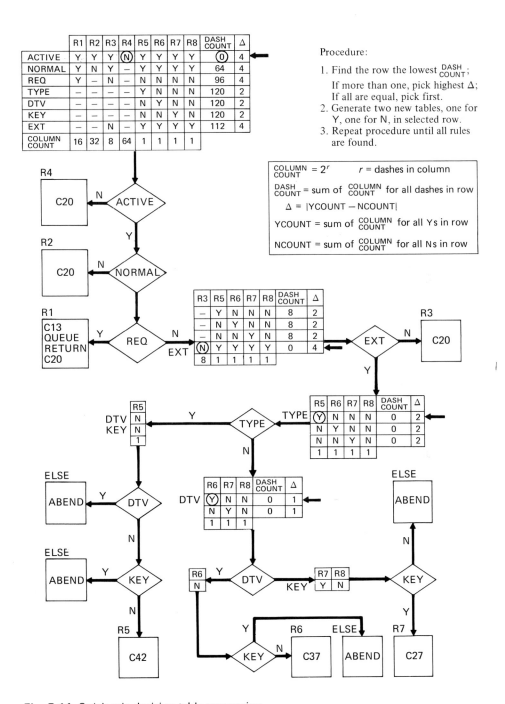

Fig. 5.11 Quick rule decision table conversion.

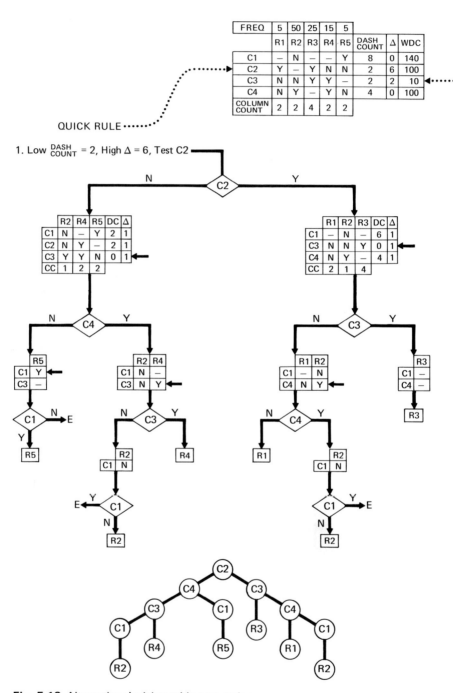

QUICK RULE ⋯⋯⋯

1. Low $_{COUNT}^{DASH}$ = 2, High Δ = 6, Test C2

Fig. 5.12 Alternative decision table conversions.

DELAYED RULE

1. Low WDC = 10, Test C3

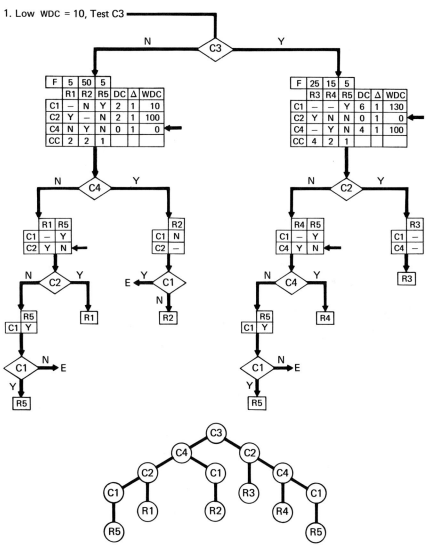

TABLE 5.1.   ALTERNATIVE CONVERSION EXECUTION TIMES

Quick rule				Delayed rule			
Rule	Freq	Tests to Reach rule	Time	Rule	Freq	Tests to Reach rule	Time
1	5	3	15	1	5	3	15
2	50	4	200	2	50	3	150
3	25	2	50	3	25	2	50
4	15	3	45	4	15	3	45
5	5	3	15	5	5	4	20
Total time			325				280

Space saved by quick rule: none
Time saved by delayed rule: 13.8%

of the two programs is compared in Table 5.1. Although the difference is small for the example, it can be significant for larger tables. The difference in storage requirements in Fig. 5.12 is nil; it, too, can become significant for large tables. Further improvements are possible (such as combining the two terminal tests of Cl into one test and a branch to that test from the other limb of the tree). Methods for making a number of such improvements to both the condition tests and the action commands are given by Myers [21].

As a general guideline, use the delayed rule process in preference to the quick rule. The quick rule is applicable mainly to large tables when storage space is very restricted. Always check design specifications to be sure that no unusual timing requirements are present. Sometimes there will be a need to execute a process within a few microseconds when a given condition exists. Test that critical condition first. The remaining conditions will form a decision table that can be treated with either of the two conversion methods.

5.4.4   Machine-Dependent Code

Higher-level languages seek to make programs independent of machine peculiarities. Although a language may achieve this objective, its compiler implementation may cancel out the advantage. The compiler takes advantage of the machine features available to it and may optimize the object code by inserting machine-dependent features in it. Restrictions on the program may result, the most serious being loss of compatibility.

Compatibility implies identical behavior with respect to selected conditions; i.e., machines A and B are compatible for programs which produce identical results on both. Machines A and B may be physically different and still be compatible. The most common loss of compatibility occurs when B is an improvement over A, having additional instructions and faster versions of A's instructions. Any program which depends on the execution time of A's instructions may fail on B because B's execution times are not proportional to A's. Any program produced by B's compiler may not run on A because it contains object code instructions A cannot recognize. The latter problem can be avoided by using A's compiler, whose output should run on both A and B. However, even this option may be unsuitable. If B is a parallel processor and A a serial processor but they both have the same instruction set, A's compiler will produce a program that will run properly on B, but it will not take advantage of any of the speed improvement due to parallelism. Since speed may be the only advantage of B, the machines are, for practical purposes, incompatible. Other incompatibilities arise from different word lengths and data representations (which lead to different results for the same instruction sequences) or unique access mechanisms. Special hardware, including microcoded instructions installed for unique application requirements, may also result in incompatibility when it has the effect of replacing a standard machine instruction with one unknown to the compiler.

Compatibility considerations are most important when a program must run on several machines. Once this was an unlikely concern since most users had only one machine. More recently it has become an issue. The user may have several different machines. And quite often the development team may find it economical to employ machine A to code and debug programs for delivery to a user with machine B.

Several coding techniques are to be avoided except under severe pressure to improve real-time performance. The use of "tricky" code has already been referred to as poor programming style. *Tricky code* is any nonobvious use of the available instruction set without an accompanying explanation. It includes operations on the command portion of instruction codes (e.g., turning an ADD into a NULL command by changing its bit pattern as though it were data) and the use of obscure side effects (e.g., creating an arithmetic overflow to indicate a logical condition). It also includes any sequence of instructions that an experienced programmer would be unable to interpret. Tricky code, if necessary, is made useful by adequate comments in the program listing. One weakness of tricky code is that it is so dependent on the exact environment for which it is designed that it must be replaced if the environment changes. Another coding technique that lacks flexibility is the use of absolute values for addresses, tables names, variable names, or certain types of constants. Symbols are preferred for any values that could conceivably change. A single compilation will correct all occurrences of a modified symbol. Much more complicated editing is required to find and update all instances of an absolute value (particularly if the value is ever the result of a computation, such as a FORTRAN Computed GO TO).

Programmers need not avoid all machine-dependent code because of these exposures, but they should certainly be aware of the effects of machine dependency and consider them in their implementations.

5.5 RELIABILITY

An error-free debugging run merely demonstrates that, for the program and data supplied and for the environmental conditions at the time, no errors were detected. It does not mean that the program will run correctly every time it is used. Some remaining sources of error can be the following.

- Bugs in sections of the program that were never exercised.

- Bugs placed in the program during operation by

   operating system actions, some of which may be legal, some caused by operating system errors;

   other problem programs which modify storage areas containing your program or data;

   machine errors;

   read or write errors while the program is being moved;

   operator loading errors.

- Changes in the program due to

   incorrect arrangement of source program cards;

   a temporary modification used to bypass an abnormal termination condition;

   hardware facility changes.

- Changes in your data caused by malfunctions in your program.

- Lack of agreement between object code and program documentation.

- Confusion due to use of the same name by several programs to refer to different files.

- Machine dependencies in the program that are not satisfied by the hardware.

Experience with third-generation computers shows that machine errors rarely affect program execution. Either none occur or those that do are corrected before they can do any harm. It is also true that full-scale operating systems adequately isolate multiprogramming regions so that interference

among programs is uncommon. Although such errors may occur in prototype systems under construction, it is more realistic to assume that operational problems are due to the programmer, the operator, or the data controller. It is the people in the system who make errors.

Defensive coding is required to minimize program failures after the
program is released for general use. *Defensive coding* anticipates problems
that can arise when the program is running and protects the program from
the consequences. There are four levels of response to operational problems.
In the simplest case, errors that occur can be ignored with the full knowledge
that they are irrelevant. Relevant errors can often be corrected or ame-
liorated by calling an error routine. This response permits the program to
continue. Catastrophic failures cannot be corrected immediately, so a recovery procedure is required. Finally, when recovery is not possible, the program must be taken off-line for maintenance or modification.

5.5.1 Preventing Failures

No amount of care short of wiring the program into hardware will prevent
all possible program failures. Even a wired program can fail because of an
open connection or a missed beat in the timing controls. It is generally
impossible to predict how reliable a program will be. Looking back on the
performance of an obsolete program, one might figure out how reliable it
was, but that information is not much help in predicting the reliability of
a different program. By taking steps to minimize failures, the programmer
can give the user high confidence in the inherent validity of the program.
Failures will be relatively infrequent and will most often be caused by
factors external to the program.

The general objective in writing a defensively coded program is to make
the object code do what the specification calls for and prevent it from doing
anything else. An unprotected program might take this form:

```
SUM = 0;
SUMSQ = 0;
DO I = 1 TO N;
    SUM = SUM + A(I);
    SUMSQ = SUMSQ + A(I)**2;
END;
MEAN = SUM/N;
DEV = (SQRT (N*SUMSQ - SUM**2))/N;
```

This string of code calculates the mean and the standard deviation of the
N numbers in the vector array A. No restrictions are placed on the size
of the numbers, the sign of the numbers, or the value of the denominator.

Under normal circumstances, the A(I) values might be positive integers so that no problems would arise. Assume that the A(I)s are all less than 999. They represent the number of disk accesses per inquiry for various types of inquiries in an information system. Further assume that they are stored sequentially—in a machine that operates on variable-length strings. A special mark designates the end of each value field in memory. Now consider the possible errors (which are unlikely but can occur).

- Machine fails to recognize field mark and reads a value greater than 999 for A(K).
- Because of an erroneously large A(K) in SUM but not in SUMSQ, the square root argument is negative.
- An interrupt from another program is incorrectly processed and, incidentally, sets N to zero.

Each fault causes the code to be mathematically incorrect. To avoid getting hung up in the computation, test for illegal conditions before each critical function.

```
   ...
SUM = 0;
SUMSQ = 0;
DO I = 1 TO N;
    IF A(I)<999 THEN
        DO;
            SUM = SUM + A(I);
            SUMSQ = SUMSQ + A(I);
        END;
    ELSE RETURN (DATA);
END;
ARG = N*SUMSQ - SUM**2;
IF ARG<0 THEN
    DO;
        ON ZERO-DIVIDE GO TO Z1;
        MEAN = SUM/N;
        DEV = (SQRT (ARG))/N;
    END;
ELSE RETURN (ARG);
   ...
```

The tests inserted before each expression check the input data. The set of permissible values is the *domain* of the function represented by the expression. The set of possible results is the *range* of the function. Testing that the result of a calculation is within range is useful for debugging, and it may be useful during execution when the result is an input to several other routines. Nevertheless, to protect against external problems occurring between the time a result is generated and the time it is used again, it is recommended that domain tests be performed prior to critical routines [24]. In the example, tests are inserted every few instructions. In practice, domain tests are placed only at the head of critical blocks of code because too many tests add so many instructions that reliability may be adversely affected. A tradeoff is required between the number of tests and the risk that an error will prevent completion of the program.

A valuable logical range test is one that can verify the reasonableness of a result before the data used to produce the result has been erased. It permits the faulty section to be tried again immediately. Retries will succeed if the source of the problem was transitory. The longer the sections of code to which such logical tests apply, the fewer tests will be needed in the overall program. Applicable logical tests include hash totals,[4] crossfoot comparisons, recalculation by an alternative method, trend analysis of sequential results, etc. Each test is placed in the section of code where the tested condition occurs. When the section is a subprogram, the best action to take may not be evident from looking at the subprogram. The test results should be passed up to the higher-level program for action because the higher-level program has more information on the global state of affairs.

Implicit in defensive coding is the need for exhaustive condition analysis. In dealing with decision table conversion, the Subtask Detach Processor example illustrated how, in DEVCOD, it was necessary but not sufficient to test only one device code to determine which device routine to execute. To be sufficient, as indicated by the ELSE results of Fig. 5.11, additional tests would have to verify that only one device code had been turned on.

---

4. A *hash total* is a number calculated by some simple reproducible manipulation of the data to be checked. Various operations, such as squaring the original data or adding the low-order digits to the high-order digits, produce hash totals. "Casting out nines" is a common form of hash total used by schoolchildren (and others) to verify arithmetic operations. It is based on a rule of modular arithmetic that relates the sum of the digits in two operands to the sum of the digits in the result of an arithmetic operation. The method calculates a *check digit* for each operand. The check digit is the remainder obtained by dividing the operand by nine. The same check digit is obtained by repetitively subtracting nine ("casting out nines") from the sum of the digits. For example, the check digit for 12345 is 6; for 327856 it is 4. The check digit of a sum or product is the same as the check digit of the sum or product of the check digits of the operands.

Operand		Check Digit	Operand		Check Digit
327856		4	327856		4
+ 12345		+ 6	× 12345		× 6
340201	→1←	10	4047382320	→6←	24

Defensive coding requires the full set of tests to exhaustively determine that only legal actions are performed. Structured coding, by its nature, encourages completeness, so it is an inherently defensive technique.

5.5.2 Handling Errors

Error routines are short programs that are used only when an error occurs. Many errors are handled by the operating system. Errors peculiar to your program are, your responsibility. Usually a separate routine is written for each type of detected error. For historical purposes large systems should log all errors in order to identify weak points requiring redesign. Therefore every error routine should produce an error message for the log and, in serious cases, for the operator. When no action is required, an error signal can be ignored, except in those machines which leave the signal on until it is turned off by the program. When an action is required, the error routine should do everything it can to correct the error so that the program can continue. It is not important that an error routine takes a second or two if it can make a 30-minute job run to completion. Based on their infrequent use, error routines need not be coded for performance, but it is essential that they be logically sound. They must be designed to ask, "What set of conditions could have turned on my error indicator?" and then, "How can I correct the erroneous conditions?"

For many *solid errors*—unrecoverable malfunctions—there is no corrective action other than to back the program up to a previously correct state and restart it. Transient errors due to a temporary malfunction that is unlikely to occur again should be circumvented by repeating the block of code in which the error occurred. One retry is sufficient for electronic transients, such as parity errors in the central processing unit. (Some machines automatically retry an instruction on which an error flag was raised.) Transient errors in bulk storage devices can be due to physical causes, such as a speck of dust. Physical movement may dislodge the dust, but it may take a couple of hundred tries to get a good reading. The number of retries, then, should be a function of the likelihood that additional attempts will succeed. If nothing succeeds, the error routine should stop the job, record the state of the system at the point of the error, identify the nature of the error, and write all this information out to the log and the recovery subsystem.

5.5.3 Recovering from Solid Errors

Jobs should be designed to run from a correct starting point through a series of correct intermediate points to a correct conclusion. Effective input data control supplemented by good operating and library procedures can get the job started right. Very short jobs (and one-time jobs) can be allowed to run without intermediate check points on the basis that the entire job can be done over cheaply. Longer jobs require periodic checkpoints to reduce the cost of error recovery. The number of checkpoints depends on the cost of checkpoints and the number of opportunities in the program for logical checkpoints to be taken. Checkpoints can usually be placed at the end of major blocks of code on the assumption that, if the code was carefully checked internally, the end of the block could be reached only through correct execution.

Program checkpoint is a term applied both to the point in a program at which correctness tests are made and to the data saved at the time the tests are made. A checkpoint is *taken*—i.e., written to a storage device—when the correctness tests are executed successfully. If the tests fail, all the work done since the last checkpoint was taken is thrown away. The last checkpoint is read in and the program is restarted from there. The *checkpoint/restart* process is the recovery procedure that makes it possible to finish a job if it can possibly be finished. Two types of checkpoint/restart procedures exist. One ignores the internal logic of the user program and takes checkpoints at the convenience of the operating system, usually at the end of every job step. A time-sharing system does this when the dispatcher interrupts one user program and rolls it out of memory in its entirety in order to give time to someone else. Many I/O subsystems save input and output records until all processes and transmissions associated with the data are completed normally. The second type of checkpoint can be supplied only by the user because it involves knowing exactly what correctness tests make sense and where they belong. After every *n* transactions, a checkpoint is taken at the end of normal transaction processing. Either the complete system status can be saved or, on the basis of the user's knowledge of the situation, only the data needed for recovery is saved. Each subsequent transaction is subjected to the usual error checks, and if an uncorrectable error occurs, the processing is terminated with the appropriate error output. The program may be restarted automatically or resubmitted at another time in accordance with the type of error and the effort required to get around it.

If the spacing of checkpoints, *n*, is 1, the program is never more than one transaction away from a usable checkpoint. If $n = N$, the total number of transactions, there are no checkpoints taken. If $1<n<N$, the program will have to redo, on the average, $n/2$ transactions when a restart is required. The value of *n* should be selected so that the total checkpoint time plus the recovery processing time for a predicted rate of error is substantially less than the recovery time for the same rate of error if there were no checkpoints.

More important than checkpoint processing time is data control. If $n = 1$, the only changes to data sets since the last checkpoint were due to the interrupted transaction. By suitably logging all changes, the program can reconstruct the data set as it appeared when the checkpoint was taken. If $n > 1$, data set recovery is much more difficult and time-consuming. In fact, it may be necessary to save the data sets as well as the program status every time a checkpoint is taken. In information systems with large files, checkpointing every transaction (or every time a subprocess within a transaction processing job finishes) is generally preferable to trying to reconstruct files. Copying the files at checkpoints is out of the question. At most, files might be duplicated as they are modified in order to protect against loss of a hardware storage unit.

5.5.4 Maintenance

Modern computers are very reliable. Those that have full operating system facilities appear to the user to be virtually free of transient errors because of built-in error retry and recovery support. As a consequence, most operating errors encountered when running under an operating system are solid errors. They can be temporarily bypassed, but eventually the program (or data) must be fixed. Programmers writing new systems programs that interface directly with the hardware have a tougher job than those whose programs interface with an operating system. The hardware interface has both transient and solid errors and offers few clues as to which is which. In late 1967, a new time-sharing program faced such a problem. Experimental test sessions had run quite successfully, so the system was opened for regular use by up to six local terminal users who had a variety of accounting and analytic problems to solve. Everything went well for two months. Then the administrative manager complained that he was getting wrong answers on some of his financial calculations. The problem had the appearance of a transient error in the hardware timing because various digits were changed randomly during processing. Extensive diagnosis found nothing wrong in the vendor's hardware or software. Finally, for reasons no one ever discovered, it turned out that when the system found a 9 in a particular position of an input, it executed a completely unexpected set of code before getting back on the track. Because the inputs were free-form statements, the troublesome position appeared to be random when it wasn't. The moral of the story is that when an error occurs, suspect everything; do not exclude improbable causes without investigation.

The sense of urgency surrounding production computing exerts pressure on people to try to make corrections as fast as they can after an error is detected. This is not always necessary. Data-dependent errors may be easy to bypass. The affected transaction can be fixed up manually, and the program will run correctly until a similar data state arises. Some real-time inputs are so redundant that, as long as most of them are processed correctly, occasional errors can be ignored. When the error cannot be ignored, the program has to be stopped and taken off-line to be fixed. An immediate temporary fix is often applied in the form of a *patch,* a machine language instruction sequence that is most often inserted by replacing the first faulty instruction with a branch instruction. The transfer goes to the patch, which ends in a branch back to the next good instruction in the original program. This technique can avoid reassembly by leaving all the original addresses alone and placing the new code at the end of the load module. The same approach is often taken with more elaborate patches at the assembly language level. Here a GO TO is used to reach the patch. Clearly, this is a violation of GO TO–free structured code.

Proliferation of patches is invariably the source of an increasingly large flow of error reports. New errors are constantly showing up in the patches themselves. In their haste to correct the error, the programmers debug the patch only against the conditions causing the error. They do not debug it for all program states, as described in the next chapter. One more danger from patches is that the programmer, concentrating on the local conditions surrounding the error, may write some code that changes the design of the program in another area. A simple illustration occurs when an error is due to the fact that the program finds the wrong number in a register.

```
PLUS1    X = X+Y;
PLUS2    Y = X+Y;
ASSIGN   A = Y;
...
CALC1    DO I = 1 TO A;
```

The number assigned to register A is $X_0 + 2Y_0$. If A was intended to be $X_0 + Y_0$, the ASSIGN step should follow PLUS1. Yet if the whole program looks like

```
PLUS1    X = X+Y;
PLUS2    Y = X+Y;
ASSIGN   A = Y;
...
CALC1    DO I = 1 TO A;
...
CALC2    DO I = 1 TO A;
```

and the A in CALC2 should be $X_0 + 2Y_0$, patching ASSIGN simply shifts the logical error to a new location.

To maintain reliable operation, make the lifetime of patches as short as possible. As soon as the patch is made, it should be fully described. Then the same error should be analyzed and fixed at the source program level. If the fix in any way modifies the design specification, it too must be corrected after appropriate coordination with the user. At the first opportunity, the new source program should be recompiled and should replace the patched version. To avoid confusion as to which copy of the program is the current one, each new version should have its own unique name or label. The source program correction should be fully debugged as though it were a brand new program. In making the fix, the programmer should refer to the program package documentation—in particular, the dictionary of names and symbols, the "where used" list of cross-references, the table of program calls, the memory map, and the current program listing. Through these documents, he should verify that the program fix has no undesirable, uncorrected side effects.

REFERENCES

1. Burge, W. H., *Recursive Programming Techniques*. Reading, Mass.: Addison-Wesley, in press.
2. Vaszonyi, A., *Problem Solving by Digital Computers with PL/I Programming*. Englewood Cliffs, N.J.: Prentice-Hall, 1970.
3. Flores, I., *Computer Programming*. Englewood Cliffs, N.J.: Prentice-Hall, 1965.
4. Corbato, F. J., "PL/I as a Tool for System Programming." *Datamation,* Vol. 15, No. 5, May 1969. Also E. E. David, Jr., "Some Thoughts about the Production of Large Software Systems." In P. Naur and B. Randell (eds.), *Software Engineering*. Brussels, Belgium: NATO Science Committee, January 1969.
5. Sammet, J. E. "Programming Languages: History and Future." *Communications of the ACM,* Vol. 15, No. 7, July 1972.
6. Nicholls, J. E., *The Design and Structure of Programming Languages*. Reading, Mass.: Addison-Wesley, in press.
7. Backus, J. W., "The Syntax and Semantics of the Proposed International Algebraic Language of the Zurich ACM-GAMM Conference." *ICIP Proceedings, Paris, 1959.* London: Butterworth's, 1960.
8. Iverson, K. E., *A Programming Language*. New York: Wiley, 1962.
9. Dijkstra, E. W., "Cooperating Sequential Processes." In F. Genuys (ed.), *Programming Languages*. New York: Academic Press, 1967.
10. Weinwurm, G. F., and H. J. Zagorski, "Research into the Management of Computer Programming: A Transitional Analysis of Cost Estimation Techniques," SDC Report TM-2712. Santa Monica, Cal.: System Development Corporation, 1965.
11. Sackman, H., *Man-Computer Problem Solving*. Princeton, N.J.: Auerbach, 1970.

12. Sammet, J. E., "Problems in, and a Pragmatic Approach to Programming Language Measurement." *AFIPS Conference Proceedings,* Vol. 39, 1971, Fall Joint Computer Conference. Montvale, N.J.: AFIPS Press, 1971.

13. Mills, H. D., "Top Down Programming in Large Systems." In R. Rustin (ed.), *Debugging Techniques in Large Systems.* Englewood Cliffs, N.J.: Prentice-Hall, 1971.

14. Linger, R. C., and H. D. Mills, *Structured Programming.* Reading, Mass.: Addison-Wesley, in press.

15. Allen, F. E., and J. Cocke, "A Catalogue of Optimizing Transformations," IBM Research Report RC3548. Yorktown Heights, N.Y.: IBM Research, 1971.

16. Parmelee, R. P., T. I. Peterson, C. C. Tillman, and D. J. Hatfield, "Virtual Storage and Virtual Machine Concepts." *IBM Systems Journal,* Vol. 11, No. 2, 1972.

17. Guertin, R. L., "Programming in a Paging Environment." *Datamation,* Vol. 18, No. 2, February 1972.

18. Morrison, J. E., "User Program Performance in Virtual Storage Systems." *IBM Systems Journal,* Vol. 12, No. 3, 1973.

19. Montalbano, M., "Tables, Flowcharts, and Program Logic." *IBM Systems Journal,* Vol. 1, No. 1, 1962.

20. Pollack, S. L., "Conversion of Limited-Entry Decision Tables to Computer Programs." *Communications of the ACM,* Vol. 8, No. 11, November 1965.

21. Myers, H. J., "Compiling Optimized Code from Decision Tables." *IBM Journal of Research and Development,* Vol. 16, No. 5, September 1972.

22. Press, L. I., "Conversion of Decision Tables to Computer Programs." *Communications of the ACM,* Vol. 8, No. 6, June 1965.

23. Pooch, V. W., "Translation of Decision Tables." *ACM Computing Surveys,* Vol. 6, No. 2, June 1974.

24. Ogdin, J. L., "Improving Software Reliability." *Datamation,* Vol. 19, No. 1, January 1973.

6
Debugging, Documentation, And Delivery

The best way to write a correct program is to leave out all the bugs. This is completely serious advice. No programmer is ready to believe that he or she intentionally seeds the program with bugs; yet all programmers rely heavily on machine runs to debug their programs. In so doing, they become lax as coders and make up for it as debuggers. When they are done (i.e., when the rate of discovering bugs drops to zero for at least one run), they believe the program is error-free. They are wrong. Dijkstra has explained that testing can show only the presence of bugs, not their absence [1]. A zero discovery rate is no proof that the program is error-free. All programs contain some errors before debugging and retain some fraction of the errors after debugging. It behooves programmers to avoid making errors in the first place so that the number of residual errors will be very small. The tools that help them program without error are top-down structured programming and, where applicable, correctness proofs. A proper attitude is also important. Programmers must exercise due care and constantly check their work in process because they know it is their responsibility to eliminate errors. They cannot delegate this responsibility to the computer or a check-out compiler. They cannot ignore this responsibility on the basis that the user can get by with a low-quality program. With the right attitude, programmers will produce logically sound programs which they know will generate the right answers except for minor syntactic or typographical errors in the code. They will still have to debug their programs, but they will feel confident that in a few runs, with adequate desk-checking in between, they can check out their packages.

6.1 DEBUGGING

Debugging is the process of running an ostensibly correct program with a variety of input data to demonstrate that the program correctly satisfies its design specifications. The term is used here only to refer to the tests run by an individual programmer on his or her own code. When tests are run by others for the purpose of detecting errors in the integrated work of several programmers, the process is called *testing* in this text and is covered in Volume 2. (As noted in Chapter 2, this definitional distinction is made to emphasize the difference between the self-discipline necessary for accuracy and the management control necessary for overall project assurance.)

The modifier "ostensibly correct" is used in the definition of debugging because a programmer will generally not try to run a program until he thinks it is correct. He is almost always wrong; yet he is usually surprised when bugs are found during the first attempted execution. Misplaced optimism further leads him to believe that the bug or bugs that caused the run to fail are the only ones in the program. So he fixes what he sees and requests another run. The second run produces a new list of bugs, including some that went unnoticed in the output from the first run. The programmer hastily fixes the obvious bugs in the second run and resubmits the job. The process, as described, is sequential. It tends to correct errors in the order of appearance in the output, not in the order of importance. In rushing back for a second computer run, the programmer is likely to overlook several bugs reported by the first run. Important errors may remain uncorrected for several runs, with the result that no pattern of behavior can be traced to explain why the program is failing.

A more productive debugging procedure starts with the assumption that bugs exist in both the logic and the syntax of the program. Each run is made to locate all the bugs that can be found by the testing methods employed. Prior to the next run, the output is completely analyzed and all recognizable bugs are fixed. An exception to the rule occurs when serious logical bugs are found. To avoid confusion, these should be fixed one at a time in the manner of a controlled experiment. Debugging is complete when all the necessary tests have been executed without error. This procedure emphasizes thorough desk-checking between computer runs. It makes better use of programmer time when computer turnaround is slow. By its very thoroughness, it helps the programmer find logic errors if they exist.

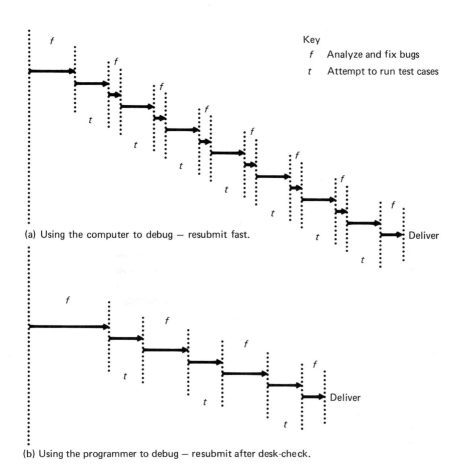

Key

f   Analyze and fix bugs

t   Attempt to run test cases

(a) Using the computer to debug — resubmit fast.

(b) Using the programmer to debug — resubmit after desk-check.

Fig. 6.1 Alternative debugging procedures.

A comparison of the two methods of scheduling debugging runs (Fig. 6.1) shows that the opportunity to get fast turnaround does not necessarily result in faster program unit completion. Elapsed time from start to finish of the debugging phase is shortened by balancing the time between runs against the amount of analysis performed at the programmer's desk. Thorough desk-checking is done with the intent of making the next computer run the last one. Effective desk-checking is analytical, not computational; the programmer checks logic, spelling, and punctuation and then seeks causes for unanticipated effects. At most, the programmer might calculate some simple sums to verify scale factors or arithmetic operator placement.

More complex formula evaluation should be left to the machine. An interactive terminal makes it convenient to let the machine carry more of the load.[1] Lazy programmers let the machine carry too much of the load. No matter how convenient it is to get access to the machine, computer runs should be used to supplement, not substitute for, programmer thinking.

6.1.1   What to Look For

The normal behavior of a program is to transform a set of inputs into a set of outputs according to the logical procedures in the program. Abnormal behavior implies that a bug exists. The most obvious abnormal behavior is either an incorrect output or a program halt before the output is reached. Incorrect output suggests that a bug exists in the program logic or the test data. Abnormal termination suggests either a logic bug or an error caused by something in the environment. In either case, the symptoms of the bug are usually observed after the bug has occurred; that is, the error caused the abnormal behavior through a chain of events [2]. It is necessary to work back from the point of termination to find the cause of the problem. Or one can work forward from the start of the test to determine what events could have produced the symptoms. Either way, debugging involves *tracing* the execution of the program and *dumping* the contents of the machine registers and memory which represent the state of the environment at significant points.

   If programmers write defensive structured code and apply whatever formal proving technique they can, they should not expect the first bugs encountered to be in the logic. It is more likely that there are mechanical or typographical errors in the source code. A good compiler will find many such errors automatically. An assembler may not. It is necessary to check the code carefully for proper use of names—spelling, insertion of blanks, substitution of hyphens for underscores, upper for lower case, I for 1, O (oh) for 0 (zero), etc.—and punctuation—correct use of delimiters, colons for semicolons, semicolons for commas. When the code is correct typographically, look for logic errors, starting with common mistakes. For instance, is the control index in a DO loop wrong so that the number of calculations was "off by one"? Are storage references off by one? Was a bit address off by one when flags in a mask were checked? Is the output wrong because the correct results were overlaid with other data? Were the variables initialized to fit the test data? Were the effects of binary to decimal conversion taken into account when integer values were computed? Did truth values (bit flags) get used as integers in arithmetic? Every programmer

---

1. The use of terminals as program development tools is discussed in Chapter 7.

knows better than to make these mistakes, but they occur anyway, just as grammatical lapses occur in conversation.

All these errors are obvious. They should be corrected during desk-checking, although it may take a couple of machine runs to detect them all. More serious bugs, as outlined by Schwartz [2], include deadlocks between subunits, timing idiosyncracies, and pointer errors, all of which occur at later stages of debugging and are particularly hard to detect. Finally, there are problem logic errors. These include incorrect procedures for processing the input, as well as correct procedures for doing the wrong job.

6.1.2 Locating Bugs

Two assumptions about computer programs help to guide debugging.

1. Program execution is logical and therefore traceable.
2. Abnormal termination occurs reasonably soon after the causative error.

Because the program is logical, it is possible to recreate each step that led to the final environment state. Because the bug is likely to be closer to the terminal state than to the initial state, a backtracking search should be faster than a forward trace. By examining the output, the programmer can use inductive reasoning to explain why the achieved result is different from the expected result. A logical explanation leads directly to the source of the error. Yet backtracking does not always work where the bug causes infinite looping or where, say, a pointer error leads the program off on a tangent. In those cases, the symptoms found when the program halts are meaningless. Such situations call for reconstructing the test and executing it step by step to determine exactly where control was lost. Looking at it another way, if the program, P, is supposed to transform A to A', then

P is correct if, for all A, the output is A';
P has bugs if, for any A, the output is not A'.

If examination of the output shows that it could be the result of procedure, P', acting on A, then backtracking should show where P turned into P'.

If the output shows no reasonable relation to A, then program, P, probably got detoured into an unrelated and possibly meaningless sequence of instructions. Forward tracing will be required to debug P.

Forward tracing on early computers was often done by "single stepping" through the program. The programmer sat at the console and controlled the execution of the program, one instruction at a time, examining the status of the machine registers after each execution to see if they contained the expected values. Today programs are so big and machines are so fast that single stepping is almost universally prohibited. Instead, the programmer must devise tests to bracket each error, finding the smallest block of code enclosing the error, and then scan the offending block off-line. Well-structured code is easier to debug this way because it has a clean block structure. Experienced structured programmers debug their source language directly, often relying on their associates to read the code, checking for logic errors, before requesting machine runs. They succeed in doing so, with few machine traces and dumps, because the structured code supports logical analysis. Unstructured code lacks the clues available in easy-to-read structured code, where all logic transfers are related to meaningful functions.

6.1.3   Debugging Aids

When necessary, programmers use debugging aids to trace the program and dump the machine state to reduce the detective work. Traces can report the problem status (a) whenever a transfer is made (to isolate information in a single, physical string of code) or (b) whenever a subroutine is completed (to isolate a logical block of the program). The latter choice is preferred because it provides more meaningful data. Selective dumps can be requested at similar points or on termination to show all or part of the problem data, including the program itself. The dump will show the changes made to the data during the run and will also reveal unexpected changes made to the program. Frequently the programmer must supplement the vendor-supplied or library debugging aids by writing drivers, generators, and program stubs.

Drivers and generators are external aids which support a debugging run. External aids do not affect the internal structure or performance of the programs they support. Rather, they provide the external stimuli and data sets on which the program operates. Stubs, like trace and dump commands, are aids inserted in the program being debugged. Internal aids are potential sources of difficulty. They must be designed so as to be *transparent* to the program; that is, the behavior of the program should be the same when the aids are present as when they are absent. The aids must be easy to identify so that they can be removed after they have served their purpose. (In some systems, debugging aids are intentionally left in the code. The cost of the additional, inactive code is justified on the basis of savings projected when the system is modified.) Particular care must be taken with internal aids which produce messages or otherwise manipulate data. There must be no confusion between the data belonging to the program and the data or data space reserved for the aid.

A *driver* is a program (or, in some systems, a hardware device) which produces the inputs and responses normally obtained by a program from its environment. The driver is designed to provide inputs in the form, quantity, and time-dependent spacing appropriate to the problem. It may generate the inputs or, more likely, obtain them from a prepared file. When the program being debugged has to refer to status indicators, timers, or other service functions, the driver supplies all the responses. Depending on the need for realism, the driver can vary from a simple, completely deterministic program to a complex super–operating system capable of representing an entire hardware-software environment, such as a distributed information network with simulated terminals and network controllers. In the context of debugging, a driver is usually small and simple; yet there are occasions when a programmer working in a large system will be using a complex driver. This is particularly likely to occur when the system program is intended for a yet-to-be-built machine.

A *test case generator* is a program (or manual procedure) for preparing a set of test cases that meets the criteria established by the programmer. As noted in the next section, the generator must be able to produce various numbers of test cases for each type of test to be run. That requires simple statistics to handle frequency distributions and random number generation to create arbitrarily different data items. It also requires the ability to recognize range limits, data types, and errors of various kinds in order to be able to generate test data that includes appropriate errors. In addition to generating test data, the same program may generate data files of various sizes, up to and including full-scale copies of actual data files to support debugging of references to bulk storage or timing of I/O operations.

The normal function of a *program stub* is to take the place of a missing block of code so that the whole program can be executed at an early stage. In a top-down implementation, for example, the program may have been developed to the depth of three levels, and although all the fourth-level routines have been named, only one fourth-level routine exists. A debug run at this stage should be able to demonstrate that all fourth-level blocks can be reached from the third level and that the existing fourth-level block works correctly. Therefore, dummy routines are prepared for each incomplete fourth-level block. The dummy routines are attached to the higher-level structure as stubs which can be invoked by higher-level programs and which can pass data and control back up the line. The simplest stub is a nonfunctional dummy which produces a message when it is invoked. The message might be: "Routine C44 was executed and returned control to C20." Such a message shows that the program flow reached the C44 stub and continued to the next block in line—in this case, C20. More complicated functional stubs can supplement the acknowledgment message with other data needed in the debugging run. If the stub represents a program that returns values for subsequent use, a set of canned values can be passed on. Variable action can be simulated by having the stub pass the values only when triggered by a counter or a random number generator in the stub. In fact, the stub can be a skeleton of the routine it represents and actually perform some of the routine's functions (as long as there is no risk that the incomplete routine can interfere with the rest of the program). Eventually the stub will be replaced by the actual routine.

When the planned debugging process results in a mass of output data, it may be necessary to write a *data reduction program* to analyze the outcome of each run. Data reduction can often be avoided, however, by planning tests which produce only a small amount of carefully selected, informative output.

In large organizations, it often pays to develop standard debugging aids and procedures. Each programmer can then plan debugging runs with emphasis on diagnosis rather than on tools [3]. The cost of a uniform approach is reduced when the necessary aids are available on the open market in a form that meets the minimum requirements of the organization [4]. Some managers maintain that drivers and test case generators should always be developed by individuals other than the programmer of the model being debugged. This procedure ensures objectivity. Although such a rule is not always followed for debugging, it is an excellent guideline during testing.

6.1.4   Planning a Debugging Run

The debugging stage of program development focuses on quality. The purpose of debugging is to demonstrate that the program is correct and ready for delivery. The demonstration, however, should be cost-effective. Debugging runs should be planned so as to find and fix all bugs with a minimum expenditure of programmer and machine time. Desk-checking is part of a cost-effective plan. Several other techniques are covered in the following paragraphs.

6.1.4.1   Test case data

Quality depends on running appropriate tests in a controlled environment. Since a program may be sensitive to certain data values as well as data ranges, test cases should be set up for a variety of values. As shown in Fig. 6.2, the input test cases should be representative of the expected problem data. Valid input values should span the domain of the program. The distribution of test values should be the same as the expected distribution of actual values. If the problem data has a lot of values beginning with an A, the test data should have a similar preponderance of A-values. This criterion checks editing routines and unusual biases in the program being debugged. At the same time, there should be a random sample of other values to see that the program responds correctly. After covering the domain

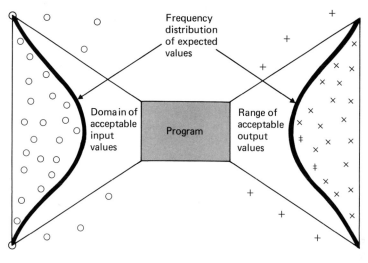

KEY

   ○   Value in test case

   ×   Output of successful test

   +   Output of failed test

   ⧺   Output of failed test determined from analysis of results

Fig. 6.2 Selecting test case data.

of allowable inputs, construct additional tests using input values at and beyond the domain boundary. The boundary values show that the program behaves properly at extreme points. Values outside the domain are generated to test the error detection capability of the program.

The test data generated for data files need not be so carefully varied as the input data. Data files that are merely referenced or moved, without having their contents processed, can contain arbitrary data as long as the record and field lengths are correct. If the data is edited by the program under test, the file must have appropriate data in the fields examined by the edit routine, but the data can be arbitrary everywhere else. Only if the data in the file is processed in detail does it need to be generated the way inputs are. Even then the tests can be rigged so that only a few predesignated records in the file can be called for processing. An alternative approach uses a data file with arbitrary contents, but whenever the program calls for a record to process, a debugging driver pulls a suitable item from a test case input file and substitutes it for the record obtained from the data file. By separating the access process from the data generation process the alternative simplifies data generation but may interfere with debugging of time-dependent functions.

None of the generation techniques listed uses an arbitrary sample of actual data. Any sample of actual data will contain some useful test data, but it will omit a lot. Errors may be common in the actual environment, but it would be purely accidental for a random sample of actual inputs to contain all possible errors. Therefore test case data must be created, not borrowed from the machine room. That is not to say that a scenario based on actual data cannot be a useful supplement to a thorough test plan. Such a scenario is recommended because it tends to uncover problem areas due to interactions among data items or due to operator actions. The scenario test should follow normal debugging. In fact, the user will normally run a scenario test as part of the acceptance and field installation procedures. Troubles found in the scenario test are generally so situation-dependent that they are not anticipated in the spec. Normal debugging gets the program up to spec. The scenario test detects plausible situations outside the scope of design of the program. Since the program meets spec at this point, the corrective action can take three forms.

1. Ignore the problem on the assumption that, if it occurs, it can be handled manually.
2. Change the spec to accommodate the newly discovered situation and revise the program accordingly.
3. Devise controls or editing procedures to prevent the newly discovered situation from occurring.

The last approach leaves the debugged program intact but may require a new program to sort or separate the inputs so that they cannot interact to cause a problem.

A scenario test used in a particular payroll program illustrates the pitfalls and planning required for effective debugging. The payroll in question was for salaried employees. (The author was responsible for information systems and the computer center at the time.) Each employee was paid a base salary plus overtime and shift premiums, less taxes, deductions, contributions, and certain authorized charges for company services. The payroll program consisted of a series of simple tests to see which additions or deductions applied to each employee. The input was the employee's time card. The output was a paycheck plus a payroll voucher explaining it. Other outputs kept accounting records and an updated master pay file. Each separate routine was tested with a small sample of typical data generated by the programmer. Then the routines were assembled into a payroll program and tested by feeding the program a handful of actual pay cards for the previous week. This test was successful, but unfortunately, the sample input contained no overtime or unusual deductions. Only the main pay calculation and the tax computations were exercised. The inadequacy of the scenario test became obvious when the current week's payroll was run in parallel, using both the existing program and the new program. The current week contained a holiday, and since it was the end of an accounting month, it involved a number of monthly deductions. The new program failed on this run. The holiday routine was incorrectly coded, giving the employees who worked that day regular pay instead of double-time pay. Several employees with many deductions ended up with less than the minimum allowable pay. The run also disclosed a deduction for sports equipment that was allowed at one location but was never mentioned in the statement of requirements. The first two bugs should have been detected by planned tests prior to the parallel run. Each was a specified function for which explicit tests were feasible. The last bug could be detected only in the scenario presented by the parallel run.

The relative amount of work involved in debugging is quite a bit less for top-down programming than for bottom-up programming. In top-down implementations, each level of the design is debugged as it is built. The highest level of the design interfaces with the external problem environment. The test data at that level is the set of inputs described in the requirements document. As lower levels are built, all the existing test cases can be reused. The only new ones needed are those that test functions introduced at the lower level. In this way, the library of test cases grows with the system, and a high degree of consistency can be expected in the test results. By contrast, bottom-up programming requires unique drivers and test data for each separate block of code. Many redundant test cases have to be written, differing in small ways to fit the requirements of the block of code they serve. Then, after the blocks are debugged, they are integrated into a program unit, and additional test cases must be written to test their behavior in the aggregate.

6.1.4.2 Controlled debugging

Now that a set of test data exists, it can be run against the program to see which inputs produce outputs within the range of the program. But indiscriminate use of the test cases will not explain why some of the outputs fall outside the range. Control must be exercised so that each test attempted provides an unambiguous cause-effect relationship. In addition, the tests should be arranged so as to provide new information with each subsequent test.

A procedure for controlled debugging might follow this sequence.

1. Test each program function separately for all applicable single values.
2. Test each program function separately for several different sequences of the applicable data values.
3. Test all functions at once with all applicable single data values.
4. Test all functions at once with several different sequences of the applicable data values.
5. Test all functions at once with an actual sample of data (scenario test).

Step 3 can be approached one function at a time from step 2 although it should not be necessary in a program unit. Such integration procedures are more applicable to larger systems, where the interfaces among units may be poorly defined.

Part of a controlled debugging process involves getting as much out of each run as possible. Thus execution time should be measured since it will be useful later. Eventually it is necessary to estimate the average kernel execution time, the time to process one input transaction, the number of instructions executed (and maybe the instruction mix) per transaction, the number of file accesses per transaction, the time spent waiting for I/O or CPU, and many other performance characteristics of the program. Much of this data should be a by-product of debugging. Similarly, a map of instructions executed by the totality of test cases is useful. It provides clues as to where the kernel path lies and where dead code remains. It also gives a check on the adequacy of the debugging plan. Output lists should be obtained showing what files and programs were referenced by the program in test, where key variables were stored, how memory was allocated, what resources were used. Finally, a count of the number of runs required to debug a given module should be kept. All this data has value either as an aid in debugging or as an aid in evaluating and controlling the finished product. Obtaining the data, however, may be costly. Some of the data is automatically provided by assemblers, compilers, and operating system services—at least for many large commercial machines. The rest requires special support programs. The cost of test recording and analysis programs is usually too high to be absorbed by a single program unit but not too high to be justified by an organization with many programmers.

Since few installations guarantee a dedicated machine during debugging runs, tests must be planned so that they do not interfere with other users. When the program unit is meant to run as a problem program under the control of an existing operating system, overall system protection can be provided by the operating system. However, when the unit being debugged is an element of the operating system, the normal protection features may not be available. For instance, on machines with interrupts, problem programs normally run with all interrupt mechanisms enabled. Any unusual event gives control to the operating system, which may disable the interrupts temporarily while it takes care of the event. When a new unit of the operating system is being debugged and it has to operate in the disabled mode, the errors it makes may be left in place to impact other programs. There are three typical solutions to this problem.

1. Embed the program in a protected problem program which simulates the interrupt-handling behavior of the host computer; i.e., build a complex driver.
2. Debug the program only when the entire machine can be dedicated to the one job.
3. Debug the program on a virtual machine which is isolated from other active virtual machines by a virtual machine operating system.

The first of these solutions is attractive because it also addresses another problem of particular importance in real-time systems, namely, being able to reproduce a test. When a bug causes a normal batch program to blow up, the test can be repeated identically, using the same setup and input data. This is not possible in a real-time system when the bug was due to the occurrence of particular data values at a particular time. Usually the only way to reproduce an identical set of conditions is to build a driver which simulates the entire environment, including clock time. In normal practice, this problem is minimized in the design requirements by specifying only elapsed time limits on program unit execution. Individual units can then be debugged as ordinary problem programs in a batch system. Only the integrated real-time system need be exercised by the simulated environment driver.

The second solution is preferred by programmers because it minimizes the interactive effects of multiprogramming. However, the computer manager tries to avoid dedicated service because it is so hard to schedule, and even if the user is willing to pay a special rate for the service, it is an inefficient use of computing resources. The third solution is an acceptable compromise. It permits multiprogramming at the same time that it provides an isolated virtual machine for the private use of the debugger.

6.1.4.3 Evaluating the results of a run

The first place to look for potential problems is the error listing provided by the system programs used in compiling or operating the job. Many systems programs give a wealth of information about a run. Sometimes it is hard to interpret, yet often it points to important mistakes that were overlooked but can be easily corrected.

Test case inputs, whenever feasible, should produce values that can be hand-calculated. Simple integers often can be traced through the program with pencil and paper. Consequently, some integer values should be among the test cases. Correct results for these cases will be readily recognized in the output. This is true even when the program is too intricate for easy manual calculation. The programmer can still trace the process, making approximations along the way. The result will be a ballpark result that, in most cases, will be in the range of the process.

A result in the range of acceptable answers is not necessarily correct. Only when the result agrees with a hand-calculated value can it be assumed correct. In other cases, there is the possibility, as indicated in Fig. 6.2, that the program malfunctioned but still ran to conclusion and yielded a result in the range of the process. Therefore, additional criteria are needed to verify the results. These criteria are *reasonableness tests*. In establishing the accepted range of results, the programmer has laid down the first criterion, namely, that a result must be within the range. The second criterion also exists in a sense; i.e., if the result is in range but the input that produced it was not in the program domain, the answer is not reasonable. Beyond these obvious rules are criteria based on subdivisions of the domain and range and relationships which connect the subdivisions. This leads to conditions such as the following.

- All outputs in field A should be different from the inputs in field A.
- All inputs of the form 1XXX use file LIBA and should produce at least one output message containing the input value and a value from LIBA.
- All inputs less than 999.99 should produce outputs between 100.00 and 999.99.
- Query inputs are not allowed to change any files.

Some of the relationships produce clearly recognizable outputs. Others require some manual cross-referencing to indexes or file listings. The last example requires a support program that keeps track of WRITE requests to the system files in order for the indicated condition to be detected.

Note that these examples are stated in terms of inputs and outputs rather than of detailed internal logic. The use of externalized test cases makes it easier to relate errors to source statements. This is desirable because source program debugging is relatively more efficient than object code debugging. The higher-level source statements make more sense to the programmer. As a result, source debugging tends to be both faster and more accurate. Consequently, many compilers include the ability to relate object code to source code. The cross-reference allows the programmer to use an object code error indication as the pointer to a suspect block of source code [5].

The debugging cycle should terminate after a fairly short time. If it drags on because one or more tests continually fail even after fixes have been made, something is seriously wrong. This is the time to ask for help. Ask an associate to study the source program to try to detect errors for which you may have a blind spot. If this doesn't work, consider throwing the source code away and starting the program all over again. The rationale for the latter step is that the problem indicates a flaw in design that continued debugging runs will not correct.

Programmers who plan their debugging runs carefully should expect to reach a point where all the planned compilations and tests have been executed correctly. If their plans are reasonable, then

1. all specified functions are tested;
2. a sample of exceptional cases is tested;
3. all or most of the code is executed;

even though no attempt has been made to exhaustively test all possible program paths.

Sometimes they never get there. When should they give up? The number of debugging runs for a typical program subunit depends so much on the situation that it is dangerous to set a rigid guideline for abandoning a troublesome job. Some experienced structured programmers who believe in the value of desk-checking find that they need one or two runs to detect "stupid" errors in their syntax, keypunched source code, and logic. When these are fixed, they expect the program to run to completion correctly the first time they try it. By preparing their test cases in a batched sequence, they can execute all the tests in one run and be finished. Only a few people are consistently as good as that; however, several managers of large systems programming shops find that three to four runs after cleaning up syntax and obvious logic errors represent a reasonable average for planning purposes.

6.1.5 Conducting a Debugging Run

In the planning of the debugging phase, both quality and cost are important. To keep the cost low, the programmers must learn how to work with the computing facility and how to schedule activities so that they are productive while waiting for computer output. Most computer rooms have preplanned work loads. Many organizations support business information systems on the same machine used for debugging systems programs. The business applications have interrelated deadlines planned weeks and months ahead. It is so difficult to adjust the schedules for that work that debugging is given a low priority and turnaround suffers. Even in machine rooms solely dedicated to the support of systems programmers, turnaround can be poor. Here the work load that justifies a dedicated machine includes the integration and test runs needed by large systems. This eats up so much time, as indicated in Volume 2, that little remains for short jobs. Turnaround can be improved somewhat by using terminals for remote job entry (see Chapter 7), but RJE affects only access to the computer; it does not change the work load.

The consequence of heavy work load is that the operations manager has to increase work flow by multiprogramming, batching inputs, setting priorities according to job length, etc. Once the methods are working smoothly, they cannot be disrupted; i.e., the manager cannot afford to give a programmer hands-on access to the machine—only the trained operators can keep the work flowing. The impact on the programmer is not serious. Hands-on debugging does not normally give the most for the money. The console debugger spends most of the time thinking. Meanwhile, the whole computer is tied up. There are only two conditions under which this approach should be allowed.

1. The whole facility is required to debug the program (certain real-time runs, runs requiring unique hardware configurations).
2. The amount of progress in each debugging run justifies the loss of normal throughput (a situation which is credible only for expert programmers).

Few individual programmers are assigned units of work that qualify for hands-on time. On the other hand, many programmers can justify interactive debugging from a terminal. This mode of operation allows many users to share the facility, so throughput can be maintained. Interactive debugging speeds up progress because it both eliminates turnaround delays and facilitates tracing, as discussed in Chapter 7.

An effective working relationship between programmers and the computing facility involves the following.

- Observing the facility rules.

  Submitting machine time requirements early so that they can be considered by the operations scheduler, who usually allocates time weekly, attempting to retain the flexibility to handle emergencies as they arise.

  Estimating the running time of the program so that the operators can put each job request in the appropriate queue and so that they can recognize when the program is stuck in an infinite loop.

  Requesting enough time to avoid termination due to a timeout.

  Filling out the facility forms correctly (for billing, for file security, for addressing the output, etc.).

- Submitting complete and unambiguous run packages.

  Writing out all instructions for the keypunchers and computer operators. Their efficiency depends on their ability to execute their instructions without having to guess what is wanted.

  Writing or printing legibly.

  Requesting listings of the input deck to be checked for accuracy against source material.

  Seeing that all pages, cards, tapes, disks are numbered or labeled so that there is a check on job completeness, sequence, currency.

  Designing the run so that it records its status and runs to completion, bypassing errors as necessary, if at all possible. This returns the most information and reduces the number of reruns.

- Cooperating with the operators.

  Staying out of the machine room.

  Assuming that failed runs are the programmer's fault, not the operators' fault; yet, if investigation shows an operator error, discussing it with the operators so that they can avoid repeating it.

  Not asking operators to fix a run when it terminates abnormally; at most, providing clear, simple instructions to tell the operator how to clean up the run and produce status reports.

  Being friendly. The operators are often the key to success when extra time or special support is needed.

Once the mutual working relationships between programmers and the computer facility are healthy, programmers will have a good feel for the type of service to expect. It is then possible to adapt to the facility turnaround cycle. Suppose that the facility normally delivers one run a day; i.e., a job submitted on Monday will be in the computer output basket at 8 a.m. Tuesday and will be delivered by the mail room by noon. Programmers might adapt to that schedule by going to the machine room at 8 a.m. to pick up yesterday's job, work on the output all day, and deliver another run on the way home. They might break an assigned program unit into subunits and lay out a work plan that keeps two subunits active. Using the mail service, they would submit subunit 1 and start work on subunit 2. By balancing the work load, programmers are always busy although switching from one subunit to another may be confusing at times. At least one and, preferably, four or more hours should be devoted to a subunit before switching to another to be able to concentrate effectively. Another way to use the time until a run is available is to plan additional tests and to decide how to evaluate the output of the run in progress. This is less desirable than the overnight or balanced schedules because it allows programmers to start debugging before thinking through a comprehensive test plan. A fairly long fixed time should be allowed for desk-checking before resubmitting a subunit; in fact, some managers advocate a computer service policy based on completing each computer run as fast as possible, then not accepting a second run of the same job for a fixed period. As indicated, the recommended work period is at least an hour, preferably much more. What does this mean in an installation where batch processing is done with less than a one-hour turnaround? In effect, programmers could get eight or more runs a day. Should they attempt to work on another subunit between runs? No. The risk of error is too great. In such a situation, programmers are better off doing nothing. Of course, there is often productive work to be done on the subunit in test—documentation, optimization, etc. And there is the opportunity for self-improvement—studying relevant manuals or texts, analyzing problems in the subject area. In the long run, it is more productive to utilize short intervals in these ways than to try to cleanse the mind of subunit 1 and refresh it with everything pertinent to subunit 2, only to reverse the cycle in an hour.

It may now be evident that debugging is not simply a process of correcting source code. The process involves a system of several elements: the programmer, the program, the keypunchers, the operators, the mail service, the machine, the other programs on the machine. Programmers are responsible for delivering a correct program unit; therefore they have to correct all errors, regardless of where they come from. Programmers are as responsible for detecting keypunch and operator errors as for catching their own mistakes. If a card deck is dropped and picked up out of sequence by the mail clerk or the operations control clerks, it is the programmer's job to recognize the problem and fix the program. If the problem is recurrent, the programmer should work with the manager of the computing facility to improve the service. In the meantime, the programmer must work around the problem to produce a correct program.

6.2 DOCUMENTATION

As suggested in Chapter 2, it is important to remember that a program exists only in its documentation. It is this concept that leads experienced professional programmers to say that the only valid documentation of a program is the actual code listing. Since that is unreadable for anyone but an expert, the professionals are willing to back off and accept the source code listing in addition to the object code listing as long as they are sure that adequate procedures exist to guarantee that the two listings are compatible. That means that no changes can be made in the object code. Any changes in the program must be made in the source statements, which, when retranslated, produce a new object listing, making the previous version obsolete.

Still, this is a very rigorous definition, one that may not be practicable. At the least, interim patches are allowed until recompilation is feasible—anywhere from daily (where computer time and dissemination procedures allow it) to monthly or less often to correspond to new releases of a parent system.

There are two common obstacles to successful use of source program listings as primary documents.

1. The people who must be able to read the documentation are not always able to read source or object code.

2. The procedures necessary to ensure compatible documentation are not foolproof.

The first obstacle can be overcome either by training the user to read source language or by expanding the program documentation to include narrative, tables, flowcharts, more or less like the design specification document. User training is never more than partly successful. It takes time and money to do it right, and even then the training may not overcome the user's natural distaste for reading precise listings. People who are interested in programming can read listings the way they read books. But people whose association with programs is peripheral to their main interest—such people as computer users, hardware designers, operators, system engineers—find programs about as interesting as telephone books. Their minds go blank when they see the listing. In much the same way, people with limited background in mathematics skip the equations that appear in technical books, whereas mathematically sophisticated readers find the equations more informative than the text. Since the objective of the program is to serve the user, program documentation should cater to the user's needs. It should be easy for the user to read according to his criteria, not according to the programmer's criteria.

6.2.1 Basic Program Documents

A straightforward way to generate a program document that will satisfy the user is to expand the design specification to include program detail. The resulting program documentation can be reorganized into three separate documents: user's guide, operator's guide, and logic manual. Especially complicated programs may also require a general information manual, but it is usually possible to put an adequate summary of a program unit in the three basic documents. Each of the three documents is expressed in the style and language most suited to the audience. Users get more about objectives and program function. Operators get more about environment, setup, and the dynamics of running a job. Systems and maintenance programmers get the program listings. In this way, each document is tailored to fit the reader. Each is smaller and more manageable than the sum of the parts and can

Document Contents	Design Specification	User's Guide	Operator's Guide	Internal Logic
Title and identification	x	x	x	x
Preface—how to use the document	x	x	x	x
Table of contents	x	x	x	x
Description of program				
Function	x	x	x	x
Performance	x	x	x	x
Background information	x	x		x
Inputs				
Description of each input type	x	x	x	x
Organization of input stream			x	x
Volume of transactions	x	x		
Files				
Description of each file	x	x	x	x
List of logical file relationships	x	x	x	x
File size	x	x	x	x
Physical organization of files	x	x	x	x
File protection requirements	x	x	x	x
Purge instructions	x	x	x	x
Vital records procedure	x	x	x	x
Outputs				
Description of each output type	x	x	x	x
Retention and disposition		x	x	x
Storage medium	x		x	x
Error correction		x		
Installation statistics			x	
Program statistics	x			x
Interfaces				
Entry and exit points, linkages	x	x	x	x
Tables used or set	x		x	x
Data used or set	x	x	x	x
Macros and programs referred to	x		x	x
Method				
Overview	x	x	x	x
Algorithms	x	x		x
Accuracy	x	x		x
Restrictions	x	x		x
Error handling			x	x
Time dependencies	x			x

Fig. 6.3 Program documentation.

Document Contents	Design Specification	User's Guide	Operator's Guide	Internal Logic
Usage				
Submitting a job		X		X
Specifying processor options		X	X	X
Preparing input data		X		
Interpretation of output data		X		
Job setup			X	
Initiation, termination, recovery			X	X
Operator messages			X	X
Run time estimate		X	X	X
Operating schedule	X		X	
Distribution of output data			X	
Maintenance				X
Programming language	X			X
Development hardware/software	X			
Operational hardware/software	X	X	X	X
Test specification	X			X
Sample program				X
Self-initiating loader				X
Documentation specification	X			
Standards, conventions	X			X
References	X	X	X	X
Responsible individuals	X	X	X	X
Management and control data				
Reports	X			
Development schedules and estimates	X			
Justification and evaluation criteria	X			
Source listing—current version				X
Object listing—current version				X
Flowchart—method	X	X		
Flowchart—operations			X	
Flowchart—program	X			X
Tables	X			X
Record layout	X			X
Storage map				X
Machine-readable code (cards, tape, disk)				X

Fig. 6.3 (continued).

be used for quick reference without searching through a mass of unrelated data. Figure 6.3 is a checklist of topics showing which items belong in each separate document.

Although no one document format is necessarily better than all others, it is good practice to standardize on one format throughout an organization or a large project. People can get used to the standard format. They will use the documents more effectively as they learn where to look for the answers to each type of question that may arise. The programmers, too, will benefit, since the standard form will become a checklist which protects them against omitting important data. In effect, Fig. 6.3 is an outline for program unit documentation. It is a subset of the data to be found in program system documents. Walsh [6] provides a complete set of documentation "models" for software from the subprogram to the program system. Local standards based on her models would be effective for most organizations.

Final program documentation differs from the design specification. Obviously, the final documents will be able to record data that was unavailable at the time the specification was written. Similarly, the final documents can omit data that was used to guide development but is no longer applicable. The detail in the final documents is more thorough as a consequence of the work done during development. In fact, every manifestation of the entire program, including the machine-readable code, must be recorded in one or more of the documents or it does not exist. Comparing the final program with the early specification, then, is comparing what exists to what was intended.

Some of the topics documented help to explain the program; others help to demonstrate that it meets the intent of the spec. In the first category are the code listings and the "as built" versions of the method, usage, graphics, etc. In the second category are the test specification as implemented, the sample program, the standards employed, etc. (The sample program really serves three functions: it demonstrates that the program meets spec, teaches the user and operator how to work with the program, and verifies that the program has been delivered intact and in the correct sequence.) Continuing verification that the program satisfies the spec can be obtained by gathering statistics on program performance, cost of operation, and maintenance requirements. Analysis of factors such as these will show whether the objectives set in the original justification for the program have been achieved.

6.2.2   Document Quality Control

All the criteria for readability and ease of use that apply to writing design specifications apply to final program documents. The fact that some hard-to-use items *must* be present, such as the code listings, simply means that supporting and explanatory material is needed to supplement the essential data. There is no need to go overboard. The proper amount of program documentation is the *minimum amount* that embodies the program and explains it adequately to the intended set of users. Within that guideline, it is possible to convey both facts about the program and reasons for its being built in a particular way. Whenever the program as built varies from the letter of the spec or exhibits unorthodox features, a brief explanation should be given. The reasons are most often explained by showing the assumptions, constraints, safety factors, and tradeoff analyses that influenced the development process. Given this information, the user is able to evaluate the program and determine whether it is acceptable under the conditions that apply in the operational environment. Of course, if the job has been done properly, the assumptions, etc., will realistically reflect the operational conditions.

Experience is the best guide to the documentation appropriate to each situation. While acquiring experience, a designer/programmer has an effective means of evaluating the documentation needs of a particular user: ask the user what he wants. Close cooperation with the user will show what style and format are most acceptable to him.

In both Fig. 6.3 and the Subtask Detach Processor design specification (Chapter 4), there are references to maintenance and change activity. Rarely does a programmer supply guidance in these areas without being reminded by a checklist to do so. The reason is simple: programmers do not usually have to maintain their programs, but if they do, they need no guidance since they can remember enough about the program structure to modify it. It is some other programmer, charged with maintaining the program, who is penalized if such guidance is omitted. Nevertheless, it is the original programmer's responsibility to write a maintainable program that will do its job over a reasonable lifetime, not just during the acceptance test. A maintainable (and modifiable) program has a structured modular design, which is described in the program documentation. Without the description, the advantage of the modular design may be invisible to maintenance programmers.

Maintainability features are described rather simply by the following means.

1. Thoroughly commenting source listings.
2. Carefully cross-referencing narrative to graphics and listings.
3. Naming modules and displaying them clearly (as in the one-subunit-per-page format of structured programs).
4. Describing how to make changes, where hooks are located, what linkages are permitted, and what type of change requires recompilation of the entire program unit.

All the pertinent data should be arranged in an easily referenced format. In addition to the table of contents, there should be descriptive page headings, paragraph titles, and figure legends. Picture an operator, John Jones, with a backlog of jobs to run and an abnormal termination on one of the active programs. He has only one opportunity to restart the failed program, and then he must throw it off the machine in order to keep the job stream flowing. If he cannot find the meaning of the ABEND operator message, he will stop searching. To support Jones and to increase the chances that the program will run to completion, the programmer should provide an operator's guide which has message identifiers in bold type pointing to recovery actions in 1-2-3 order. No space should be wasted on "ifs," "ands," or "buts." State only one recovery sequence per case in a way that cannot be misinterpreted.

Since the program documents are the whole outcome of a programming task, they should be carefully protected. All work in process should be locked up in a safe place each night; otherwise it may be swept up with the trash. Work in process should never be just a collection of loose paper. It should always be a collection of named, dated, related subunits of source code. The best way to keep track of it is to put it in a loose-leaf binder with a current table of contents showing not only the names of the entries but also their hierarchical relationships.

As soon as a subunit is finished, a copy should be made. The copy should be kept separate from the original in a vital records file, the purpose of which is to permit recovery from a catastrophe. This procedure is exactly like the checkpoint procedure placed in a program although the vital records are handled manually. One hopes that the vital records file will never be needed, but in case of fire or theft, it is available to replace the lost originals. Obviously, the vital records should be physically separate from the originals. For small programs of no great complexity, the copy may be in a file cabinet in the same room as the original. Complex programs of high urgency warrant more protection. Copies of the debugged portions should be stored in fireproof units in another room or another building.

Backup copies of the finished program, after delivery to the user, should also be placed in vital records storage. A general rule for key programs with a long life is to have one copy in the computer room, a second nearby in a fireproof vault, and a third at a distant location. The importance of computer programs (and other permanent records) has led to the offering of vault space for a fee by a number of commercial security firms. Such firms can usually deliver the vital records within a day of a request.

Some programmers are able to store their work in computer files using a development support system. The on-line library is a big help in maintaining control of the developing program, but it is not a substitute for a hard-copy vital record. Entire projects can be wiped out by disk failures, or they can be delayed by major computer outages. To protect against such disasters, the same vital records program that applies to an off-line project should be followed when using an on-line library. One shortcut is feasible. As long as the programmer has a working hard copy, the vital records can be stored in machine-readable form; i.e., a tape or disk copy of the library can be stored. Rising costs of paper make high-density magnetic media more attractive each year.

Given a sound vital records procedure, some programmers find it helpful to retain all historical copies of their work. There are two advantages to this approach. It permits falling back to an earlier set of specifications when a proposed change is canceled, and it provides the manager with a basis for analyzing how the programmer works.

6.2.3   Documentation Aids

The development and production of program documentation can often be simplified by the use of computer-aided text processing. As is true with any computer-based support system, text processing can be justified when the number of users makes the cost per user reasonable. Therefore these aids are normally found in large organizations that have their own computers. Text processing should also be used by any organization that has a large enough work load to justify a contract with a computer service firm. Where they are available, documentation aids offer several benefits.

- Consistent, legible output
- Simple procedures for correcting errors
- Simple procedures for modifying documents
- On-line storage of documentation
- Fast output of updated documents

The greatest value from on-line documentation aids is obtained when a document is subject to frequent and extensive changes over a long period of time. Because the document is stored in the machine, it can be treated like a data file. The file, consisting of paragraphs, sentences, words, characters, can be updated by adding, deleting, or changing any element of the record structure. Only the modified portion of the text is affected. A programmer can rearrange paragraphs, correct spelling, substitute a new name for every occurrence of an old name, reword instructions to the operator, etc. All such changes are made without retyping the manuscript. For protection, the old text is kept until the new text has been completely edited and released by the programmer. Finally, when the time comes to print the updated document, it is done at computer output speed. In some systems, the output looks like ordinary line printer output. Others produce output in upper and lower case. The most sophisticated systems pass an output tape to a photocomposer, which produces printed output in multiple fonts with the quality of a good book [7].

Text processing systems are capable of handling source code, tables, narrative—anything that can be entered one line at a time. They are not generally designed to handle two-dimensional data effectively. Therefore special programs are used for flowcharting or other graphics [8,9]. The input to these programs is often prepared as a set of descriptive statements giving the location, symbol type, and wording for each block in the chart. The statements can be keypunched and submitted to a batch processing program, which produces the flowchart on a line printer. Subsequent editing can be done statement by statement. Also available are interactive flow-charting programs which use a graphic display. The programmer can enter the descriptive statements via a keyboard and then move the blocks around or modify them by pointing at the affected block with a light pen. Again, the significant value of either type of system lies in its facility for updating an existing chart. Small programs may not need such an aid if the original flowchart is simple. The sheet affected by a change can be redrawn by hand as fast as the flowcharting program can do it (considering turnaround time). Large programs make better use of such an aid since the computer is able to correct all cross-references throughout the flowchart as fast as the programmer can update a single sheet.

Note that the process just described draws the flowchart as directed by the programmer. Since it includes only the logical features the programmer wants to record, it can be as easy to read as the programmer makes it. Two other flowcharting schemes are less likely to produce useful output. One of them simply creates a block in the flowchart for every statement in the source code. The other "decompiles" an object program into what, one hopes, is a representation of the program logic. Both tend to cloud the program logic with excessive detail. The statement-by-statement approach is generally recommended only when a flowchart at that level of detail is required by contract. The decompiler may be useful to analysts interested in the structure of undocumented object code, but there is no justification for using it as a principal documentation aid in development projects.

An important documentation aid that should not be overlooked is not an automated process. It is simply the advice and assistance of competent people. Those programmers who do not write well or who are not careful about details can still prepare good program documents. All they need do is ask someone to read the draft document and critique it for clarity and completeness. The readers should represent the audience of the documents so that they can criticize vocabulary and organization from the standpoint of an actual user. Technical editors (and many experienced secretaries) are able to help also because if the language is confusing to them, it will be confusing to others, regardless of the accuracy of the content. The final document should always pass the test of effectiveness in actual use.

6.3 DELIVERY

The programs referred to in this text are not built for the personal use of the programmer. With the exception of temporary aids the programmer may construct in the course of a project, the programs are intended for someone else. The recipient can be another programmer or a project manager who will incorporate the program in a larger system. The recipient can also be the person who will use the program to produce results in daily operations. In either case, the program package is delivered to the recipient. Delivery can take several forms.

1. The program package (all documentation, including a machine-readable version of the code) can be handed to the recipient. The package is printed, copies are made, and a meeting is scheduled at which the formal delivery is to be made. The recipient then conducts acceptance tests. Delivery is complete when the acceptance tests succeed and the recipient formally accepts the package. Note that the time for all this activity should be included in the schedule for developing the program unit.

2. The machine-readable code, stored in an on-line library, can be relabeled to show that it now belongs to the recipient. In practice, a copy of the code is assigned to the recipient as a "released" program. The original is kept in the library as a working copy for maintenance and upgrading. The program documentation is hand-carried to the recipient. Delivery in this form can be authorized by preparing the right control cards. It can be acknowledged by showing the new ownership in a current listing of the library contents.

3. The programmer can be reassigned to the receiving department. This type of delivery requires that the programmer put on a new hat and act like a user rather than a developer.

Ultimately, all deliverable programs will reach an end-product user who will need the full program package.

6.3.1 Acceptance

When the job was initially assigned, the programmer assumed responsibility for building a program unit that would satisfy the requirements statement. Job *assignment* was a transfer of responsibility from the user to the designer/programmer. Program package *delivery* transfers responsibility from the programmer back to the user. The assignment scenario goes something like this:

User: This statement of requirements represents what I want. Can you do it for x dollars in y weeks?

Designer/Programmer: Yes, I have studied the requirements and estimated the job, so I can do what you want as long as you don't change the requirements. In addition, you should recognize that, according to my interpretation of your needs, I will deliver the program package that will do precisely the following things:

   ...

User: All right, your interpretation of the requirements statement is accurate; however, I can't promise that no changes will occur.

D/P: In that case, let's establish a change control procedure on the basis that you will pay the time and cost due to any change in work scope.

User: Agreed. I am willing to have you take over the implementation responsibility on this job.

D/P: I accept the responsibility to satisfy your stated requirements. I will do it my own way without interference from you, and I will follow what I consider to be good commercial and technical practices.

Having reached mutual agreement, the two can separate. It is the programmer's sole responsibility to perform the job. The only control the user can exercise during the development phase is whatever was spelled out in the requirements; i.e., the right to make changes, receive reports, critique technical decisions, etc., should be stated and agreed to at the start.

Now the programmer owns the job. The goal of the development effort is to transfer ownership of the completed program unit back to the user.[2] The user will not accept the program package unless it satisfies the requirements. As long as the user legitimately refuses to accept responsibility, the programmer is obligated to keep working toward the goal. Of course, no

---

2. Ownership may remain with the programmer under certain circumstances. Permanent assignment of ownership to programmers is most common in vendor shops that build general-purpose systems programs or user shops that support long-lived administrative applications.

one wants the project to go on forever, and the user's need for the program will grow more urgent as time passes. There must be some mutually agreeable way to effect delivery. One is to write a contract between the parties defining the terms and conditions under which the programmer's obligations are discharged. (The basic types of contractual agreements will be covered in Volume 2.) The second way to resolve delivery questions is to include the specification of an acceptance test in the statement of requirements. Since the statement of requirements was mutually agreed to by both parties when the job was assigned, the acceptance test spec can be treated as the one and only benchmark for acceptance at delivery. In other words, if the program package satisfies the statement of requirements *and* the program passes the acceptance test, the user *must* accept the package, relieving the programmer of further development responsibility. If at this point the program is unsuitable for the user's current needs, it is the user's responsibility to lay out new scopes of work to correct the situation. The acceptance test should be designed to provide a clear demonstration of all the functions and performance measurements stated in the original requirements statement. A list of the items to be demonstrated should be included in the statement of requirements. Each item should be observable and measurable. For example, acceptance of a compiler might be based on the following criteria.

- Correct processing of up to five samples (provided by the user) of each permissible statement type in the language.

- Correct compilation of three sample programs (provided by the user and edited for correctness by the programmer) in the language.

- Demonstration that symbol table size, treatment of illegal statements (as defined by the language), number base conversions, and other functional features have been provided, as called for in the requirements.

- Demonstration that the compilation rate (in statements per minute) meets or exceeds the performance requirement for the test programs.

Tests of this type produce results or measurements that are compared with predetermined standards. Therefore the user must know in advance what the result of the compilation should look like. Either the user or the programmer can work out the standard answers. To minimize the effort, each test is usually designed so that the results can be evaluated by inspection. The code generated by the compiler will not be examined in detail. Instead, the source program selected for use as a sample will be one that gives known results for certain inputs. Then the compiled program can be executed with the same inputs to see if the expected results are obtained. Similar methods can be used to test the correctness of a single statement processed by the compiler.

Vague or ambiguous test criteria must be avoided because they can only lead to disputes between the user and the programmer. Thus a criterion that a program be "efficient" is not acceptable. If efficiency is important, it should be quantified in terms of processing speed or program size or instructions executed per transaction, etc. "Quality" is another unacceptable criterion. It is a subjective term that cannot, in general, be defined satisfactorily. Finally, it is improper to include anything in the acceptance test specification that is not also in the requirements list. The programmer is supposed to satisfy only the requirements statement. It is unfair to measure results by any other standard. Therefore, if no performance requirement was established, the running time of the program is not relevant to delivery and acceptance. If certain I/O devices or library programs were not included in the required environment, they may not be attached as part of the acceptance test. And if the requirement called for a COBOL compiler without specifying the level of language, the user cannot object if the delivered program handles only the minimal acceptable subset of American National Standard Institute COBOL. Such situations will not arise if the statement of requirements comprehensively identifies what the user wants.

Conducting the acceptance test requires some prior planning, too. Even though the programmer will have completely debugged the program unit before offering the program package for delivery, there is no assurance that the acceptance test will succeed on the first attempt. Machine failures, bad data input, operator mistakes, or test case errors can cause an acceptable program to fail the test. A reasonable amount of time should be set aside for acceptance testing so that a few reruns and some rework of the tests can be accommodated. Nevertheless, there should be rules for determining when the test is over.

1. The duration of the test period should be predetermined.

2. The criteria for reinitiating the acceptance test after a failure should be predetermined (e.g., can a single item be rerun, or must the entire acceptance test period be started over?).

3. Given the fact that the acceptance test can uncover the need for changes in the program, rules for allowing changes during the test period should be established.

4. Rules should be established for resolving disputes between the user and the programmer. These include technical rules regarding how measurements are to be made and how results are to be interpreted, as well as administrative rules for arbitration or management decision.

5. The criteria for success should be stated in terms of which tests (or what percentage of test cases) must succeed to justify acceptance.

Rules for completion require successful execution of a known set of tests within a predetermined time period. Either failure to meet the quantitative success objective or failure to finish on time shows that the programmer did not do the job properly. The acceptance test is over. The programmer is responsible for fixing the deficiencies in the program unit so that a new acceptance test can be scheduled. A clean distinction between the development work done by the programmer and the acceptance test itself helps reaffirm the programmer's responsibility. Only when the acceptance test succeeds does responsibility transfer back to the user.[3]

After acceptance, the programmer is relieved of responsibility. However, a new assignment related to the maintenance or modification of the delivered program unit may be given to the same programmer rather than to one unfamiliar with the package.

6.3.2 Conversion and Installation

Acceptance has been described for the simplest type of delivery, in which the program package is handed over as though it were a library book or some similar off-the-shelf item. The deliverables meet the user's statement of requirements, but they have not yet been installed in the user's operating environment. This is the normal type of delivery for vendor-supplied program packages. They are tested and delivered to a library, which is not the ultimate user but only an intermediate repository. Customers order the program package from the librarian on the basis of the description in an offering circular or library catalog. When the vendor guarantees that the program meets the specifications in the descriptive literature, the customer will not run an acceptance test. A *suitability test* is in order to see that the program, as built, will be useful in the customer's shop. A suitable program is one that will satisfy existing needs without a great deal of modification or installation expense. In effect, the vendor has placed the program in the library on a "take-it-or-leave-it" basis, an arrangement that is entirely satisfactory to the customers since the value of suitable programs far exceeds the vendor's price.

Programmers who work for just one user must go through additional steps to complete the delivery of a program package. Not only must the acceptance test succeed, but the program must also be installed in the operating environment so that it can be run by the user's personnel. The

---

3. *Responsibility* is used here in the sense of carrying out an assignment. In a larger business sense, the user never relinquishes responsibility for the job; he merely subcontracts performance to the programmer. If the job is never done, it is the user who suffers the major loss.

personnel must be trained to use the program. Procedures must be developed or adjusted to fit the new program's operating principles. Parallel operations may be required to show that the replacement program can be used without disrupting ongoing operations. A cutover date must be set so that everyone involved will know when the new program will be activated. All of these things should be done as part of the development phase; therefore they should be included in the programmer's plan of action.

There are many people associated with an operational program. All of them should know those aspects of the program's behavior that affect them. The information they need is in the program package, but they have to be told that the program exists, and they have to be taught how to use the package. The minimum training procedure is to post a notice on the bulletin board describing the program and giving references to the documentation needed by each class of user. A more personalized touch is to send the affected people a memo explaining how they can find what they need. The next level of effort is to send each of them the appropriate documents, perhaps with a study outline. Finally, there is actual training via meetings, classes, or hands-on exercises. In general, the activities at any level incorporate all the activities at lower levels; i.e., running a class does not relieve the programmer of preparing notices, memos, and self-study aids. Note that, since training the user is part of program implementation, the programmer must be sufficiently well rounded to be able to write and teach.

In a typical data processing installation, at least four kinds of users can be found.

1. Systems support programmers
2. Application program users
3. Computer operators
4. Casual users

A development programmer will transfer responsibility for a system program, such as a utility or a compiler or an operating system extension, to the systems support programmers. They will run an acceptance test and then try it out gingerly a few times with real job streams, preferably after normal working hours. When they are satisfied that the new program is compatible with the rest of the environment, they will add it to their system library. Then they will set a date several weeks in the future, at which time the new feature will be made available to all users. Responsibility for the program can transfer to the systems support programmers at any time after they add it to their library up to the date of release. In the meantime, the users will have to be trained. Some programs, such as the facility aid Sort described in Chapter 3, are used only by the support programmers and computer operators. Training them is simple. It usually requires only enough time to review the user instructions and run the program from the operator's console. Compilers, on the other hand, are used by many programmers and nonprogrammers outside the computer department. Getting the word to these people takes all the mechanisms described above.

Casual users are not as amenable to classroom training as are people who make heavy use of a program. With interactive terminals available, anyone can walk up to a terminal and start to exercise a system program, particularly an interactive language processor. For this reason, interactive systems need good self-teaching aids built into the programs directly and included in the user manual.

Responsibility for a system program transfers from the developer to the systems support department. This is a feasible arrangement because the systems support people are normally responsible for making the facility effective, and they can accept ownership of the tools that contribute to facility effectiveness. Application programs are often treated differently, particularly in business data processing installations. Payrolls, personnel records, accounting, etc., are routine jobs that process sensitive data, including specially controlled documents, such as blank checks. The best judge of the condition of the payroll program is the payroll department. Similarly, each of the other business programs is best managed by the functional department responsible for the input and output. Therefore the program developer will transfer responsibility to the application program user. The application program user needs assurance that the application will be properly processed with no disruption of service. Thus transition to the new program must be so smooth that no one notices that there has been a change—except, of course, for improvements [10,11].

All application programs in a business data processing environment tend to be man-machine systems. The input data is prepared manually according to fixed procedures. The job is broken into segments so that control totals are available for manual review between segments. This arrangement is desirable because of the generally high level of input data errors for which no automated editing logic can be devised. Corrections may be entered manually between segments (although this practice is not encouraged). Then the output is distributed to a multitude of addressees, each of whom edits the results. In a payroll, for instance, manual entries on an employee time card can easily be misread, and the resulting errors may be compounded by the timekeeper and keypuncher who prepare input for the computer. Some of the errors are caught by programming. Others cannot be detected, but they will cause an overrun in total hours or total pay for the organization. When an overrun occurs, a payroll accountant has to study the detailed listings to figure out what caused it. If possible, an adjustment is entered on the spot. In this way, the payroll can be run to completion so that every employee can be paid on time.

Manual procedures in the payroll govern not only computer operations but also source recording (the time card), data preparations (timekeeper's calculations, keypunching), analysis of intermediate results (accounting review and adjustment), handling of accountable documents (controlling the blank checks and the printed checks), distribution of accountable documents (the pay checks), and distribution of accounting reports (payroll listings, exception reports, tax data, etc.). All these procedures exist in some form before a new program is introduced. Occasionally the new program is transparent to the system, so all of the existing procedures are unaffected. More often the new program changes the procedures, adding some, deleting others, and shifting the responsibility for some to new departments. The new program can be tested in a simulated environment, but the new payroll system must work correctly in the real environment. The programmer responsible for installing the new program must see that the new procedures are published and that all the people interfacing with the system understand the procedures. But since the programmer may not be well qualified in the *system* aspects of the application, the actual training may be conducted by the payroll experts in the functional area.

After everyone has been properly briefed, it is possible to attempt to run the application using the new program. No payroll manager, however, will be willing to jump in all at once. Since no excuses are allowed for failing to pay the employees, there must be a safe backup for the new program. This requirement leads to a conversion plan consisting of a period of parallel runs. Initially, the new program will be verified by the acceptance test, using a scenario representing real data. Second, both the existing and the new program will be run, using actual data for the current pay period. The pay checks will be printed by the existing program only. A careful comparison of the outputs from both runs will be made by the payroll department to verify that the new program produces correct results. Several more pay periods will be run in parallel to prove out the new program with respect to exceptional inputs that occur in one week but not another. The ability of the new program to accumulate year-to-date totals and to produce month-end or quarter-end reports is tested by making the conversion plan span multiple accounting periods. After a predetermined number of parallel runs (at least one, preferably three or four), the pay checks are printed by the new program instead of the existing program. If this works without any problems, the new program can be substituted for the old one. At each stage of the conversion plan, segments of the new program that require new manual procedures may be substituted for their counterparts. In this way, the payroll system makes a smooth transition. The end of the conversion plan completes the delivery process, and responsibility for the program package passes to the payroll department.

Although the example treats a payroll, a similar conversion plan must be incorporated in the program development plan any time the system incorporating the new program must operate without interruption or disruption.

When a system program passes its acceptance test and is added to the library of software resources in a facility, it can be released to the users. The term *release* implies that the program is known to function in accordance with the program documentation. There is no guarantee that the program will do the user's job. The user must determine that by studying the documentation. A stronger guarantee is made for an application program which has gone through a successful conversion. When the application program is substituted for its predecessor subsystem, the owner can say that an updated application system has been *installed*. Installation of an application system implies that, as long as everyone follows instructions and does his or her job, the system will perform the application properly. Thus an installed payroll system will produce the payroll as long as the time cards and other inputs conform to procedures. The employees and timekeepers do not have to learn anything about the *program* in order to use the *system*.

6.3.3   Postinstallation Activity

Delivery of an operational program relieves development programmers of further responsibility unless they are assigned the continuing responsibility for maintenance and modification of the program. Nine times out of ten such a continuing assignment will be made for installed programs. It occurs less frequently for released programs and least often for general-purpose programs released to a vendor library. In the latter case, a maintenance group may pick up the assignment while the development programmer moves on to another task. Inspection of the program documentation in a data processing facility often reveals a substantially better level of documentation for vendor releases than for in-house installed systems. The vendor programmers recognize the need for handing over good documentation to a maintenance group in the vendor shop. The in-house programmer, expecting to be assigned to do maintenance and understanding the program well enough without detailed writeups, puts less on paper. It is not good practice to allow skimpy documentation. The hoped-for savings are more than lost when problems develop in a system after the original programmer leaves the organization.

Regardless of who is assigned to support a delivered package, certain guidelines apply. As indicated in Chapters 4 and 5, change control procedures are required to maintain the correlation between the object program and the program documentation. All changes should be tested and documented, as was the original program, and the updated version should *replace* not *patch* the current version. No changes to the object code should be allowed except those that pass through the change control procedure. This rule is not always easy to enforce. If a payroll system crashes in the middle of a run, it is normal for the support programmer to fix the problem in order to complete the run. Under the pressure of the moment, paying the employees outranks other considerations, so the programmer will patch up the system and get it going again. He will make an effort to record the patch adequately so that a formal correction can be made the next day, but when, as is often true, the trouble occurs at three in the morning after a full workday, the programmer is likely to be a little sloppy. Some installations handle this situation by building into their job control system a procedure which allows a change to be made to a program already in the job stream but does not allow the change to be placed in the library copy of the program. Appropriate flags and messages remind the operator the next time the job is requested that it required a patch the last time it was used. This alerts the operator to look for a certain type of behavior. It also reminds the facility manager that a permanent fix is required to correct the error known to remain in the library program. This procedure works well with the type of error that occurs infrequently and is easy to fix. Severe errors cannot be treated so casually. When they are first encountered and the diagnosis shows them to be severe, a repair plan should be laid out that explains (a) how to run the program until the fix is available and (b) when the fix is scheduled.

A job control system can help pinpoint the cause of operational problems in other ways as well. By keeping part of the program documentation on-line, specifically the names of the data elements, files, and other programs referenced by each program, the job control system can detect mistakes in the job control cards before the program is dispatched. An attempt to reference a nonexistent file or a data element that is someone else's private property will hang up most programs at a point where the nature of the error is not obvious. If such errors are caught before the job starts, diagnosis is easy and the job, once started, will run to completion. Coupled with assiduous use of data editing and file label checking in each application program, this sort of job control is a major facility aid. An informal analysis of a weekly payroll system in the author's organization showed machine failures to be rare. They were usually due to the mangling of checks by the printer. Program errors were also rare. About once a month some combination of inputs that had never been seen before would cause an output error. A fair number of changes were caused by new payroll requirements or changes in tax regulations. By far the largest number of errors, on the order of 200 a week, were pure and simple mistakes in the input data. Most of them were caused by someone who failed to follow the published procedures. The combined job controls and programmed edits were able to detect and correct almost all of these data errors.

Once the program is running smoothly in the operating environment, it is natural to ask whether it is doing a good job. Whoever is paying for the use of the program will be interested in throughput, with the hope that cost can be reduced. The facility manager is always looking for ways to reduce the running time of current jobs to make room for new jobs. The user will also think up useful new functions as time passes. Questions along these lines justify periodic, planned evaluations of program performance. Various methods of measuring program performance described in Volume 2 can be used to determine the response time of the program (running alone and running in the normal multiprogrammed environment), the resources used by the program (system resources and file activity), and the functions exercised in the program (instruction execution trace). Knowing this, the user and the programmer can answer the following questions.

- How well does the program meet the original requirements? That is, how well did the programmer design the system?
- How well does the program meet the current requirements? That is, are modifications necessary?
- What program design changes would improve performance?
- What is the cost per input transaction?
- What is the average elapsed time or response time per transaction for each use of the program?
- How much storage is used? Is storage a problem? Should files be reorganized? Should data be purged to archives?
- Who uses the program and how often?
- How many errors occurred per run and of what type?
- What other programs interface with this one? That is, would a redesign of the system logic improve program performance?

The purpose of evaluating points such as these is to build a base of knowledge for making future decisions. Certainly, other factors being equal, an inexpensive program used once a month is not as good a candidate for performance improvement as an expensive program used every day. Yet the monthly program may get the attention if detailed performance data is not available. Precisely that happened in a facility which had a weekly payroll program that was old and rickety but serviceable. The payroll manager got the general manager's attention and sold a proposal to rewrite the payroll program at a cost of eight programmer-years. The result was a better payroll program that processed all the employees in one hour instead of one-and-a-half hours. Meanwhile the same organization had a bill-of-materials (BOM) program that ran two hours every day to handle supply control for an engineering lab. The program had to be completed by 7 a.m. daily to expedite the delivery of parts needed by assemblers throughout the plant during the day. Unfortunately, the complex linked list file structure of the BOM program was hard to use, and many errors occurred which delayed processing and interfered with the expediting activities. The savings potential for an improved BOM program far exceeded those for the payroll, but no one had collected the data to show it. So the payroll was revised and BOM was not.

The conclusion to be drawn from this example is that improvements should be made to programs only when they are necessary. The mere fact that performance and function *can* be improved is insufficient justification for spending time and money [12]. Improvements are necessary only when one of the following conditions applies.

1. The program cannot perform its job without the change.
2. The tangible savings or added value due to the improvement exceeds the cost of the improvement by a substantial and verifiable margin.

When the first condition applies but the second does not, it may be appropriate to abandon the program rather than improve it. The decision depends on the importance of the program. (In another context, a necessary program change is any change the programmer is directed to make by the user or the programming manager.) Tangible savings and added value can be achieved in several places.

1. In the machine room, by reducing running time or resource utilization.
2. In the application system, by reducing the number of people required or by cutting the cost of data preparation or by reducing the time required for a person to do a job within the system.
3. In the business, by increasing net profit by creating a new source of revenue or enhancing the marketability of a current product offering.

Proposals for program improvement should take into account the broader system view to ensure that no potential benefits are neglected.

6.4 PROGRAMMER MEASUREMENT

Project development guidelines place great emphasis on documented statements of requirements, design specifications, and deliverable program packages. The value of formalizing such procedures is that the user and the developer can mutually determine when the job is complete and whether it satisfies the requirements. The documents clearly show who is responsible for what and how changes may be made in a nondisruptive manner. Taken together, the documented procedures permit control and measurement of project and program performance. Indirectly, they also permit measurement of programmer performance.

In the absence of accepted norms for programmer performance, the quantitative data obtained from a single program unit is of little value. The fact that a programmer wrote a 1000-statement macro assembler in six weeks is not a good predictor of what the same individual can do on a different job. It is not even a good indicator of productivity on that job. Unless the instruction rate is related in some way to program quality and problem complexity, the productivity rate of 667 lines per month is meaningless. It could represent an outstanding job if a consensus of other programmers was that it should have taken six months; it could represent poor work if other programmers saw it as a 250-line task that could have been done in two weeks. Since no job is ever done twice (except in laboratory tests), there is no basis for comparing the conventional wisdom of experienced people.

How, then, does a programming manager tell how well a programmer is doing? There are three sources of information available for this purpose.

1. The programmer's estimate for the program unit assignment.
2. The average experience of all programmers in the organization over a long period.
3. The trouble reports on the delivered programs.

The programmer's estimate represents the target he was working toward. A large variance between actual and estimated results (either in project objectives or program performance) shows that the programmer really did not understand the problem or, perhaps, lacked the technical ability to do the job. Similarly, if the typical experience in the organization is that a program unit takes a weeks, has b lines of source code, used c computer runs for debugging, etc., a significant variance for a specific unit bears investigation. Note that, although the guidelines are stated in quantitative terms, the only significant information is the existence of a large variance. The variance is a flag alerting the programming manager to the fact that there is something unusual about the task. A danger signal does not tell whether the variance is due to problem complexity or programmer inadequacy. The manager has to determine that by studying the situation in detail. Trouble reports are a clearer indicator of programmer performance. Presumably the programmer thought the program met the user's requirements and the local standards of quality when it was delivered. Trouble reports, either by their volume or their content, indicate subpar quality. Of course, trouble reports requesting new functions cannot be charged against the programmer.

Taking these measures into account, the manager can work with the programmer to reinforce weak areas in his or her training. Thorough discussion of the things a programmer did wrong or failed to do, when coupled with instruction on the right way to do the job, will help the programmer grow as a professional. The conscientious programmer will seek out this help. Yet some, like people in all areas, prefer to avoid measurement. They are afraid it will show how poorly they are doing and will hurt their careers. Therefore they do not record plans and objectives if they can avoid it. Managers have to overcome this pessimistic fear of measurement by demonstrating the constructive side of the story. There are two standard techniques.

1. Make it a point to review successes as well as failures. When measurements are merely criticisms, the programmer will react badly. Measurements can also lead to a pat on the back. Every opportunity for praise should be seized.

2. Discuss performance measurements in the context of programmer development. When the manager can show the programmer how to do a better job next time—enhancing the programmer's chances for advancement—the advice is welcome. A discussion in which the emphasis is on berating the programmer for the bad job done this time will be resented.

A well-rounded measurement plan, then, not only ensures that useful, high-quality programs are delivered but also that the individual programmers enhance their capability for future assignments.

REFERENCES

1. Dijkstra, E. W., "Structured Programming." In J. N. Buxton and B. Randell (eds.), *Software Engineering Techniques.* Brussels, Belgium: NATO Science Committee, 1970.

2. Schwartz, J. T., "An Overview of Bugs." In R. Rustin (ed.), *Debugging Techniques in Large Systems,* Courant Computer Science Symposium I. Englewood Cliffs, N.J.: Prentice-Hall, 1971.

3. Schofield, P. B. "Minimodules." In T. O. Barnett (ed.), *Modular Programming.* Cambridge, Mass.: Information and Systems Press, 1968.

4. *IBM OS TESTRAN System Information Manual,* Form GC26-3796. White Plains, N.Y.: IBM Corporation.

5. Gaines, R. S., "The Debugging of Computer Programs." Working Paper 266. Princeton, N.J.: Institute for Defense Analysis, 1969.

6. Walsh, D. A., *A Guide for Software Documentation.* New York: McGraw-Hill and Inter-ACT Corporation, 1969.

7. VanDam, A., and D. E. Rice, "On-Line Text Editing: A Survey." *Computing Surveys,* Vol. 3, No. 3, September 1971.

8. Rubin, M. L., *Handbook of Data Processing Management,* Vol. 1: *Introduction to the System Life Cycle,* Appendix B, "Automated System and Program Documentation," P. Zuckerman and R. C. Dickenson. Princeton, N.J.: Brandon/Systems Press, 1970.

9. Chapin, N., "Flowchart Packages and the ANSI Standard." *Datamation* Vol. 18, No. 9, September 1972.

10. Canning, R. G., *Installing Electronic Data Processing Systems.* New York: Wiley, 1957.

11. Rovone, P. E., *Developing Computer-Based Information Systems.* New York: Wiley, 1967.

12. Marienthal, L. B., "The Internal Isolation of the DP Department." *Datamation,* Vol. 17, No. 1, January 1971.

7
Using
On-line
Terminals

Individual programmers working on a program unit are generally restricted to the computer facilities provided by their organization. The facility manager is charged with serving various users. In most locations scheduled business and engineering production jobs have priority over programming development. Furthermore, the facility manager tries to saturate the computing resources in order to hold down costs. The result is relatively slow turnaround for program compilation and debugging. It can range up to several days in some business data processing facilities. Even in large systems programming shops, where the computers are dedicated to programmer support, debugging turnaround can average a day or more because of the queues that develop in heavily loaded systems. Since the *apparent response time,* as far as the programmer is concerned, is the total time from submission to receipt of results, (Fig. 7.1), it is little comfort to the programmer to know that the actual job processing time on the computer was only a few seconds.

7.1 REMOTE JOB ENTRY

Programmers using batch service have to plan their work, as discussed earlier, to adapt to the prevailing turnaround time. Since both programmers and application users find that slow turnaround wastes the high-priced time of professional personnel, many organizations justify the use of *remote job*

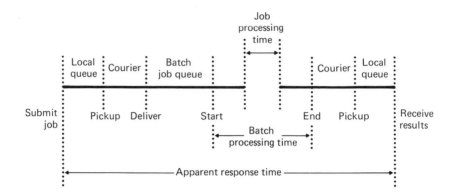

Fig. 7.1 Centralized batch service.

entry (RJE) terminals. The function of the terminals is to bypass the delivery service and, in some cases, keypunching [1]. High-speed terminals, such as card readers, tape drives, or small computers, located in the user area accept the same type of input—cards, tape, or disk—as is normally sent to the computer room via the courier service. Output punches or printers deliver computer output directly to the user [2].

The cost of high-speed terminals and the associated communication lines is substantial, so less expensive keyboard terminals are more commonly used for RJE. Typewriters or display devices, connected via ordinary telephone links or directly wired to the computer, can be used by individual programmers to enter modest amounts of data. Provided that bulk programs and data sets are passed through the normal batch service once and retained in the facility library, subsequent changes or execution commands can be entered from the terminal. Intermediate results, if terse, can be printed or displayed at the terminal. Final high-volume results can be delivered by the courier. Alternatively, small programs can be entered originally from the terminal, stored in a temporary library, edited from the terminal, and finally dispatched to the main batch stream by terminal command. The programmer has continuous access to individual lines of code (corresponding to punched cards in a program deck) and can modify them at any time. This mode of operation is called *conversational remote job entry* (CRJE). It is not truly conversational since only the programmer says anything; the computer listens and records. As in all RJE, the input is stored in a temporary area. When the programmer dispatches the stored program for execution, it is not immediately executed; it is merely added to the end of one of the current batch job queues (Fig. 7.2).

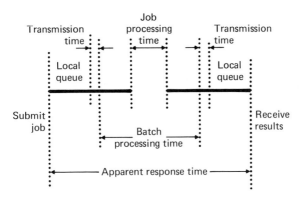

Fig. 7.2 Remote job entry (RJE).

7.2 INTERACTIVE ON-LINE TERMINALS

RJE reduces turnaround time and, depending on the type of terminal, can support one or more programmers in each user location. This type of service is batch-oriented; i.e., a programmer cannot interact with the program during execution. Interactive programming is also feasible, particularly with low-speed keyboard terminals. A programmer sitting at a terminal can establish a link to the computer by a sign-on procedure, which provides all the functions (except master resource management control) needed to operate the computer. In this mode, the programmer bypasses all the intermediaries and becomes the computer operator.

On-line terminals form a broad class. All input/output devices that can be in constant communication with the central computer are on-line terminals. That definition includes the operator's console, bulk storage devices, readers, and printers, as well as remote terminals. In common usage, however, "on-line terminals" has come to mean "user terminals" as distinct from basic system components. Within the class of user terminals are *interactive on-line terminals,* which permit the user to interact with and control the progress of the jobs submitted from the terminal. Now it is possible to picture each programmer with a private terminal. As Teager [3] points out, the programmer's effectiveness improves for the following reasons.

- Two-way conversation is possible. When the programmer keys in a statement, the computer can analyze it and point out syntactic or even logical errors.
- Turnaround time can be reduced to almost instantaneous response. The programmer can decide, at any point, to substitute some actual values

for the program variables and see what results a block of code will produce. The answer will be printed in a matter of seconds for most simple strings of code in a language supported by an interpretive translator. Large programs that must be compiled can usually return results in less than half an hour, as compared with a whole day when using the normal delivery service.

- Storage and retrieval of the program and its supporting documents can be done on-line. With the right type of library support, the programmer can have fast access to all the data, including history, needed in the project.

- A good record of how programmers spend their time can be obtained by monitoring terminal utilization. Therefore managers can sample developing programs and keep track of time spent on each module to determine when a programmer might need assistance.

Interactive terminals cannot be simply plugged in and run as a remote card reader can. The interactive capability must be supplied by special systems programs which handle terminal interruptions and prepare meaningful responses. Thus a good interactive terminal capability always requires extensive total system planning.

The major benefits of interactive systems—man-machine interaction, turnaround time, storage and retrieval, and management information—can be analyzed in terms of their relation to individual conceptual ability and span of attention. People are most effective when they are working on one thing at a time, completing small tasks in short periods. For example, a typist concentrates on the character being typed. In fact, so many speed-typists can tell when they have hit the wrong key that one manufacturer made a significant product improvement by adding a one-character storage buffer to electric typewriters. This allowed the typist to correct a character error before it was printed. Typists are much less likely to catch errors when they scan completed pages. Similar effects can be observed among programmers. One who writes source statements on coding sheets and then reviews the listing prepared after the statements are keypunched misses many errors. As a result, the first attempt to compile fails and the programmer gets a long list of syntactic errors back. The same programmer, using a terminal, will see typing errors immediately, backspace, and correct them. Then, with computer assistance, he can debug simple statements or small blocks of code, correcting additional errors while the purpose of each statement is still fresh in his mind. The number of computer interactions increases but each interaction contributes more to the progress of the program.

The value of immediacy carries over to the full extent of the material currently occupying a programmer's attention. Note that the programmer, though able to understand the entire scope of a program unit in general terms, concentrates on only one piece of it at a time. The piece being worked on will be only as detailed as the programmer's conceptual ability allows.

Structured programming and top-down implementation are ideal for terminal users. Top-down implementation produces one-page executable programs that are conceptually manageable all the way from the top to the bottom. In other words, every page describes a portion of the program at a level of detail that the programmer can understand. A question arising in a low-level module can always be answered by referring to the higher-level parent, which is itself of a convenient size for terminal use. (Trouble in a bottom-up module may not be resolvable until late in the development, at which time the entire set of available modules may have to be examined to find a solution.)

By eliminating turnaround delays and supporting man-machine interaction, the on-line terminal permits the programmer to focus on a complete analysis of a small portion of a problem. The complexity of the piece at hand is always within bounds, even though it is part of a highly complex program. Under these conditions, the programmer is more likely to find good solutions rapidly. Programs should be done sooner and have higher quality. Sackman [4] reviews a number of experiments in the effectiveness of time-sharing and reaches a similar conclusion. His analysis of ten studies conducted between 1967 and 1969 showed that time-sharing jobs took about 20% fewer man-hours than did the same jobs when run through batch services. Some of the experiments were graded with respect to student performance and student understanding of the problem. Time-sharing gave slightly better results. In all the experiments the subjects preferred time-sharing to batch service.

The results reported by Sackman are by no means conclusive. Their applicability to systems programming is unclear because the experimental problems were designed to test programming procedures rather than programming ability. They consisted of math-oriented problems that would take 5–40 hours to complete. No group activity was studied. The test results are valid for the university and laboratory problem-solving environment. They may be valid for systems programming, but then again, they may not. A typical program unit takes 4–6 weeks and involves much structure and file activity. Math problems, therefore, may not be suitable test vehicles for predicting programmer performance. Another drawback is that, in common with all programming experiments, the variations in individual performance are large—larger than the variations between on-line and batch performance. Thus there is no assurance that the programmers in a given organization will automatically achieve the benefits of time-sharing achieved in the experiments. Programmers must adjust their style to take advantage of the capabilities of interactive time-sharing.

Fortunately, programmers who favor interactive on-line terminals believe they can do their work faster, better, and cheaper than with batch services or RJE. This belief is based on tangible factors involving turnaround time, etc., which can be evaluated in a cost analysis. The belief is also strongly grounded in the apparent *symbiosis* between the programmer and the on-line system. The symbiotic relationship allows the programmer and the machine to cooperate in a mutually beneficial way. As a result, the programmer is a better analyst, reaching conclusions in a more direct way. Many students, engineers, and scientists who have used interactive time-sharing systems to solve problems attest to the power of symbiosis. Each response from the computer stimulates them to think of an appropriate follow-up, so they quickly converge on an answer to the problem. Fast feedback is the key. In a batch system, the computer output returns too late to feed the creative fire that is sustained at a terminal. Although there are plenty of supporters for this belief in a problem-solving environment, there is no hard evidence that symbiosis can be achieved in a program development environment. Neither is it a relationship achievable by all programmers. This suggests that interactive time-sharing should be used primarily during the portion of the development cycle that is most like problem solving, namely, the actual coding and debugging stage.

7.3 COSTS OF ON-LINE SUPPORT

Intuitively, interactive on-line terminals are attractive even though the quantitative data available cannot prove it. The nonquantitative judgments of programmers lead many of them to like the idea of using terminals. They like the fast response. They like the reinforcement the conversational mode gives them when they are trying to decide what to do next. They like the way the interactive software forgives their mistakes and helps them make progress in spite of minor errors. And they like the flexibility inherent in the direct connection the on-line terminal provides to the computer; it lets them do things that are not worth the effort in the batch system. On the assumption that programmers perform better when they like their working conditions, interactive terminals should be made available when the price is right.

Gold [5], in one of the studies summarized by Sackman, gave some thought to the cost-justification question. His experiment dealt with solving a business management problem. Students had to learn how to use a computerized simulation model of the construction industry and then devise a set of decision rules that would maximize the profits of a small-scale builder. The students using time-sharing spent an average of 16 man-hours to produce a paper profit of $444. Batch users took a little over 19 hours on the average to net \$244. Time-sharing appeared to lead to a better solution. The computer time for the time-sharing users, however, was 344 seconds, compared with only 72 for the batch users. When the values were plugged into the formula

$$\text{Cost} = (\text{Resource hours}) \times (\text{Resource cost/hour}),$$

time-sharing and batch operations broke even at a wage rate of just under \$12 per programmer-hour. In other words, the lower cost of batch compute time would be offset by shorter job completion time only when the programmer-hours saved by time-sharing were worth more than \$12 each. This figure corresponded in 1969 to the earning rate of mid-range professionals (e.g., engineers or researchers with five years or more of experience) and their managers.

Streeter [6] carried the cost analysis further and looked at the question from the viewpoint of a facility manager. As Director of Computer Systems in the IBM Research division, he obtained data from his customers, scientists in the research laboratory. In this environment scientific effort is the primary product, and the value of user time is high. Streeter placed a value of \$30 an hour (in 1972) on this factor. He then evaluated total problem-solving cost as a function of computing system costs, communications costs (connect time for remote terminals), cost of user's time, cost of delays (elapsed problem-solving time), and auxiliary charges (keypunching). Using a sample program, he measured the costs of each factor for several configurations, including a small personal computer (IBM 1130), a large scientific batch processor (IBM S/360-91), three time-sharing systems (IBM S/360-67 TSS, IBM S/360-67 CP/CMS, and a hybrid IBM S/360-67 TSS with S/360-91 OS), and one time-sharing system used in batch mode (IBM S/360-67). Total cost of solving the test problem was highest for the personal computer because it was so slow and tied up the user the whole time. The lowest cost was attained by the hybrid system, in which the Mod 67 permitted interactive data entry (CRJE) connected to a batch system (RJE). The other services were comparable in cost, about midway between the lowest and highest figures. The straight batch systems were penalized by large elapsed-time delay costs even though their computing costs were low.[1] The time-sharing systems had better elapsed time but considerably higher computing costs because of time-sharing system overhead.

Computer costs were predictably low in batch operating systems which can be tuned to minimize the amount of operating system overhead per

---

1. Delivery costs were ignored except as they contributed to delay costs or user time. Users delivered their own work to the computer room. Presumably users were idle during delay time.

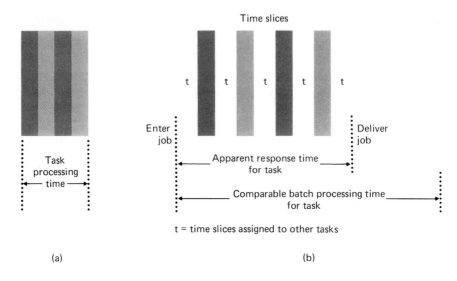

Fig. 7.3 Time-shared service: (a) work slice as the sum of time slices; (b) time slices versus batch.

user transaction. Multiprogrammed batch operating systems increase the overhead ratio in order to maximize computer resource utilization for multiple batch job streams operating in restricted core regions. A virtual storage operating system increases the overhead further in order to relieve the user from worrying about region size. Still more systems programming support is needed to support interactive systems [7]. In batch-oriented multiprogramming, decisions can be made in between tasks. The job is a series of tasks, or *work slices,* of variable length depending on the amount of work to be done. When interactive terminals are added, certain functions have to be handled immediately; the operating system cannot wait until the current work slice comes to an end. So a schedule of fixed-length *time slices* is introduced (Fig. 7.3) which permits many jobs to be interleaved. All jobs requesting service are started at the same time. Each in turn receives a slice of time, at the end of which it is interrupted by the operating system in favor of the next job. Time slicing makes all the jobs appear to proceed in parallel compared with the serial appearance of work slicing. The shortest jobs require fewer time slices per task and are completed sooner than if they had to wait for long jobs ahead of them to be finished. The time slice is shorter than the average work slice, increasing both the number of operating system decision points and the number of times a job is interrupted before it is finished. Thus a time-sharing system has the highest overhead per user transaction of the commonly available operating systems.

Add to the pure operating system overhead the additional services provided by interactive language translators, debugging aids, and library support, and you find that the interactive time-sharing system carries a significant price tag. The use of the system is justified only when the value of the service exceeds the price tag. That means that savings must be achieved by a combination of factors.

- Less idle time on the part of professional programmers and supporting personnel.
- Earlier delivery of completed packages, enabling earlier realization of operational savings.
- Higher-quality results because the interactive service increases programmer effectiveness.

There is one more cost factor to be considered when on-line support is being evaluated. That is the cost of backup. In program development a job taking 4–6 weeks cannot afford many long delays. Normally, there is plenty of flexibility available to compensate for unexpected problems. Thus, if the batch service is suspended for a couple of days, a programmer can either find another computer or spend the time on planning, analysis, documentation, or other activities that do not depend on the computer. When the job goes on-line and all the information about the job, including the documentation, is in the computer, the programmer has no fallback position. Every day the computer is unavailable is a true day of delay. Thus, unless the system provides a manual backup, there is a potential cost of delay that must be reflected in the project estimate as a risk factor.

The various pros and cons of time-sharing that influence when time-sharing should be used are discussed in Section 7.5.2.

7.4   DESIGN CONSIDERATIONS FOR INTERACTIVE TERMINALS

It would clearly be a disadvantage if on-line services were frequently interrupted for extended periods. No time-sharing service can function successfully under such conditions. In addition, there are less severe problems associated with interactive terminals that can frustrate individual users. Wilkes [8] notes that time-sharing moves the users *into* the system; they are no longer outsiders. The users are very adaptable and will quickly learn how to take advantage of the good features of the system while avoiding the bad features. Nevertheless, the users will continue to use the time-sharing system only as long as it gives satisfactory service. Some of the factors that influence the acceptability of an interactive service are listed below. It will appear that overdue emphasis is placed on trivialities. Quite the contrary, the items have been selected because they can make the difference between an acceptable and an unacceptable interactive service. The factors are grouped into four categories.

1. Human factors affecting the user personally.
2. Terminal factors affecting the mechanical aspects of interactive use.
3. Communications factors affecting the quality of an interactive session.
4. System load factors affecting the performance of an interactive system.

7.4.1   Human Factors

The user, as a human being, demands an environment that is physically and psychologically congenial. Physical needs affect the design of facilities, terminals, and accessories. Psychological needs affect the design of languages and manuals. There is general agreement that professional workers are most productive when their working area is quiet, well organized, and pleasant. Further, productivity is influenced by the convenience and availability of tools. Time-sharing may fail to achieve this primarily because of the terminal.

Because impact terminals (typewriters) are noisy to the extent of being totally distracting, people generally do not want to be near an active terminal (unless they are operating it). This separates the user from the terminal, so he must leave his work area to use it. A carefully planned programming office could substantially eliminate this problem and provide a good office environment for time-sharing (Fig. 7.4). It is a modular design which provides optional enclosures for terminals but treats them as normal pieces of furniture. The problem of noise in a programming environment is more important than has been understood. For over two years, programmers in one facility complained of excessive noise levels. In particular, terminals were creating local disturbances on the order of 20 db over the ambient noise. Narrowing the gap by introducing a higher level of ambient noise was considered. A better solution was to provide sound conditioning of work space and terminals. Later, nonimpact terminals were substituted for typewriters. Displays were used in this case although hard-copy nonimpact printers could have been selected.

The terminal should be an extension of the user. Not all users can acquire the clerical skills necessary to make the terminal "second nature." For them the terminal is a distinct distraction. (Keyboard/display/light pen terminals seem to be much easier for professionals to use than typewriters.)

Predictable performance is essential to the user who automatically adapts to changing situations with a 2–4 week time cycle but cannot adapt to fast-changing situations. Thus, if time-sharing support is supposed to be

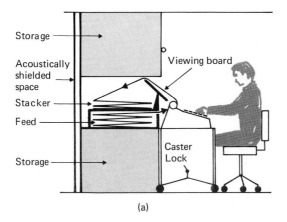

Storage

Acoustically
shielded
space

Viewing board

Stacker

Feed

Storage

Caster
Lock

(a)

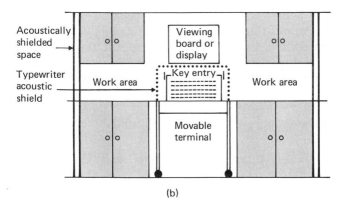

Acoustically
shielded
space

Typewriter
acoustic
shield

Viewing
board or
display

Key entry

Work area

Work area

Movable
terminal

(b)

Fig. 7.4 Interactive terminal workspace: (a) side view; (b) front view.

available for 12 hours a day, programmers will organize their behavior to
get the most done under that assumption. If, in fact, the availability is less
than 12 hours a day, they will have to reorganize their activities through
a subconscious process that converges on a new schedule by trial and error.
If the availability continues to vary, users will always be a step or two
behind. Not only will they use their time poorly, but they will blame the
computer for their wasted effort. The simple solution is to schedule each
individual time-sharing system in such a way as to guarantee its availability
(barring system failure) during the scheduled hours. This is a trivial task
on a dedicated system. It is much harder to accomplish in a multiple-use
system with priorities.

Desk calculator systems are so simple the user needs no reference material other than an instruction list or sample problem as a reminder of how to operate it. More complex systems need thorough references. It is important to design these manuals so that they can be easily used at the terminal. This means that each manual must be self-sufficient, well indexed by topic and by key word (instructions, commands, etc.), and provided with a means for hanging it on the wall or standing it on a table. It is preferable that the *console manual* be organized to reflect the sequence of operations a user normally follows. The *reference manuals* can be organized sequentially or alphabetically by function. All of these considerations are relevant to the effective use of terminals by programmers, but they apply equally well to nonprogrammers. Therefore programmers should keep these points in mind when designing interactive systems for other people.

7.4.2 Terminals

Terminal design must stress ease of use and mobility.

Many interactive languages use nonstandard character sets that can confuse the user, particularly a touch-typist. Current methods of showing what character will print when a given key is struck include the following.

1. Pasting the graphics on the front vertical face of the key.
2. Posting a keyboard pattern on the wall behind the terminal at user eye level.
3. Having the system type out a character set at the start of each user session.
4. Painting or defacing the key tops to show the correct graphics.
5. Fitting plastic caps over the keys.

Only methods 2, 3, and 5 are appropriate for terminals which serve several different time-sharing systems. If the terminal is dedicated to one system—or one character set—the keytops should be ordered to correspond with the systems standard.

The user needs help to determine the status of the system. Visual, tactile, and audible signals regarding terminal, communication, and system status are desirable or, according to the very comprehensive terminal specifications of Dolotta [9], essential. As a minimum, these signals should indicate whether an element is operating or not operating and which element is in control. It is convenient to have the visual status signals grouped in one place so that a status change is immediately evident to the user.

Stack control and paper feed precision are important. Long printouts may be requested by an operator who intends to leave the room until the printout is finished. (This is a particular problem in automated documentation systems.) Good paper-handling devices are provided, but they need frequent inspection and adjustment. A properly adjusted platen and stack are essential, even with pin feeding, to prevent paper jams and loss of data due to paper slippage. For dealing with these problems, an audible alarm is recommended to alert a nearby operator to a problem. A simple stacker can keep the work space organized and avoid paper tears.

It is natural for a user to find a graphic display suitable for some activities. Such a device is most useful when the system permits retrieval of page-length lists of command options or data which may involve a light-pen selection by a user. This configuration is typical of information-handling systems, including computer assisted instruction (which can be thought of as a special type of information-handling system). The graphic device may be a costly luxury in other systems. Here its main advantage—the page-length display—can be effectively obtained by fixing a paper holder to the typewriter carriage, as shown in Fig. 7.4. This places a recent history (about 60 lines) in front of the user and thus gives a reasonably adequate global view of the work in process. If the relative cost of graphic devices versus impact terminals favors graphics in the future, as we predict, their versatility will lead to more general use.

Storage and workspace area are needed for working with program listings. The terminal gives access only to local data in the range of 1–60 lines, according to the type of display. Moreover, retrieval of archive listings may result in only a small part of the requested data being displayed. For this reason, programmers will continue to rely on listings in hard copy for global analysis. Structured programs simplify retrieval of useful segments on-line, but even structured programmers like to have all the work to date available in handy notebooks.[2] Large organizations may reduce the cost of computer printouts by using microfilm or microfiche printers for bulk output. If so, a manually operated viewer should be installed next to each terminal to serve the purpose of global reference to the listings. About one out of every four viewers should have an attachment for making hard copies of selected pages.

There is inevitably an imbalance between the number of terminals available at a given place and the demand for terminals at that place. For this reason, almost all users of time-sharing find it necessary to move termi-

---

2. This point was brought home to the author when, on a neatness campaign, he told his programmers in a terminal-oriented shop to throw out their listings. The ensuing chaos impacted schedules. Within a week, the listings were back in place, i.e., piled next to each terminal.

nals around. This is usually accomplished by installing homemade casters, which cause the keyboard to be too high for comfort. It is more practical to cut off the legs of the terminal stand to give it the correct height when on casters. The casters, of course, should be locked when the terminal is stationary. The design should allow one person to maneuver the terminal without assistance.

A user who must wait in line for a terminal will soon find an alternative tool. The ratio of users to terminals should be small enough to reduce average queue length to zero. Since a number of different activities are involved in developing a program unit, and since on-line support is useful only in a subset of them, a programmer will not need a terminal 100 percent of the time. If more than two people have to share a single terminal, too much contention will be generated. However, if several terminals are placed in a central area (close enough so that the users are willing to walk to them), the ratio can rise to four or more programmers per terminal. Such a pool should have a minimum of three machines so that even when one is in maintenance the queue is short. The terminal room should have standard acoustic enclosures for the terminals or be large enough (and well enough decorated with sound absorbing materials) to minimize mutual interference among terminals. By insisting on casters, managers can have the option of placing the terminals anywhere they are needed on a temporary basis.

7.4.3   Communications

Communications errors can cause effects that are terribly annoying to a terminal user. Some errors interrupt transmission and can disconnect the terminal, wipe out the user's work in progress, force the user to reenter a line of data, or garble a message. Errors of this type cancel out all the benefits of being on-line, and if they occur often, they will drive away the users.

The data transmission network consists, for the most part, of voice quality lines used on demand for data transmission.[3] Two characteristics of data transmission are not consistent with good time-sharing performance. The first is noise; the second is holding time.

Noise in a voice system can be tolerated over a wide range because there is sufficient redundant information transferred in the voice signal to carry the message. Noise is less tolerable in a data system because it may take the form of a data bit and be indistinguishable from true data. Although

---

3. Rapid improvements in data transmission quality and computer network reliability, expected in the latter 1970s, will correct most of the problems referred to here.

existing hardware provides enough error control for average noise levels, it seems inadequate to cover noise in certain elements of the data transmission network, such as rotary switches. Thus long lines may give worse service than local connections. Some terminals are designed in such a way that a rather common effect of communication noise is to introduce a spurious "attention" signal. This is the signal which reverses the half duplex line; it is also used extensively as a powerful control signal. Of all possible ways for noise to appear, this is probably the worst. It can disconnect the terminal without the programmer's knowledge, and it can look like an end-of-message signal in the middle of a transmission. The burden is on the system software to store messages until the programmer (or some unambiguous program state) signifies that the message has been correctly handled. Full duplex line disciplines ease the control problem and frequently save line costs.

In the voice system, average holding times are expected to run 4–5 minutes. In time-sharing, they may run 4–5 hours, according to the length of a programmer's work session. During the hold period, little actual data is transferred, but the line remains unavailable to anyone else. The result of long holding times is saturation of switchboards in spite of network contingency reserves. Traffic capacity may not be taxed, but physical connections are used up. The cost of the hold is excessive for the individual user, who would prefer to share the facility with another paying customer. This can be handled on a limited basis by line concentrators, which are communications boxes that service several terminals at a location.

Connecting a terminal to the data transmission system is most practically done by using a common carrier modem (a device for converting digital computer data to the proper analog form for transmission, and vice versa). Alternative methods use an acoustic coupler or direct wire. The direct wire gives the best service because it bypasses the data transmission network. It is limited to terminals within a few thousand feet of the computer and may create a facility problem in stringing wire. The common carrier modem is next most reliable but bulky and difficult to position where it is both convenient and out of the way. The acoustic coupler is the least reliable but the most flexible since it can be moved easily to any phone near an electric socket.

7.4.4   System Load

Both the communication system and the computing system should be operating below saturation so that terminal response is reasonable. Streeter [6] gives an analytical procedure for determining the appropriate load on a combination batch/interactive facility in relation to the value of user time.

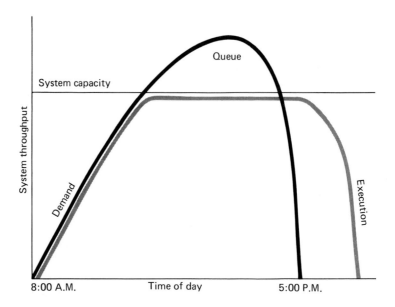

Fig. 7.5 Workload in a time-sharing facility.

As the computing load increases, user response time deteriorates at an ever increasing rate. Second, when the communications system overloads (as happens when data communications demand builds up before the physical plant of the communications utility can handle it), the user gets a busy signal and cannot get on-line to start a session. Advance planning can avoid overloads of this type by providing enough resources. A third load factor is harder to cope with. As indicated in Fig. 7.5, daily workload in a facility is not stable. When people get to work in the morning, they need time to get organized before they can use the on-line system. Therefore the system load generated by time-sharing is low in the morning. It builds up during the day, gradually displacing background batch jobs. Finally, in late morning, all the users are on-line competing for resources. Since the facility has a limited capacity, it may not be able to service all requests immediately. At this point, it is normal for the operators to adjust the amount of time allocated to each priority class of job. Batch jobs running in the background are usually deferred until second or third shift by giving them the lowest priority. Other users will see their response time erode, first because of the heavy load, and second because they may not claim the highest priority for service. Naturally, a queue develops. At first it is not noticed because of a noontime slump in usage. Later in the day, users whose service is too slow and all users attempting to get on-line to start a work session will look at the clock on the wall and decide not to waste any more time at the terminal. They go home. Then, as work in process ends, the system load drops precipitously. If the users are free to do their work either in batch mode or on-line, they can, of course, prepare a batch run for overnight service before they go home. In practice, this takes extra management attention because (a) most time-sharing systems lock the user into one mode of operation, and (b) most programmers, hoping to get their work done on-line, wait too long to prepare a batch submission before quitting time. *Without management attention a time-sharing system may actually reduce the programmer's time on the job.*

Time-sharing systems share with multiprogramming systems the difficulty that system crashes are much more expensive. In a sequential batch system, only the current job is lost when there is a crash, whereas in time-sharing or multiprogramming a crash is much more destructive. Not only does work in process have to be recreated, but data files may have to be regenerated. The computer center management and operators must understand time-sharing if they are to provide a satisfactory service. For example, if there is a reason to bring the system down, it is necessary to notify all time-sharing users so that they can file their work before the system comes down. As another example, they must be ready for the telephone to ring as soon as something goes wrong. They must be keenly aware that a crash or an operator error that brings down the system will not only waste the machine time that has been invested in partly completed work but also waste the programmer time that has been invested. It is possible to run a very effective time-sharing computation center, but the computation center manager and the operators have just as much learning to do as the programmers in order to use time-sharing effectively.

7.5   EFFECTIVE USE OF INTERACTIVE SUPPORT

Implied in the list of benefits and design considerations are potential problems that can occur in interactive systems. All of the problems can be solved by careful planning and generous budgeting. Consequently, effective use of interactive support is not a question of feasibility; it involves only cost and utility. The results of time-sharing experiments highlight the types of *interactive support* that are most likely to provide cost benefits *and* increase programmer effectiveness.

1. Problem-solving
2. Interactive editing and debugging
3. Storage and retrieval

Common to all the cost-effective activities is the fact that they are *individual activities*. Interactive terminals, even when they can communicate with each other via message store-and-forward software, are not effective group tools. A second common characteristic is that each activity leads to user work sessions of limited scope so that the user's local interests are well adapted to the terminal's line-by-line mode of operation. In general, the criteria for cost-effective interactive support are that the support be easier to use than batch and RJE, that it be reliable, that it be available, that it not restrict the programmer's ability to meet project requirements, and that it be economical.

7.5.1   Using a Time-Sharing System

The mechanics of using a time-sharing system are complicated by the fact that the simplest time-sharing system contains a sequence of interfaces invisible to the user (Fig. 7.6).

To illustrate the point, picture the typical user (A) who intends to do a time-sharing job. First, he must locate an unoccupied terminal (B). Then he must either move the terminal to his office or carry his working references to the terminal room. To link into a computer the user must determine what the legal phone numbers are and dial one in the hope that a stepping switch will connect him to any available line. He dials eight digits and may get a busy signal after the first (line busy—D), fourth (destination switchboard busy—E), or eighth (extension busy—F). He will usually redial since in many instances the busy condition is transient. He will also get a busy signal if the computer is already saturated, i.e., if all lines are occupied. In this case, redialing won't help. If he gets a line into the computer, he may hear the phone ring, but no connection is made because the system is down, the extension is not connected to the multiplexer at this time, the destination rotary switch (E) fails to step, or the rotary is stopped on a previously disconnected line. In some cases, the line will simply go dead. When the user does get the connection signal, a high-pitched continuous tone, he must hook up the modem (C) by pressing the "Data" button (or by placing the phone handset in an acoustic coupler box, closing the lid, and throwing the coupler switch). The hookup process appears to throw a noise signal on the line that can cause a disconnect. The user who expects to get into the computer on the first try is often disappointed.

After a few tries, the user will either give up or call the computer operator (L) for assistance. This involves a different phone number. The operator may not be able to help, other than to say whether the computer is up or down. If it is down, the user will probably stop trying to get on-line since there is no way to know when the computer comes back up without spending unproductive time at the terminal.

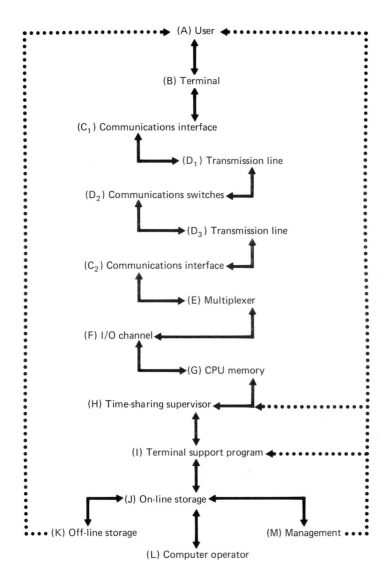

Fig. 7.6 Terminal interfaces.

A successful hookup produces a computer message on the terminal. In a well-designed system (I) this message identifies the system, provides basic guidance to the user, and prints out any system messages applicable that day. It then asks the user to *log in.* The log-in identifies the user for security and accounting purposes. It may also identify the terminal and terminal character set. The response to a log-in request is short and simple, containing only passwords and lockwords. As long as the user remembers the lockwords, he should be in good shape. It is common, however, for the response to be garbled or misunderstood by the system, so another log-in is requested. The problem is most likely to be due to data transmission errors, but lacking diagnostics, the user loses confidence in the accuracy of the passwords and lockwords, or he becomes unsure of the log-in procedure. The essential difficulty is that the user and the computer are not yet in communication, and in some cases, the system is not able to issue useful diagnostic messages. Until log-in is successful, the user cannot interpret delays as accurately as he can later. He is likely to think he is waiting for his turn when actually the system has failed to hear him.

Once logged in, the user can begin a job. At this point, the power and utility of the time-sharing system (H) are evident, and the user temporarily forgets earlier difficulties—that is, until the keyboard locks. In the simplest case, this will occur when the instantaneous work load exceeds the system capacity. The keyboard will automatically release after a while. Nevertheless, it is a significant irritant because the user is able to enter data faster and faster as the day goes on, but the system responds slower and slower as users log in. In other words, the system does not let the user take advantage of the interactive power designed into the system. (Only some systems have this difficulty. In order to eliminate this irritating feature, many systems are managed (M) so that the user gets no better service when the system is lightly loaded than when it is heavily loaded. This practice may be slightly inefficient in terms of computer usage, but it effectively satisfies the user's need to know what service to expect.)

The keyboard may lock for less evident reasons. If the system or that portion assigned to a given terminal crashes, the terminal will lock. At this time, since the communication link is broken, the user cannot do anything to diagnose or fix the situation. When the system recovers, users must retrace their steps to see where the system thinks they are. Many of these crashes seem to be due to the lack of adequate memory protection (G). One user can bomb the entire system by trying to execute undebugged code. Similarly, one data transmission error can cause a crash by modifying privileged programs. Proper protection and use of virtual stores and virtual machines control this problem. A troublesome case to handle occurs when a user requests the transfer of a block of data from bulk storage (I) to a work area. Some transfers can be quite long, and the keyboard is locked until it is completed. Sometimes the user forgets that a transfer is in progress and thinks an error has occurred because the keyboard is locked, so he may disconnect and redial. The result of the action may introduce errors that can crash the user's work area.

Many minor errors can be ignored because the user can figure them out. Mistyped characters can be retyped, garbage or garbled lines can be retransmitted, poor carriage spacing or line formatting can be accepted if the data is correct (except when producing final copies of documents). The programmer generally keeps listings from a prior run (K) to help resolve some of these errors. Some errors cannot be ignored, however. One is loss of synchronization between the carriage and the computer clock. In systems which provide automatic space control and tabbing, the loss of synchronization causes data to be misinterpreted or lost.

This compendium of problems is not intended to frighten off prospective terminal users. The types of things that can go wrong and interfere with programmer productivity should be taken into account when deciding how to use a terminal. Some conclusions drawn from this exposition follow.

- The average work session should be long compared with the time spent logging into the system.
- A programmer should expect a consistent level of service from the interactive system.
- Service problems should be reported in such a way that a programmer can decide whether to wait for service to resume or to do an off-line task.
- Local services are preferred to long-distance connections because they involve fewer interfaces.
- A copy of all necessary material should be kept separate from the on-line computer storage so that work can continue, even when the computer is busy or otherwise unavailable.
- The software support for interactive programming should be compatible with the batch system to the extent that programs and data can be run using either [10].

7.5.2   When to Use Time-Sharing Support

A summary of benefits and drawbacks of time-sharing shows that on-line support is beneficial in two situations: (a) when improved turnaround reduces the net cost of programming; and (b) when interactive programming increases programmer effectiveness. On a pure cost basis, the first situation favors RJE over interactive support. Both the cost and the savings due to RJE can be calculated, whereas neither quantity is readily determined in interactive systems. RJE is easy to introduce into an organization since it does not require any change in management or programming practices. Predictable savings can be achieved solely by eliminating the unproductive time formerly generated by slow turnaround.

Interactive terminals do require new practices and procedures. Managers will have to supervise programmers in a different way because each programmer can develop individual work habits at a terminal. In addition, the manager loses the opportunity to review work content. In batch and RJE systems there is a control point past which all work flows. This is where a manager normally would focus attention. Interactive systems lose this control point, so the manager more or less has to sample individual progress by looking over a programmer's shoulder and trying to elicit information about technical status from system statistics about resource use and data base activity. More important is the loss of an important practice that helps to ensure quality—program reading among peers. The cooperative procedure of critiquing one another's programs is a powerful tool for checking program logic, efficiency, and correctness. The best time to do it is when a program module is supposedly finished and ready for initial compilation or assembly. This point is clearly defined in batch and RJE systems. It is not defined in interactive systems. Since a programmer can interactively debug a program as it is created at the terminal, there is no obvious point at which to call in a friend to read the "first draft" program.

Therefore RJE is preferable to interactive terminal support because it costs less and fits in well with the existing practices of many managers. Some people do not agree, pointing out that they cannot afford a big, high-speed RJE terminal but can afford a typewriter terminal. Yet the size of the terminal has little to do with the recommendation. It is quite common to see a programmer who has a typewriter terminal write the program in longhand and ask a secretary to enter it from the terminal. This is an admission, for that programmer at least, that there is one task, namely, program entry, that is not cost-effective. First, the secretary does it better. Second, the programmer adds no value by sitting at the terminal and essentially copying data. Third, the whole point of the exercise is to get the program into the computer so that it can be executed by commands from the terminal, that is, RJE. The logic of this way of entering programs strikes home to most programmers after a few months of using a keyboard terminal and, particularly, after receipt of the bill for telephone charges covering their connect time. As a result, many programmers recommend that their typewriter terminals be replaced by communicating card or tape machines. These devices are slightly more expensive. They have two modes of operation; one is identical to the original terminal, and the other is a stand-alone mode. In the latter mode, the machine is an ordinary typewriter augmented by its own memory. As data is typed, it is stored on a magnetic card or tape. Limited stored programming allows the user to correct errors. Thus a draft can be developed and corrected off-line. When the draft is ready, the same machine can be switched to the on-line mode, and the programmer can log in and read the whole program in at maximum speed from the card or tape cassette. The savings in connect time generally pay for the extra features.

7.5.2.1 Problem-solving

The story is not complete, however, since there remain some functions that a programmer can (or could) do better at a terminal. As noted above, there are specific individual activities in which interaction contributes to productivity. The most important is problem-solving. When faced with a problem that has an analytic solution, a programmer (or engineer, scientist, student, etc.) can use both the arithmetic power of the computer and the techniques of trial and error to achieve the symbiosis that makes interactive terminals popular. The computer makes it feasible to try out tentative ideas for solution that would be unjustified if they had to be worked out by hand. The speed of the system makes it possible to try several approaches in less time than it takes to investigate one by hand or via a batch service. Interaction in problem-solving pays off. But note that the context of problem-solving is very narrow. Someone who sits down at a terminal to solve a problem expects to get up and leave with the answer within a short time, certainly less than a day. There are no large data sets or programs involved except those borrowed from a public library. There is no need to become an expert in the mechanics of the system support regarding long-term storage or linking to a batch system. In other words, a problem solver gets the benefits of symbiosis without suffering any of the distractions of being a machine operator. At most, the user will have to practice using the keyboard to avoid sloppy mistakes.

Problem-solving is typically the kind of activity examined in the published time-sharing experiments. It represents a relatively small portion of the working hours of most of the users. In fact, so many problem solvers are casual users of time-sharing that the major interactive systems stress ease of use and provide many on-line teaching aids for the inexperienced user. Only a few people have continuing need for terminals. Often they do not care whether the tool they use is a small computer or a large one; however, economic factors may convince them that a low-cost subscription to a commercial time-sharing service is better than having any in-house facility dedicated to time-sharing. They can select one or more service bureaus based on the languages offered, the cost of subscription, the user support offered, and the reported reliability of the service [11]. Since problem-solving sessions are short, reliability over periods up to eight hours is important. Longer-term issues, such as "What happens when the service is halted for a week while a new computer is being installed?" are less critical to problem solvers since they can dial a different service during the interval.

Among the problem-solving activities of interest to programmers are the following.

- Design tradeoff analyses
- Program performance modeling
- System throughput modeling
- Schedule planning and analysis
- Budget variance reporting
- Programming technique comparisons
- Mathematical algorithm development
- File organization analyses
- Test design

Thus the advantages of interactive problem-solving can affect a program unit in many ways.

7.5.2.2   Editing and debugging

Data entry and data editing are best done by secretaries. This rule applies to program entry and program statement entry as well. As pointed out before, programmers are not noted for their skill as machine operators. They cannot compete with trained clerical people in keying data. Therefore, the primary users of interactive documentation aids are not programmers.

Only when it is convenient to enter data in conjunction with another task does it pay for a programmer to do it personally. Thus a problem solver can afford to enter problem data and solve the problem on-line. Similarly, a programmer who wants to debug a program or a portion of a program can afford to enter small amounts of code at the terminal. It is interesting to watch programmers work at a terminal. They are clumsy compared with typists when it comes to correcting typographical errors; yet they are better at rearranging blocks of code and at building a logical program flow. The difference in proficiency is probably due to the fact that programmers pay attention to the content and context of what they are looking at. This permits them to see logical block structure and data flow. Typists are trained to concentrate on the accuracy and position of what they are typing.[4] Program-

---

4. Users of documentation aids, such as the IBM Administrative Terminal System [12], which use sequential line numbers to locate lines of text can observe the effect of clerical versus professional training. Given an existing text to be updated by a list of changes, a typist will correct the first text line first, changing all subsequent line numbers. It is then necessary to calculate where the next change will fall. This procedure is slow and tiring for most typists. A programmer, after one session, will correct the last line first, realizing that this will preserve the remaining line numbers. Each will say the other is proceeding in an illogical manner.

mers are responsive to cues produced by a debugging compiler containing information about the input. They are not responsive to such visual cues as a lack of agreement between two strings of characters. Therefore, programmers should plan a work session that is loaded with content-dependent decisions and actions. Debugging is such an activity. The editing associated with debugging is also an effective use of the programmer's time.

In order to debug from a terminal, users need help from the interactive system. When the input is higher-level language source code, it is necessary to be able to execute program fragments; otherwise, the interactive system is no different from an RJE system. This can be done by an interpreter or a very fast compiler which keeps track of declarations and assignments from previous compilations. The interpreter is easier to build and appears more natural to the programmer. It is fast. It allows statement-by-statement modification, and it detects many input errors. However, it may not be compatible with the batch compiler that will be used to build a production version of the program. Incompatibility of debugging and production tools requires that the debugged program be tested again in batch mode after compilation. An interactive compiler may also be incompatible with the corresponding batch compiler. It is less natural because it forces the programmer to worry about the entire compilable module instead of the one or two source statements of interest. Object code debugging can also be done on-line with proper debugging aids [13, 14]. It is harder because some of the logical flow of the program may be lost when the original source program is compiled. Optimizing compilers which rearrange code to achieve speed are quite likely to produce object code which contains no clues to the logical purpose of the program. In summary, the best tools are those that allow the same source statements to be carried from initial interactive entry through all subsequent processes. In the absence of the best tools, additional time should be scheduled to compensate for the difficulty of working around small incompatibilities.

7.5.2.3   Storage and retrieval

There are three ways that an interactive system can be very helpful to a system programmer when it has a storage and retrieval capability.

1. Answer questions
2. Cue the programmer
3. Control temporary storage

Standard reference material should be printed for distribution; however, data which is of interest to a number of people and which changes frequently can be stored in the computer. Programmers can then get the latest data by asking for it. Some information, such as the status at the moment of the computing center facilities, can be handled this way or even displayed automatically to each user who logs in. Other data, such as library indexes, cross-reference tables, schedules, etc., can be stored for selected reference by authorized people. Documentation on released programs or instructions on how to use certain procedures can be made available.

Among the items stored for terminal users can be various development aids. One that is helpful in many large organizations is a library of templates used to cue programmers. The *template* is a standard format containing blanks to be filled in by the user. Templates can be used to describe allowable queries, standard reports, display formats, etc. Programmers can ask for a template by name, fill in the blanks (following the instructions displayed with the template), and let a behind-the-scenes program generator carry out the rest of the programming job. Other cues are simple instructions telling a user what to do next or menus listing the capabilities available to the user or explanations teaching how to use a capability.

Storage and retrieval capabilities in an interactive system can save and protect programs under development. During a work session, the support system will automatically save the user's work space periodically to protect against a system crash. It will also allow the programmer to make a copy of something as a backup in case of an accidental unrecoverable error. On completion of a work session, the support system will allow the finished work to be (a) retained or dumped to a cheaper storage medium, (b) relabeled as a released program, or (c) retained as working data *and* relabeled as a released program. By having several levels of labeling plus access codes, the system can help managers control who uses programs at various stages in their development or modification.

7.5.2.4 Summary

Lawrence [15] ranked six methods of providing support for program development, with emphasis on reducing development time. In order of preference they are

1. High-speed automated batch—RJE
2. Conversational automated batch—CRJE
3. Interactive coding of program blocks—batch test with control from the terminal
4. Interactive coding of program blocks—interactive test with debugging aids
5. Fully interactive coding and testing with incremental, compatible compiler
6. Standard closed-shop batch

In the ranking, cost is not considered. If it were, standard batch would look more attractive to some facility managers. Lawrence placed fully interactive systems low on the list primarily because no such systems existed at the time he wrote the paper. Although the same ranking applies to projects using top-down structured programming and those using a bottom-up approach, Lawrence recognized that the scope of terminals was limited to small blocks of code; therefore he considered top-down structured methods as the norm against which he measured performance. He also recognized that the data on which he based his conclusions is going to change, so further experiments will be required in the future to improve the ranking of recommended systems in the light of advanced technology.

7.5.3   Planning an Interactive Work Session

Before we leave the subject of interactive terminals, it is necessary to say a few things about how to lay out a work session. An appropriate start might be "Select a pencil and a piece of paper," since the trick to using a terminal is to get organized. A terminal is an individual's tool. As such, it lacks the disciplinary and social rules that lead to conformity in groups. A programmer trying to use a batch service quickly learns from the bulletin board or a buddy or a computer center specialist how to submit a job. Failure to learn means no service. The same programmer sitting at a terminal has no one to turn to and must be more self-sufficient. While the programmer is floundering, the terminal is providing service—plenty of service, with a corresponding bill; however, this service is not productive. Not until the programmer's manager measures results against costs is it evident that a problem exists.

There is no need to flounder. There are two steps to successful use of the terminal: (1) learn the interactive system; (2) organize each work session in advance.

Learning an interactive system is best done by using the terminal. A good interactive system is forgiving and helpful. It has built-in training aids. The novice should become familiar with the manual of operations and then start trying things out. At first it will be natural to use only a subset of the system capabilities, getting them wrong. As proficiency grows, the programmer will refer to the manual to find easier ways to express various functions —learning by doing. Instructors and managers can assist by suggesting a set of tutorial problems of increasing difficulty.

Organizing a work session is easy for someone who understands the pros and cons of terminal usage. A good work session will minimize the amount of connect time necessary to maximize the programmer's productivity. This entails off-line preparation of all the materials that are to be used during the work session but which do not require interactive support.

- Preparing a scenario of the work to be done, keeping it within a few hours, if possible.
- Collecting the appropriate references and listings, including necessary log-in codes and access codes.
- Arranging the work space to hold the references and still have room to make notes.[5]
- Providing reading and writing materials for keeping busy during long compute intervals in the session.
- Providing enough of the right kind of typewriter paper to last the whole session.
- Verifying that the correct typing element is available on the terminal typewriter.
- Checking the keyboard tops on the terminal (if removable) to ensure that they are appropriate.
- Ensuring that a system manual is available.
- Preparing an alternative task that does not require a terminal.

Now the programmer is ready to sign on and initiate the work session. If the system is overloaded (i.e., if a busy signal is received or the first 10–12 responses are intolerably slow), there is no value in waiting. The programmer should get off the terminal and turn to the alternative task.[6] At appropriate points, say an hour or two apart, additional attempts can be made to sign on. The programmer should stop trying when it is so late that the planned work session cannot be completed in one shot that day.

Once on-line, the programmer should make an effort to optimize the session. This is why a scenario is required ahead of time. It schedules the work session activities so that all fast-response activities are grouped together where possible. The fast-response activities include data entry, editing, interpretive execution of one or two statements, fetching data from work space in core, moving data into core from bulk storage, and other things which take only seconds. Nothing productive can be done between such commands. By grouping as many of them together as possible, the programmer can concentrate wholly on the terminal interaction. This part of the session is fast-paced and busy, so the programmer feels that progress is being made and, consequently, feels good.

------

5. Put coffee cups and ashtrays where they cannot fall over and mess up the working materials.

6. Another individual may take the programmer's place and sign on successfully to a different interactive system. The first programmer would still get a busy signal.

Slow-response activities, such as compiling, executing a program block or larger unit, or printing a long output on the typewriter, take minutes. An activity that takes more than one minute but less than thirty is frustrating. There is not enough time to do anything useful, and it is just plain boring to sit there waiting to issue the next command. By grouping them together it is possible to get periods of 30 minutes or more during which only minor attention to the terminal is required. The programmer can use this time for a related productive task.

Terminals encourage bad programming habits. It is uncomfortable to sit at a terminal without using it. Programmers tend to do the job in small increments just to keep the terminal busy. This has the effect of increasing input errors, debugging errors, and compilations. Programmers violate that rule of debugging which says "Find all the bugs before recompiling." They prefer to treat each bug as it is discovered, generating one compilation per bug instead of one compilation per program. It is the individual programmer's responsibility to fight the temptation to program badly. One way to solve the debugging problem is to end each scenario at the end of a major debugging run and then not to schedule another work session for 3–4 hours. In the interval, thorough desk-checking can be done.

The terminal pays off when it increases programmer productivity. The payoff depends on the ability of the programmer to work in a professional manner.

In "The Quiet Revolution," Winkler [16] points to the undeniable trend toward increasing use of communications-based systems in all aspects of industrial and social activity. From the householder's terminal for shopping, bill-paying, or entertainment to the corporation's terminal for order entry, information storage and retrieval, or machine tool control, there is more and more reliance on communications-based systems by choice. With the sudden onset of the international energy crisis in 1973 and the consequent restrictions on travel, it is clear that many things will be done via communications by necessity. The massive increase in the use of interactive terminals is a good reason to learn how to use them effectively.

REFERENCES

1. Aron, J. D., "Real-time Systems in Perspective." *IBM Systems Journal,* Vol. 6, No. 1, 1967.
2. Theis, D. J., and L. C. Hobbs, "Trends in Remote Batch Terminals." *Datamation,* Vol. 17, No. 17, September 1971.
3. Scherr, A. L., *An Analysis of Time-Shared Computer Systems.* Introduction by H. Teager. MIT Research Monograph No. 36. Cambridge, Mass.: MIT Press, 1967.

4. Sackman, H., *Man-Computer Problem Solving.* Princeton, N.J.: Auerbach, 1970.

5. Gold, M. M., "Time-Sharing and Batch-Processing: An Experimental Comparison of Their Values in a Problem-Solving Situation." *CACM,* Vol. 12, No. 5, May 1969.

6. Streeter, D. N., "Cost-Benefit Evaluation of Scientific Computing Services." *IBM Systems Journal,* Vol. 11, No. 3, 1972.

7. Corbato, F. J., C. T. Clingen, and J. H. Saltzer, "Multics—the First Seven Years." *AFIPS Conference Proceedings,* Vol. 40. Montvale, N.J.: AFIPS Press, 1972.

8. Wilkes, M. V., *Time-Sharing Computing Systems.* New York: American Elsevier, 1968.

9. Dolotta, T. A., "Functional Specifications for Typewriter-Like Time-Sharing Terminals." *Computing Surveys,* Vol. 2, No. 1, March 1970.

10. Hobgood, W. S., "Evaluation of an Interactive/Batch System Marriage Reveals Ideal Mates." IBM Research Report RC3479. Yorktown Heights, N.Y.: IBM Research, July 29, 1971.

11. Hillegass, J. R., "Piecing Out the Timesharing Puzzle." *Computer Decision,* Vol. 5, No. 2, February 1973.

12. *Administrative Terminal System Application Description Manual,* Form H20-0297. White Plains, N.Y.: IBM Corporation.

13. Grishman, R., "Criteria for a Debugging Language." In R. Rustin (ed.), *Debugging Techniques in Large Systems.* Englewood Cliffs, N.J.: Prentice-Hall, 1971.

14. Balzer, R. M., "EXDAMS—*EX*tendable *D*ebugging *A*nd *M*onitoring *S*ystem." *AFIPS Conference Proceedings,* Vol. 34. Montvale, N.J.: AFIPS Press, 1969.

15. Lawrence, L. G., "Remote Computing for Program Development." *Proceedings of 5th Australian Computer Conference.* Brisbane: Australian Computer Society Inc., 1973.

16. Winkler, S., "The Quiet Revolution." *IEEE Spectrum.* In press.

8
Conclusion to Part 1

In seven chapters, guidelines have been presented that can help an individual programmer improve his programs when working alone and when working as a member of a team. These guidelines are far from a complete list of techniques for professional programmers. Mainly, they represent the procedural steps that allow a programmer to work effectively in any environment. Such procedures establish basic standards of quality for all programming activities. But procedures cannot be substituted for brains. Programmers must also know how to solve problems, how to write code, how to use tools, and how to make tradeoff decisions. These things are learned through education and experience. The references in this book will act as pointers to sources of technical details. Through experience, each programmer can develop the judgment necessary for adapting the guidelines in this book plus the techniques learned elsewhere to the job at hand. That judgment is the distinguishing mark of the competent professional programmer.

8.1 SUMMARY OF GUIDELINES

The brief review of the guidelines in this chapter will serve as a reference aid and will reinforce the relationships between guidelines and concepts. Six basic concepts were introduced in Chapter 2.

1. Individual conceptual ability. The maximum size of a unit of programming is determined by the programmer's conceptual ability.

2. Span of attention–span of control. A manager's span of control is limited by the number of independent, interrelated activities he or she can handle. A programmer manages a program unit and must have a manageable span of control.

3. Complexity. The complexity of a system is proportional to the square of the number of its units.

4. Software versus hardware. One important way in which software differs from hardware is that all important design decisions occur early in the software development life cycle.

5. Documentation. A program system exists only in its documentation.

6. Change. Change is inevitable; therefore systems must be adaptable.

These concepts, which apply equally well to programs and projects of all sizes, suggest several guidelines for individual programmers.

1. Know your own capabilities; divide your assignments into manageable units.

2. Concentrate on only a few things at a time.

3. Manage your task *and* your program so as to minimize complexity.

4. Design each phase of your effort before you start implementation; i.e., draw a flowchart before coding.

5. Document your work so that someone else can use it.

6. Be flexible; schedule time to respond to changing requirements, and design your programs so that they can be modified easily.

All six of these guidelines apply to the programmers addressed by the two volumes of this book. In fact, Part 2 goes into much more detail on the concepts because they are so pervasive in team projects. If you think the concepts do not apply to you—if you say to yourself, "Well, I don't have to do all the documentation shown in Chapter 6 because my programs are used only a few times"—remind yourself what a programmer's job is. The programmers who constitute the audience of this book develop programs for the use of others. Only in Chapter 7 did we discuss writing programs for one's own use, and we were then careful to refer to the activity as "problem solving." A programmer should always think in terms of building a product to be delivered to a user. Thus handing over documentation is part of the job. The programmer has responsibility for the quality and the effectiveness of his product, but he is not the primary judge of the product's success. The user is. Therefore the product must be delivered in a form the user understands. That is why good documentation is so important. Each of the concepts applies in a similar manner to the programming job.

8.1.1   Problem Analysis and Planning

In Chapter 3 an example illustrated how a vaguely stated requirement can
be reduced to a precise statement of a programming task. The reason for
using an example instead of a checklist or a procedure is that problem
analysis is situation-dependent. Each case is different. The approach used
in the example shows how to get started.

- Find out what is required.
     - What is to be delivered?
     - Who needs it?
     - Why is it needed?
     - When is it needed?
     - What is the operating environment?
- Study the requirement, try to understand it, and then formulate ques-
  tions to get more detail. Ask for specific answers.
     - What are the inputs?
     - What outputs are wanted?
     - What files, library programs, operating system are available or re-
       quired?
     - What is the workload? How often is the program to be used?
     - What is the computer configuration?
- Clarify constraints.
     - How much time and money can be spent satisfying the requirement?
     - What is the performance requirement for the end product—what
       program size, running time, response time, resource utilization?
- Talk to anyone who can help answer your questions—the user, other
  programmers, the operations team, and consultants on technical topics.
- Sketch out a rough design of a program and the procedure for using
  it to satisfy the requirement. Keep it simple.
- Lay out your implementation plan. Estimate development cost and
  schedule.
- Verify with the user that your approach is acceptable.
     - Does it solve the problem?
     - Does the user want to redefine the requirement now that he sees
       what his original request will produce?

Are there growth requirements your program cannot handle because you have proposed the literal minimum response to the requirement?

- Obtain the user's authorization to proceed.

This approach is obviously iterative. You keep asking questions until you understand the requirement—indeed, until both you and the user understand the requirement in sufficient detail to agree that the end product will be satisfactory and is worth building. The approach is the same whether the user is your manager or a customer, whether he knows anything about programming or not.

In planning the effort involved in building a single program unit, be careful to allow enough time for design and debugging. The temptation to rush into coding must be resisted if you are to maintain a consistent level of quality in your end products. Initially, assume that a normal distribution of effort allocates the scheduled time as follows:

35% to design,

30% to coding and documentation, and

35% to debugging.

Increase the time allotted to design and/or debugging to cover unusually difficult logic or control requirements. When you are implementing from the top down, design, coding, and debugging are not separate, sequential activities; nevertheless, if you track how you spend your time on a daily or weekly basis you should observe a split comparable to the distribution of effort on a comparable bottom-up job.

The total time required to build a program unit depends on the problem, your capability relative to the problem, and the tools you use. Your estimate should consider your experience with similar problems. To the extent that the present requirement is clearly the same as one you have done before, you should do the new job at least as fast. Furthermore, if the job is to convert an existing program to a new form, you should take advantage of the existing design and even some of the code to shorten the schedule for conversion. In general, each new task will be new to you. Be aware that a task may look like one you have done before yet be sufficiently different to require a completely new approach. Make a formal estimate for each task rather than follow your intuition. The formal estimate should be based on the structural attributes of the problem, modified for your know-how and the uniqueness of the problem. The result of the estimate should be further adjusted to allow for any abnormal working conditions in your facility.

8.1.2   Program Design

Program design is described in Chapter 4 as a process of discovery and resolution which results in a documented specification. Design starts with *what* the user wants and shows *how* the solution will be provided. The process deals with increasing amounts of detail as problems are encountered at each step due to technical obstacles, inconsistencies in the problem statement, or changes in the requirements. Because many design decisions may affect the user's requirements, the designer has to keep the user fully informed. Otherwise there is a possibility that the resulting specification will be written to the designer's interpretation of the requirements instead of the user's. The user should always be asked to concur in the key decisions which will control the character of the delivered program.

The design process is similar to analysis, but design is much more detailed. Design starts with data analysis.

1. Verify the available data.

    a. Distinguish between facts and other data.

    b. Test the suitability of algorithms to be used.

    c. Identify assumptions, constraints, safety factors.

    d. Identify relationships in the data that were not explicit in the requirements.

2. Explain to the user what your end product will do, given your interpretation of the data.

    a. Show where you have modified or extended the user's original data.

    b. Show what alternatives are available if he does not accept your interpretation. Show the effect of using the alternative data.

3. Select an approach that is consistent with the user's goals.

    a. Evaluate the relative importance of programming cost, schedule, resource requirements, and other development factors.

    b. Evaluate the relative importance of running cost, performance, maintainability, functional capability, and other operational factors.

    c. Evaluate the relative importance of training, growth opportunities, and other human factors.

    d. Analyze the tradeoffs among all the factors to select the implementation approach.

4. Develop mutual agreement with the user on your interpretation of the requirements and your approach.

It is a good idea to incorporate the agreement in the specification. Then, when you deliver the program, it will be easier for the user to see that you have done what was called for.

The specification should of course follow the principles of good program design. You should develop it by stepwise refinement, testing each step to see that it brings the program closer to the objectives you have set.

- Execution speed
- Modularity
- Maintainability
- Precision
- Ease of use

The specification document should be the minimum set of narrative, graphics, and tables that completely describes the design so that both you and the user can understand it. Furthermore, the specification should be organized so that, as you build the program, you can concurrently extend the specification, making it the final program documentation.

The requirements imposed on an individual programmer who is working as a member of a team are discussed at length in Part 2. A special case of working within a large system arises when a programmer is assigned to program an intelligent controller. The interest in distributed intelligence started to gather momentum in 1973 when programmable devices and communications services became available at prices that were attractive. As a result, system designers started to remove or "off-load" some functions from central computers by placing them in remote controllers. The resulting task for the remote controller programmer looks like the first-stage tasks pictured in Fig. 1.2. There is a big difference, however. The application program or the terminal control program specified for the remote controller is really a module of a much larger system. The decision to distribute the system and transfer the module to a remote controller has been made for the benefit of the overall system; it does not make the module independent of the rest of the system. Therefore, if you are asked to program an intelligent controller, always treat the task in the context of the larger system to which it belongs.

8.1.3 Coding

There are three dominant guidelines in Chapter 5.

1. Program in the highest-level language applicable to the job. Fine-tune the critical portions of the object code by hand where necessary, but

do not sacrifice the advantages of high-level languages: readability, ease of use, maintainability, transportability.

2. Implement from the top down where possible. By building the program as you design it, you maintain better control of the logic flow. You can test your partial product. You can make changes with less effort.

3. Follow the rules of structured coding.

All these guidelines can be applied in all circumstances if you understand them. Used blindly, the rules can lead to inefficient end products. Used properly, with appropriate complementary techniques, the rules can give you the benefits of high-quality code without interfering with your program's performance.

The following complementary techniques can help you do your best job.

- Select a higher-level language by a weighted analysis of language attributes in the context of your task.

- Design the program in executable code so that you can test your logic and the program's performance as you go.

- Use an indented paragraph-like format to make the code easier to read.

- Limit the amount of code on a page, but make each page correspond to a proper flowchart.

- Use pronounceable, mnemonic names in the program.

- Ask another programmer to read your code and critique it.

- Store your work in process in an on-line library.

- Use library routines whenever they fit your requirements with no more than nominal tailoring.

To get the best performance out of your program without endless tuning of the end product, keep several guidelines in mind.

- Optimize code by arranging routines and computations so as to minimize the total number of executions.

- Package code so as to maximize local contiguity and minimize paging in a virtual-storage computer (or overlays in a real-memory computer).

- Allocate enough real memory to your job to hold your working set of pages.

To protect your program against computer errors or software changes, write defensive code.

- Document the program well and keep the documentation current.

- Write straightforward programs without tricky code.

- Use the protective mechanisms provided by the operating system.
- Include tests in your routines to protect them against incorrect inputs.
- Provide checkpoint/restart capabilities for your program.

Having observed these guidelines in coding the program, do not discard them after you deliver the end product. The same quality control is required when the program is maintained or modified. At all times, the program should be well structured, properly tested, and fully consistent with the most recent copy of the program documentation.

8.1.4 Debugging, Documentation, and Delivery

The lessons of Chapter 6 regarding debugging can be summarized in six points.

1. Assume that your code has bugs.
2. Plan controlled debugging runs to save time and encourage thoroughness.
3. Use your head to find logical errors; use the machine to find coding errors.
4. Develop an environment for your program to facilitate debugging.
   a. Test cases for each function
   b. Data files that represent the problem domain
   c. Operational scenario
   d. Stub messages and drivers
   e. Data collection and reduction routines
   f. Real-time simulator, if necessary
5. Predict the outcome of each proposed run so that you can interpret the actual results and explain out-of-range items.
6. Look for multiple bugs after each run rather than fix the first bug you find and rush back to the computer.

If you have asked an associate to read your code ahead of time, many bugs will be eliminated before you run formal test cases. The formal debugging runs are your responsibility. They disclose errors in your work that you must fix before your end product can be integrated with a larger system. The process of integration and test of the larger system is a topic deferred to Part 2.

Let us restate the guidelines for documentation: The deliverable program is contained in its documentation, which is the minimum amount of narrative, graphics, and tabular information, including the program source and object listings, that will permit you and the user (or the user's representative) to operate and maintain the program. The minimum program package is generally more than you would need for yourself but less than a line-for-line description of the object code. The package includes at least the design specification, a user's guide, an operator's guide, and an internal logic manual for programmers. Each document has certain minimum entries.

- Program title and identification data
- Preface explaining how to use the document
- Table of contents for the document
- Description of the program
- Description of program inputs, files, outputs
- Description of interfaces between the program and other programs or data
- Description of how the program works
- References to other sources of information
- Names of responsible individuals—your name, the user's name

In addition, each document has data for its primary reader, as shown in Fig. 6.3.

When the program package is complete, the program is ready for delivery. The assignment is not completed until (a) the user accepts delivery and (b) you have discharged whatever release and installation responsibilities you were assigned with the task. This is a critical point for you personally. Your manager, the user, and the people operating your end product look to you for a quality job. They hold you responsible for ensuring that the program does what your program package says it does. You accepted responsibility for doing your best as a professional programmer when you accepted the assignment. If the program fails in any respect, it is your fault. Normally, your manager measures your performance and your potential for greater responsibility in terms of how well you do on current assignments. He has no abstract way of looking at a program and giving it a score. The only practical measures he can apply are based on observing you and others and making comparisons. His inputs include a few quantitative items, such as how long you took to do the job and how many lines of code you delivered. Qualitative inputs are more readily available, including praise or complaints from the user. In fact, a qualitative evaluation of how well your programs do their job is likely to dominate your manager's opinion of your performance. Therefore, always keep sight of the operational objectives of your program. Test every decision by asking, "Will this decision improve the ultimate end product?"

8.1.5   Using Tools

Many references to tools are scattered through Chapters 1–7. Properly used, these tools can help you increase your productivity. Since every tool has a cost associated with acquiring it, learning how to use it, and actually using it, a decision must be made on each task as to which tools, if any, you should adopt. Obviously, the benefits of the tool must outweigh the costs. Fortunately, acquisition and learning costs are paid only once, so the use of a tool on several jobs tends to increase the tool's value. Standardization on selected tools within a programming department tends to maximize the tools' value. In most departments, for example, standard languages, library support systems, flowcharting programs, subroutine libraries, and similar development tools are specified. A manager must give permission for any deviation from the standard. This approach creates a common level of understanding for everyone in the department. Programmers can easily move from job to job within the department without having to go through a long learning process. In large shops, a support systems group can be set up to maintain and enhance the tools, further reducing the cost of using them.

On-line terminals represent a special class of tools which are both expensive to acquire and demanding in their use. Chapter 7 explains the potential benefits of various on-line terminal applications and shows the constraints these applications place on the programmer. The following five significant uses of on-line terminals are listed in the order of probable net value to a programmer.

1. Remote job entry to reduce turnaround time
2. Interactive problem-solving for design, analysis, simulation, or forecasting
3. On-line documentation: preparation, storage, retrieval
4. Interactive editing and debugging
5. Interactive program development from start to finish

The five applications are ranked to favor RJE, which is easy to use and gives a big assist to programmer productivity without making the programmer overdependent on its availability. A system which requires all work from the initial design to final delivery to be done on-line offers much more function than RJE; however, one needs practice to use it well, and it limits programming to those periods when the system is up and running. Chapter 7 includes a scenario for using an on-line interactive terminal as a guide to proper use of your time. The scenario requires only that you (a) learn the interactive system and (b) organize each work session in advance. By following the scenario, you can make an interactive system at any of the five levels of sophistication a tool that supports you rather than a master you must serve.

8.2   PREVIEW OF PART 2

Part 1 has been addressed to the individual programmer. Each section could have begun, "When you sit down at your desk to develop a program unit, consider the following guidelines. They will help you do your job." Simple and straightforward guidelines really will help the individual programmer because he can adapt them to his behavior patterns independently of what his associates may do. This is possible only because the programmer is working on a single program unit, thereby avoiding many of the consequences of complexity. When many programmers work as a team to build a program system, the communications among them and the interfaces between the elements of the system begin to dominate the job. These interactions must be controlled to permit each programmer to concentrate on his assigned area of responsibility. The management procedures that make large systems feasible are the subject of Part 2.

To many people, the burden of management, planning, and control in a large system seems too big compared with the effort involved in building one program unit. Some additional cost to integrate separate program units can be understood, but a system cost more than double the cost of the program units, with much of the extra cost paying for nonprogrammers, seems unreasonable. Part 2 starts by explaining why such costs are natural and should be expected. The first chapter defines a system. Drawing on the concept of complexity, the chapter outlines the characteristics of a system. Different degrees of difficulty are assigned to logical, data, and control interactions in order to define an arbitrary measure of complexity. Then the measure is applied to a simple example to show how complexity can be reduced by judicious design decisions. Some guidelines are also provided to show how system workload is related to system size.

The second chapter of Part 2 expands on the idea that every element of a system contributes to its complexity. Thus you have to understand total system behavior in order to manage a system or subsystem. Behavior is examined from three points of view.

1. The system as a system of people
2. The system as a hardware/software system
3. The system as a system of tools and techniques

In each case, it is clear that there are many nonprogramming factors which affect the programming process. Most of the factors can delay that process.

All of them can force the programmers to modify design decisions to accommodate needs external to the program.

The process itself is laid out in detail in the third chapter, which presents a system development life cycle that is the software equivalent of the engineering life cycle found in hardware projects. The cycle spans (a) concept formulation, (b) project definition, (c) project implementation, (d) operation, maintenance, and upgrade, and (e) termination. By plotting the manpower required each month on a project, one can draw a life cycle curve. Chapter 3 compares the shape of this curve for a traditional hierarchical project implemented from the bottom up with that for the same project implemented from the top down. Both curves are compatible with the recommendation in Part 1 that individual programmers implement program units from the top down. Top-down implementation is also recommended for systems, but it may not always be feasible, particularly on very large projects.

The life cycle curve is a useful management tool. Its use as a resource and schedule planning aid is shown. One can easily see the effects of various schedules, especially crash schedules, in the life cycle curves. In addition, the curve identifies points at which responsibility shifts from designer to programmer to tester to maintainer. These hand-over points represent changes in the character of the project which call for changes in management technique and support tools used.

Subsequent chapters in Part 2 cover the stages of the life cycle in more detail. Data in Part 1 is not repeated. The new material in Part 2 shows how groups function and how they are managed. In addition, those activities which are a trivial part of one-person jobs but are significant in team projects are explained. For example, problem analysis in Part 1 deals with the definition of a problem on a specific computer; the corresponding topic in Part 2 is expanded to consider the total system. Trade-offs between hardware and software, between function and performance, and between function and cost are considered. Negotiations among competitive users, in which the programming manager is the mediator, are introduced. The volume covers the effects of competition by treating the programming group as a contractor who must submit a proposal to win the right to build a system. This leads to sections on how to prepare a proposal and how to manage contractual responsibilities.

Teams are made up of people, who need leadership and who must work constructively together. Managers are appointed to provide leadership and organize the team. A major chapter is devoted to the responsibilities of a programming manager. It offers guidelines for making decisions in the system environment. The attributes and advantages of various types of organizations are discussed. Finally, a section is devoted to such personnel issues as recruiting, training, evaluation, and most important, fitting each person to an appropriate job. This chapter follows the one on system analysis and proposal preparation since, if you win a contract, your first responsibility is to staff the job.

In parallel with staff acquisition, a nucleus of designers can start laying out the system structure. The top-down process is not new; however, it differs from design of a program unit in that the designer is not the sole implementer. Special attention must be given to the work breakdown structure, which shows who is going to build each unit within the system. Other formal system management techniques are introduced that allow a design control group to monitor the project and keep it on the right track. Techniques used by such a group for controlling system interfaces, functional specifications, and system performance are included. Other techniques and tools for supporting the system development process—program production libraries, job control systems, measurement and prediction methods—follow in the chapter on implementation. This is not a long chapter since implementation of program units is covered in Part 1.

Considerable space is devoted to planning and control. A chapter on the general characteristics of the control loop is followed by a set of sample planning documents. It will be seen that in large systems a separate plan is needed for each type of activity.

- Technical plan
- Resource plan
- Test plan
- Documentation plan
- Implementation plan
- Support plan
- Maintenance plan

Each plan is a combination statement of purpose, checklist of activities, and commitment to perform. Most of the plans are the natural consequence of the design process.

One—the resource plan—is different. Few programming managers are good at estimating workload, budgeting costs, and setting schedules. Most are particularly weak at resource planning during the proposal and early design stages of a project. Later they can draw on their observations of actual progress to make good estimates. To help managers over the difficult early period, a quantitative estimating procedure is presented which can be used to develop a ballpark estimate. The procedure is based on the concept of individual conceptual ability.

Most programmers are also weak when it comes to assessing the status of a system development project. The complex interactions among system elements prevent a simple review of program unit status from showing system status. Lacking a precise measure of progress, the system manager has to rely on plans and controls. His key tools are change control and project reviews. The principles and the mechanics of these tools are presented in the next to the last chapter.

Finally, the support functions are laid out in terms of how a support group serves a programming group and what the programming group must do to make effective use of support groups. Management of the support functions differs from the programming groups in two ways.

1. Support functions do not change in character during the life of a project whereas programming progresses through the various stages of the life cycle.

2. A support group usually serves several programming groups; therefore the support manager must allocate his limited resources to meet competing demands.

The consequences of these two aspects of support are reflected in the discussion of (a) machine operations, (b) test support, (c) publications, (d) training, and (e) intrasystem communications.

Part 2 is a companion to Part 1, extending the programming process to group activities of all sizes. Taken together, the two volumes are intended to give the professional programmer the basic tools he needs to perform effectively in positions of increasing responsibility in a systems programming career.

ABOUT THE AUTHOR

Mr. Aron is presently manager of computer networking in IBM System Development Division. He is also Editor-in-Chief of The Systems Programming Series.

On joining IBM in 1954 he served as a technical engineer engaged in logical design of the 705 system at Poughkeepsie. There followed a short assignment to develop and teach a programming course for the SAGE Air Defense System. In 1955 he was transferred to Washington, D.C., as an applied science representative in the Federal Marketing activity of IBM, having technical and marketing responsibility for IBM support to non-defense scientific agencies. After a period as a product planner in IBM's Data Processing Division, he became Manager of Applied Science for all Federal Marketing activities. From 1962–1967 Mr. Aron was responsible for technical coordination for the Federal Systems Center, the software contracting arm of the Federal Systems Division. He became Manager of the FSC Programming Laboratory in 1968 and assumed the position of Technical Assistant to the Vice President and General Manager of the Federal Systems Center in 1970. In 1973 he organized the System Technology Department of the Complex Systems Directorate of the IBM System Development Division. He has published numerous technical papers. In conjunction with Mr. A. M. Pietransanta, Mr. Aron developed and taught the widely used IBM Programming Project Management Course.

Mr. Aron received a BS degree in Military Engineering from the U.S. Military Academy in 1948, and graduated as 2nd Lt. in the Corps of Engineers. He spent six years in the Army primarily engaged in geodetic surveying.

INDEX

Pages on which definitions appear are set in boldface type.